Regional Security in the Middle East

Throughout the twentieth century, the Middle East remained an arena of incessant conflict attracting global attention. As recent developments in Israel/Palestine and Iraq have shown it is difficult to exaggerate the significance of Middle Eastern insecurities for world politics.

This book provides an accessible yet critical analysis of regional security in the Middle East. Using a non-realist approach the author provides a comprehensive study of the pasts, presents and futures of security in the region. In doing this, the author focuses upon the question of regional identity formation, explaining how and why various regional representations came into being and explores the practical implications of a particular identity. Finally the author presents alternative future scenarios including a critical security studies perspective on the future of the Middle East as a security community.

This book recognises the presence of a multitude of contending perspectives on regional security, each one of which derives from different conceptions of security that have their roots in alternative worldviews. Topical and well-written, *Regional Security in the Middle East* will be essential reading for those interested in Middle Eastern politics, security studies and critical approaches to world politics.

Pinar Bilgin is Assistant Professor of International Relations at Bilkent University, Ankara.

RoutledgeCurzon advances in Middle East and Islamic studies

Regional Security in the Middle East

A critical perspective

Pinar Bilgin

RoutledgeCurzon
Taylor & Francis Group

LONDON AND NEW YORK

First published 2005
by RoutledgeCurzon
2 Park Square, Milton Park, Abingdon, Oxon OX14 4RN

Simultaneously published in the USA and Canada
by RoutledgeCurzon
270 Madison Ave, New York, NY 10016

RoutledgeCurzon is an imprint of the Taylor & Francis Group

Typeset in Baskerville by Wearset Ltd, Boldon, Tyne and Wear
Printed and bound in Great Britain by MPG Books Ltd, Bodmin

British Library Cataloguing in Publication Data
A catalogue record for this book is available from the British Library

Library of Congress Cataloging in Publication Data
A catalog record for this book has been requested

ISBN 0-415-32549-8

Contents

Preface and acknowledgements

Stefan Zweig once wrote that he found the best way to explain a difficult subject was to seek to understand it through telling about it to others. This book could be viewed as an attempt to gain greater understanding of regional (in)security in the Middle East through telling about it to others. Contesting such approaches that present the Middle East as only amenable to realist readings, the book argues that critical approaches to security are indeed relevant in the Middle East, while accepting that some of the items of the traditional agenda also retain their pertinence and should be addressed, but within a comprehensive framework cognisant of the dynamic relationships between multiple dimensions of regional security.

Although I have been an observer of this conflict-ridden part of the world for more than a decade, it is my interest in critical approaches to security that led me to embark on a research project of which the end-result is this book. The appeal of critical approaches to security for me could partly be explained by my aversion to all that was presented under the title International Security when I was an undergraduate student of International Relations. A lot has changed since then, but during the early 1990s, what was on offer under the label International Security was nuclear strategy and, in particular, nuclear deterrence. Turkey being a non-nuclear state beleaguered by perceived conventional threats, the emphasis put on nuclear deterrence only added to my puzzlement as to the way courses on International Security were set up. Special thanks go to my professors at the Middle East Technical University in Ankara: Mahmut Bali Aykan and Süha Bölükbaşı introduced me to Middle East politics and Hüseyin Bağcı to new approaches to Security Studies.

As a Master's student at Bilkent University I was introduced to critical theories of International Relations and gradually began to make more sense of what I had been studying in the previous four years. During my Master's studies I remember dropping a course on crisis management, not being able to grasp the exclusive focus given to superpower conflict, and feeling uncomfortable with the lack of critical reflection in the 'problem-solving' approaches to conflict resolution, the course I took in its place. My thesis supervisor at Bilkent University Nur Bilge Criss deserves special thanks for encouragement and support beyond the call of duty.

When writing up my Master's thesis I began working for a government department as a junior researcher on Middle Eastern affairs. It was during that brief period that I began to think more deeply about the need to broaden our conceptions of security, problems involved in zero-sum thinking and practices, and the ways in which security thinking was constitutive of the very 'reality' to which it sought to respond. However, I did not know how to put such thoughts into words. To learn that, I had to wait until I found out more about Critical Security Studies.

I am grateful to the British Council for awarding me the Chevening Scholarship, which enabled me to do an MSc in Strategic Studies at the University of Wales, Aberystwyth. The 1995–96 academic year was the first time a postgraduate course on Critical Security Studies was offered by Ken Booth and Richard Wyn Jones, who later became the co-supervisors of my PhD dissertation. Their enthusiasm inspired and encouraged me to undertake further studies on critical approaches to security.

Upon completion of my Master's studies, the Department of International Politics at Aberystwyth awarded me a PhD scholarship, which allowed me to lay the groundwork for this book. My gratitude is due to the Department of International Politics, University of Wales, Aberystwyth for an E.H. Carr Studentship (1996–99) and the Overseas Research Awards Scheme for an Overseas Research scholarship (1996–99). I would also like to thank the British International Studies Association and European Consortium for Political Research for travels grants, and numerous workshop/conference organisers for providing me the space to present my ideas and receive feedback.

During my years at Aberystwyth many people contributed to this study in numerous ways and I am grateful to them all. Particular thanks go to my two supervisors Ken Booth and Richard Wyn Jones who have provided invaluable intellectual insight, support and guidance over the years. I am especially grateful to Ken Booth for his perfect mix of incisive critique and encouragement. He will always be my teacher. Thanks also go to Bill McSweeney, Michael Williams, Adam David Morton, Pauline Ewan and Tarak Barkawi who commented on draft papers and chapters.

Since February 2000 the Department of International Relations at Bilkent University has been my new intellectual home. At Bilkent my first debt of gratitude goes to our Head of Department Ali Karaosmanoğlu who welcomed me to the Department of International Relations. My colleagues and especially my students in the courses War, Peace and Security, and New Directions in Security Studies stimulated me to re-think my ideas about the relevance of critical approaches to world politics. I am equally grateful to our Dean Merih Celasun for his encouragement and support. I would also like to thank my assistant Berivan Eliş for her help on compiling the bibliography. My family deserves a special mention; they shared the high moments as well as the low ones.

Parts of the argument appeared in an earlier version in 'Alternative Futures for the Middle East', *Futures: Journal of Policy, Planning and Future Studies*, 33, pp. 423–36, copyright 2001. This material is reprinted here with permission from Elsevier.

Introduction

Throughout the twentieth century, the Middle East remained as an arena of incessant conflict attracting global attention. As the recent developments in Israel/Palestine and the US-led war on Iraq have showed, it is difficult to exaggerate the significance of Middle Eastern insecurities for world politics. By adopting a critical approach to re-think security in the Middle East, this study addresses an issue that continues to attract the attention of students of world politics. Focusing on the constitutive relationship between (inventing) regions, and (conceptions and practices of) security, the study argues that the current state of 'regional security' – often a euphemism for regional insecurities – has its roots in practices that have throughout history been shaped by its various representations – the geopolitical inventions of security. In doing this, it lays out the contours of a framework for thinking differently about regional security in the Middle East.

Prevailing approaches to regional security have had their origins in the security concerns and interests of Western states, mainly the United States. The implication of this Western bias in security thinking within the Middle Eastern context has been that much of the thinking done on regional security in the Middle East has been based on Western conceptions of 'security'. During the Cold War what was meant by 'security in the Middle East' was maintaining the security of Western (mostly US) interests in this part of the world and its military defence against other external actors (such as the Soviet Union that could jeopardise the regional and/or global status quo). Western security interests in the Middle East during the Cold War era could be summed up as the unhindered flow of oil at reasonable prices, the cessation of the Arab–Israeli conflict, the prevention of the emergence of any regional hegemon, and the maintenance of 'friendly' regimes that were sensitive to these concerns. This was (and still is) a top-down conception of security that was military-focused, directed outwards and privileged the maintenance of stability. Let us take a brief look at these characteristics.

The Cold War approach to regional security in the Middle East was top-down because threats to security were defined largely from the perspective of external powers rather than regional states or peoples. In the eyes of British and US defence planners, communist infiltration and Soviet intervention constituted the greatest threats to security in the Middle East during the Cold War. The way to enhance regional security, they argued, was for regional states to enter into alliances with the West. Two security umbrella schemes, the Middle East Defence Organisation (1951) and the Baghdad Pact (1955), were designed for this purpose. Although there were regional states such as Iraq (until the 1958 coup), Iran (until the 1978–79 revolution), Saudi Arabia, Israel and Turkey that shared this perception of security to a certain extent, many Arab policy-makers begged to differ.

Traces of this top-down thinking are still prevalent in the US approach to security in the 'Middle East'. During the 1990s, in following a policy of dual containment US policy-makers presented Iran and Iraq as the main threats to regional security largely due to their military capabilities and the revisionist character of their regimes that were not subservient to US interests. In the aftermath of the events of September 11 US policy-makers have focused on 'terrorism' as a major threat to security in the Middle East and elsewhere. Yet, US policy so far has been one of 'confronting the symptoms rather than the cause' (Zunes 2002: 237) as it has focused on the military dimension of security (to the neglect of the socio-economic one) and relied on military tools (as with the war on Iraq) in addressing these threats. This is not to underestimate the threat posed by weapons of mass destruction or terrorism to global and regional security. Rather, the point is that these top-down perspectives, while revealing certain aspects of regional insecurity at the same time hinder others. For example, societal and environmental problems caused by resource scarcity do not only threaten the security of individual human beings but also exacerbate existing conflicts (as with the struggle over water resources in Israel/Palestine; see Sosland 2002). Besides, the lives of women in Kuwait and Saudi Arabia were made insecure not only by the threat caused by Iraq's military capabilities, but also because of the conservative character of their own regimes that restrict women's rights under the cloak of religious tradition. For, it is women who suffer disproportionately as a result of militarism and the channelling of valuable resources into defence budgets instead of education and health (see Mernissi 1993). What is more, the measures that are adopted to meet such military threats sometimes constitute threats to the security of individuals and social groups. The sanctions regime adopted to rid Iraq of weapons of mass destruction has caused a problem of food insecurity for Iraqi people during the 1990s. In the aftermath of the US-led war on Iraq, Iraqi people are still far from meeting their daily needs. Indeed, it is estimated that if it were not for the monthly basket distributed as part of the United Nations' 'Oil for Food' programme, 'approximately 80 percent of the Iraqi population would become vulnerable to food insecurity' (Hurd 2003). Such concerns rarely make it into analyses on regional security in the Middle East.

During Cold War years such top-down approaches to regional security in the Middle East were compounded by a conception of security that was directed outwards – that is, threats to security were assumed to stem from outside the region whereas inside was viewed as a realm of security. Given the number of inter- and intra-state wars in the region during the Cold War, it might seem an exaggeration to argue that the region was peaceful. The argument here is that the regional status quo was considered to serve the interests of Western policy-makers (and their regional allies). Indeed, with the crucial exception of the Arab–Israeli conflict, it was generally assumed that threats to regional security took the form of Soviet intervention and communist infiltration. Even those approaches that did pay attention to conflicts within the region focused on controlling the forceful settlement of disputes lest instability invites Soviet military intervention.

The military priority of security thinking in the Cold War manifested itself within the Middle Eastern context by external (as well as regional) actors' reliance on practices such as heavy defence outlays, concern with orders-of-battle, joint military exercises and defence pacts. For example, the British and US security practices during this period took the form of defending regional states against external intervention by way of helping them to strengthen their defences and acquiring military bases in the region as well as bolstering 'friendly' regimes' stronghold over their populace (at times through military intervention or covert operations) so that the 'Middle East' would become inviolable to Soviet infiltration and intervention. This top-down, outward-directed and military focused approach was reflected in the literature on regional security in the Middle East in that internal and international conflicts, alliance formation and military allocations were considered as 'key areas that reflect degrees of security or insecurity in the region' (Maoz 1997: 2; also see Inbar and Sandler 1995). Likewise, the literature understood the roles played by regional security institutions as one of either minimising the role of the use of military force in settling inter-state disputes, or defending the region against external actors. Even when regional security dynamics were studied, the intellectual framework adopted was a 'regionalised version of the global strategy/security paradigm' (Klein 1994: 14). Consequently, those regional dynamics which were motivated by domestic as opposed to external security concerns were rendered invisible in the literature on regional security (Acharya 1992; also see David 1991).

Stephen Walt's study, *The Origins of Alliances* (1987) is a good example of how Western conceptions of security were put into use in scholarly analyses on regional security. Walt's main argument in this study was that balance of power theory is less powerful than a theory of balance of threats in explaining state behaviour. 'Although the distribution of power is an extremely important factor', argued Walt (1987: 5), 'the level of threat is also affected by geographic proximity, offensive capabilities, and perceived intentions'. Focusing on alliance patterns in the Middle East, Walt sought to show that in order to maintain security in the Middle East, alliance behaviours of regional states had to be understood. Walt was particularly critical of US policy towards maintaining security in the Middle East via the construction of anti-Soviet alliances ('pactomania', 1987: 3), for he believed that regional policy-makers were not as concerned with the threat posed by the Soviet Union as were their Western counterparts. They were more concerned with the Israeli threat to balance against which they formed inter-Arab alliances. However, although critical of US approaches to security in the region, Walt's conception of regional security remained outward directed in that he understood security in the Middle East as one of making the region inviolable to Soviet intervention and communist infiltration. Walt's criticism, then, stemmed from his rejection of the argument that it was necessary to bring regional states under the roof of anti-Soviet alliances in order to secure Western interests in the region (Walt 1987: 3). Instead, he maintained that given the fact that most regional policy-makers were more concerned with each other than the Soviet threat (which was the main preoccupation of their Western counterparts) the best the United States could do, in order to maintain the security of its interests, was to understand the alliance patterns of regional states and manipulate them in accordance with its own concerns.

Walt's conception of regional security did not constitute a deviation from the top-down, outward-directed and military focused security thinking of mainstream approaches. True to his neo-realist perspective, Walt built his argument on the assumption that international anarchy conditioned regional states to endlessly seek to balance each other in the attempt to maintain security. Yet, he failed to note how their alignment behaviour was designed to counter internal as well as external threats (see David 1991 for a discussion on Third World alignment and 'omnibalancing'). In fairness to Walt, he did show awareness of how non-military factors seemed to shape regional states' alliance behaviours. He noted, for instance, how non-military dimensions of power had an impact on the threat perceptions and alliance behaviours of Arab states. He also noted that 'a different form of balancing ... occurred in inter-Arab relations' (Walt 1987: 149). What Walt meant by 'a different form of balancing' was that Arab policy-makers did not only invest primarily in the military sector in the attempt to balance each other but sought to 'attract as many allies as possible in order to portray oneself as leading (or at least conforming to) the norms of Arab solidarity' for this was how regimes gained (and lost) power and legitimacy in the Arab world (Walt 1987: 149). In the Arab world, noted Walt, 'the most important source of power has been the ability to manipulate one's own image and the image of one's rivals in the minds of other Arab elites' (1987: 149). Yet, the neo-realist perspective did not allow him to analyse the role ideas and identities play in shaping behaviour (and vice versa).[1]

What was missing from Cold War thinking about regional security in the Middle East was an understanding of regional actors' thinking; that is, what they perceived as threats and how they sought to achieve security in this part of the world. Although it could be argued that this was what Walt was also trying to do – i.e. bringing regional actors' perspective into his analysis of alliance patterns in the Middle East – by way of failing to move away from a mainstream (top-down, outward-directed and military-focused) conception of security, he ended up neglecting the security concerns of regional actors. These were concerns other than Soviet expansionism and inter-Arab rivalry (such as state building and plight of the Palestinian peoples); concerns that cannot always be understood within a framework that black-boxes the state and fails to recognise how some (mostly developing) states seek to balance against internal threats, thereby allying themselves with 'secondary adversaries' in the attempt to 'focus their resources on prime adversaries' (David 1991: 235). Walt's main contribution to the literature on regional security in the Middle East, therefore, remained showing how 'a different form of balancing . . . occurred in inter-Arab relations' (Walt 1987: 149).[2]

In his 1998 study entitled *Dialogues in Arab Politics*, Michael Barnett showed that although Walt was able to point to an 'anomaly' in inter-Arab politics, he could not explain it within a neo-realist framework, which takes identities and interests for granted and does not allow the analyst to look at the ways in which the two are mutually constituted. Adopting a constructivist approach, Barnett did away with the military focus of neo-realist approaches and pointed to processes through which Arab policy-makers sought security through 'representational politics' (1998: 2), that is, through bolstering their 'pan-Arab' image for purposes of legitimacy. In doing this, argued Barnett, 'Arab leaders deployed "symbolic power", not military power, to enhance their security and to control each other's foreign policies' (1998: 2). Arab 'symbolic politics' included Voice of Arabs broadcasts by Arab leaders (such as Nasser) who 'took to the air-waves to portray their adversaries as outside the Arab consensus as a result of policies they had recently enacted or proposed' (1998: 2).

Although Barnett's study is exceptional in showing how Arab policy-makers differed in their use of non-military instruments of security, and how a common Arab identity shaped their interests as well as practices, his study brackets 'security'. It is argued that Arab actors were concerned about internal as well as external threats to their security. Barnett's study also shows how the Arab security agenda included threats of military as well as non-military nature. Yet, there is very little discussion on how representations of threats to Arab national security were based on an inside/outside divide in that threats were assumed to stem from outside the Arab world whereas inside was represented as the realm of security.

Likewise, there is very little discussion in Barnett's study on how regime security was prioritised by Arab actors at the expense of other (non-state) actors. In other words, what the author focuses on is the non-military character of the threats faced by and the security practices resorted to by the Arab actors and the need to adopt an alternative framework to understand the dynamics of inter-Arab politics. What Barnett does not focus on is myriad Arab actors' conceptions of security, what they perceived as threats, how they sought to meet them. His approach takes issue with the military focus in Cold War approaches to insecurity insofar as the latter fail to show how Arab actors responded to internal (as well as external) threats and adopted different (non-military) practices in search for security. In other words, Barnett is interested in showing the need for a different method, that of constructivism, in understanding inter-Arab politics. He does not directly take issue with the top-down and outward-directed approach to regional security in the Middle East as adopted by Walt and other students of Cold War Security Studies.

Students of critical approaches to security have sought to remedy this neglect by adopting a broader security agenda and looking at actors other than states in their scholarly analyses (on Africa, see Booth and Vale 1997; Thomas and Wilkin 1999; on the Middle East, see Jacoby and Sasley 2002; Bilgin 2002, 2004). The critical point being that prevailing approaches to regional security in the Middle East fail to take into consideration alternative conceptions of security that coexist in the region. Hence the need for a critical perspective that seeks to enter into people's 'common sense' and poses questions about 'what it means to be "secure" in the Middle East' (Jacoby and Sasley 2002: 9) to present the reader with a critical understanding of regional insecurities.

Tami Amanda Jacoby and Brent E. Sasley's edited volume *Redefining Security in the Middle East* (2002) is a commendable attempt to re-think security in this region. Critical of single-factor accounts of Middle Eastern politics, Jacoby and Sasley and the contributors to their edited volume have chosen to look at non-military security issues such as the environment, gender and politicised religion. Yet, this study's definition of what constitutes a 'critical' approach is not radically different from the definition of 'new security' in Lenore Martin's 1998 volume *New Frontiers in Middle East Security* or Bassam Tibi's *Conflict and War in the Middle East: From Interstate War to New Security* (1998a) where the authors adopted broad definitions of security to study the Middle East while maintaining the state's central position in normative as well as analytical agendas. The point here is that adopting a 'critical' approach to security in the Middle East should involve more than adding a number of 'new' issues and stirring. Understanding the broadening move simply as one of adding more issues to governmental security agendas would be misleading in that those who drew up Cold War security agendas were never totally ignorant of the non-military dimensions of security. Although broader conceptualisations of the earlier years had been replaced, by the mid-1950s, by more military-focused approaches, economic, political and even environmental issues were never totally excluded from national security agendas in general and Middle East security agendas in particular. For instance, water scarcity has always been considered a security issue in the Middle East. Likewise, the issue of unhindered flow of oil at reasonable prices was successfully securitized by US policy-makers in the post-Second World War period. Indeed, the problem with traditional approaches to security was not only that they emphasised the military dimension of security to the neglect of other dimensions, but also that they focused on military and non-military issues from a statist perspective whilst failing to reflect upon the constitutive relationship between thinking/writing about and practising/doing security. Then, although those studies that adopted 'new' or 'critical' approaches to study regional security in the Middle East have done away with the military-focused character of the prevailing approaches, they failed to ask 'what it means to be "secure" in the Middle East' (Jacoby and Sasley 2002: 9) as viewed through the lenses of various actors. This failure to take into consideration the alternative conceptions of security, in turn, has narrowed the ethical and political horizons of security thinking and practice.

From a critical perspective, thinking differently about security involves: first, challenging the ways in which security has traditionally been conceptualised by broadening and deepening the concept and by rejecting the primacy given to the sovereign state as the primary referent for, and agent of, security. Critical approaches also problematise the militarised and zero-sum practices informed by prevailing discourses and call for reconceptualising practice. Second, thinking differently entails rejecting the conception of theory as a neutral tool, which merely explains social phenomena, and emphasises the mutually constitutive relationship between theory and practice. That is, the way we (the community of students of security) think and write about security informs practice; it privileges certain practices whilst marginalising others, thereby helping constitute what human beings choose to call 'reality'. Theory is itself a form of practice; theorising is recognised as a political activity. Finally, adopting a critical approach to security implies adopting an explicitly normative (for some, emancipation-oriented) approach to security in theory and practice.

Aims

The aim of this study is to provide an account of regional security in the Middle East from a critical perspective. The study has three more specific aims that correspond to the three tasks of critical approaches as identified above. First, it aims to present a critique of prevailing security discourses in theory and practice with reference to regional security in the Middle East and point to unfulfilled potential imminent in regional politics.

Second, the study aims to explore the constitutive relationship between (inventing) regions, and (conceptions and practices of) security. Finally, it aims to show how critical approaches might allow one to think differently about futures of regional security in the Middle East.

These aims are achieved via a threefold structure which looks at Cold War pasts in Part I, and post-Cold War presents in Part II. Part III looks at possible futures of regional security. The intention here is to emphasise the dynamic relationships between pasts, presents and futures in thinking as well as practices. Following Edward Said's (2001: 187) counsel that for thinking constructively about their future people must anchor themselves in their history and agenda, the book begins with an agenda. Chapter 1 lays out the basics of a critical security approach after briefly tracing the development of security thinking in the Cold War and post-Cold War eras. I then move on to consider Cold War pasts and post-Cold War presents of the Middle East by focusing on the constitutive relationship between geopolitical inventions and practices of security. Parts I and II are each made up of two chapters: representations (Chapters 2 and 4) and practices (Chapters 3 and 5). Chapters 2 and 4 will present alternative spatial representations of this part of the world and seek to tease out the conceptions of security in which they are rooted. The point being that each spatial representation gives primacy to different kinds of threats depending on the security conceptions of its proponents. Chapters 3 and 5 look at the practical manifestations of adopting particular spatial representations. These chapters are not intended as comprehensive accounts of Middle Eastern history but only to introduce attempts at achieving regional security. The aim is to show how representations shape practice; they enable some practices while marginalising others; they address some regional insecurities while constituting others. Part III (Chapter 6) focuses on possible futures of the Middle East. It surveys alternative future scenarios and their potential implications for regional politics. In doing this, the emphasis is put on a discussion of the potential for the creation of a security community (in line with the precepts of critical security thinking).

The adoption of the Cold War/post-Cold War divide as a juncture where pasts end and presents begin may require justification. Admittedly this is a disputable choice, not the least because it reinforces the prevalent tendency to see an unproblematic dividing line between Cold War and post-Cold War eras. As Fred Halliday (1990) noted, one's understanding of when the Cold War ended and the post-Cold War began depends on his/her conception of what the Cold War was all about. Cynthia Enloe (1993) echoes Halliday when she questions whether the Cold War has come to an end at all, say, for women who live next to military bases in the Philippines or for women in Afghanistan doing daily 'battle'. Her point is that some Cold War structures still remain despite the end of the conflict between the United States and (former) Soviet Union (see also Booth

1998a). The Cold War is bound to have not one, but 'a multitude of endings', concludes Enloe (1993: 3), each ending resulting from the pulling down of yet another structure (such as the Berlin Wall) that helped to sustain the Cold War.

The adoption of the Cold War/post-Cold War divide as defining the juncture between Part I and Part II, pasts and presents, could be viewed as an attempt to reinforce the points made by Halliday and Enloe and to provide a critique from within. Thus, the study will seek to destabilise the prevalent tendency in Security Studies literature to present the emergence of critical thinking about security issues as a post-Cold War phenomenon, the implication being that what is being criticised was exclusive to the Cold War and therefore long past and gone. Instead I will seek to present an array of spatial representations, security conceptions and practices adopted by different actors. It will be argued that just as some critical thinking existed during the Cold War, just as much traditionalist thinking remains in the post-Cold War era.

Another aim of this study is to contribute to the critical security approach by suggesting that when studying regional security from a critical perspective, both concepts – 'region' and 'security' – should be opened up.[3] Those few studies that have looked at the Middle East from a critical (or 'new') perspective (see, for example, Martin 1998; Tibi 1998a; Jacoby and Sasley 2002) have bracketed 'regional' in 'regional security'. This is rather unfortunate because, as the book will argue, regional insecurities are shaped by their various representations – 'geopolitical inventions of security'. 'Middle East' is one such (spatial) representation. Accordingly, this study pays attention to the 'regional' component in 'regional security' and seeks to explore what Simon Dalby (1991: 274) has called the 'politics of the geographical specification of politics'. The aim here is to question the politics behind the invention of the 'Middle East' as well as that of other alternative spatial representations (such as 'Arab Regional System', 'Euro–Med Region' or 'Muslim Middle East') that have been adopted by different actors. Towards this end, I will make use of the burgeoning literature on critical approaches to Political Geography (or Critical Geopolitics) (see, for example, Agnew and Corbridge 1995; Agnew 1998; Ó Tuathail and Dalby 1998; Ó Tuathail *et al.* 1998) that has emphasised the 'invented' character of regions (see Taylor 1991) as opposed to some earlier conceptions that viewed regions as 'eternal'.

The Middle East is arguably a hard case for critical approaches to engage in. It has for long been viewed as a region that 'best fits the realist view of international politics' (Nye 2000: 163); or 'an "exceptional" case eternally out of step with history and immune to trends affecting other parts of the world' (Aarts 1999: 911). 'While the rest of the world worries about new and non-traditional threats to national security', argued one author, most countries in the Middle East are still poised to counter the same old, traditional threats. In the Middle East, to use Thomas Hobbes's famous line, 'there is continuall feare, and danger of violent death' and 'the life of man' (and woman) is still 'poore, nasty, brutish and short'. The Cold War has had a revolutionary impact on the security agenda of most states in the world, with the exception of the Middle East.

(Shehadi 1998: 134)

Accordingly, it has been argued that whereas critical approaches to security may have relevance within the Western European context, in other parts of the world – such as the Middle East – more traditional approaches retain their validity (see Ayoob 1995: 8–12). The Gulf War (1990–91), the US-led war on Iraq (2003), the stall in Arab–Israeli peace-making and the seeming lack of enthusiasm for addressing the problem of regional insecurity, especially when viewed against the backdrop of increasing regionalisation in security relations in other parts of the world (see, for example, Rosecrance 1991; Hettne and Inotai 1994; Alagappa 1995; Fawcett and Hurrell 1995; Gamble and Payne 1996; Lake and Morgan 1997; Hettne and Söderbaum 1998), does indeed suggest that the Middle East is a place where traditional conceptions and practices of security still prevail.

The question is whether critical approaches can provide a fuller account of regional security in this conflict-ridden part of the world. The book will try to show that they can. Contesting such approaches that present the Middle East as only amenable to realist readings, it will be argued that critical approaches are indeed relevant in the Middle East, while accepting that some of the items of the traditional agenda also retain their pertinence and should be addressed, but within a comprehensive framework cognisant of the dynamic relationships between multiple dimensions of regional security.

Re-thinking regional security in the Middle East

Why seek to re-think regional security in the Middle East at a time when its status as a region is being questioned? 'There is no Middle East', declared one author when discussing the impact of the end of the Cold War and the dissolution of the Soviet Union and Yugoslavia on this part of the world (Kaplan 1994a). More recently, Yezid Sayigh (1999: 231–2) brought up this issue when he indicated that since the end of the Cold War it has become 'questionable whether the Middle East can usefully be conceived as a single system any longer' (also see Khalidi 1998b, 2003). Sayigh's point was that since it was Cold War balance of power politics that gave the Middle East its shape, the end of the Cold War 'raises questions about the validity of its continued definition as a region' (Sayigh 1999:

200). What the author failed to note is the fact that the Middle East as a geopolitical invention predates the Cold War (see Chapter 2). It was indeed balance of power politics, but that of Great Britain and Russia during the late nineteenth and early twentieth centuries, that resulted in the invention of the 'Middle East'. During the Cold War, the borders of the region were (re)shaped as a part of the attempt to contain the Soviet Union. The point being that the end of the Cold War need not mean the end of the Middle East as a region of world politics so far as the rationale behind the 'invention' of this region (that is, furthering the security needs and interests of external actors) remains. As the US war on Iraq (2003), which sought to change the regime thereby creating a positive domino effect on the rest of the region (and making the region inviolable to terrorism) has showed, the security rationale of the external actors that gave rise to this spatial representation remains.

Another point Sayigh makes is that it is not only the end of the Cold War but a number of other developments (including the Iraqi invasion of Kuwait [1990] and the Gulf War that ensued [1991], the stall in Arab–Israeli peace-making and the decline of 'Arabism' as a force in inter-Arab politics) that have led to the 'fragmentation of the Middle East state system and further undermined prospects for regional cooperation or integration in the security, economic and political spheres' (Sayigh 1999: 201). The author considers this an additional reason why the Middle East should no longer be treated as a single region. The issue of the lack of regionalism in the Middle East has puzzled others in that one scholar has dubbed it 'a region without regionalism' (Aarts 1999) given the lack of enthusiasm in reviving the Middle East Peace Process and the slow progress of the Euro–Mediterranean Partnership scheme. When viewed against the backdrop of increasing regionalisation in other parts of the world the Middle East indeed appears to be a 'region without regionalism'. Yet, what is significant to note is that the problem in the Middle East is not necessarily a lack of interest in regionalism per se, but rather the presence of a multitude of approaches to regional security propounded by different actors. Arabism as a force in inter-Arab politics may be on the decline,[4] but it still continues to shape and constrain regional politics via the practices of non-governmental actors. Similar points could be made about 'Islamism' and 'Mediterraneanism' as well. Although it would be premature to present the practices of non-governmental actors as 'regionalism-from-below' (in contrast to Middle Easternism, which could be considered as 'regionalism-from-above' by virtue of its major proponents being governmental actors such as the United States and some of its regional allies),[5] they nevertheless are significant forces and their understanding could help to explain the lack of agreement on a single regionalism project. Then, instead of taking the relatively little evidence of enthusiasm for addressing the problem of regional insecurity for granted and leaving aside the Middle East as a geopolitical concept, an essential place for critical approaches to begin is a recognition of the presence of a multitude of perspectives on regional security, each one of which derive from different alternative world views and different security concerns.[6]

The 'Middle East' is a geopolitical invention of external actors. It is a spatial representation that has been adopted to represent this part of the world when thinking about and organising action for maintaining its security against other external actors. In other words, the 'Middle East' as a geopolitical invention is used not because this part of the world exhibits the characteristics of a 'single system'[7] or because regional consciousness is strong (Sayigh's criteria on what makes a region), but because 'Middle East' serves as shorthand to describe a part of the world that is crucial to external actors' security concerns and interests.

This, however, is not to argue that the 'Middle East' is somehow unique or different from other regions. As the literature on Political Geography reminds us, there is nothing 'natural' or 'neutral' about geographical assumptions or language. Throughout history, the driving purpose behind the identification and naming of geographic sites has almost always been military strategic interests. Indeed, as Kären Wigen and Martin Lewis (1997: xiii) note, 'some of the most basic and taken-for-granted "regions" of the world [such as Southeast Asia and Latin America] were first framed by military thinkers'. In other words, the origins of regions have had their roots in the security thinking and practices of their inventors (see Foucault 1980; Lacoste 1998). The reason why the lands to the south-west of Asia and north of Africa have been lumped together in the mind's eye and labelled as the Middle East is because this particular representation helped British (and later US) strategists think about and organise action for maintaining security in this part of the world.[8]

Although the 'Middle East' preserved its position as the dominant representation, alternative spatial representations emerged during this period as well. Accordingly, the book will look at three other representations of this part of the world, namely 'Arab Regional System', 'Muslim Middle East' and 'Euro–Med Region'. Each of these representations gives primacy to different kinds of threats depending on the security conceptions of their proponents.[9] It will be argued that when re-thinking regional security in the 'Middle East', the students of critical approaches should pay attention to regional peoples' conceptions of security; what they view as the referent; and how they think security should be established in this part of the world. The aim is to show how difficult it is to generalise about questions of security; how peoples' ideas about security differ from one another; how they changed in the past and might change in the future. Within the context of the 'Middle East' this amounts to amplifying the voices of those whose views have been left out of security analyses and pointing to possibilities for change that exist.

The significance of questioning – what Simon Dalby (1991: 274) has referred to as – the 'politics of the geographical specification of politics' becomes apparent once one recognises that the current state of regional insecurity in the Middle East has its roots in practices that have been informed by this representation. As John Agnew and Stuart Corbridge (1995: 48) have argued, 'to designate an area as "Islamic" or "Western" is not only to name it, but also brand it in terms of its politics and the type of foreign policy its "nature" demands'.

Reflecting upon the history of US engagement with the Middle East, Douglas Little identifies representations of the region as the problem behind policy failures. According to Little, it is 'American Orientalism' defined as 'a tendency to underestimate the peoples of the region and to overestimate America's ability to make a bad situation better' that has often misled US policy-makers in their dealings with the region. Regarding the future, Little (2002: 314) writes:

> Although there is greater appreciation for the complexities of the Muslim world than a generation ago, most Americans still view radical Islam as a cause for instant alarm. Having been fed a steady diet of books, films and news reports depicting Arabs as demonic anti-Western others and Israelis as heroic pro-Western partners and having watched in horror the events of 11 September, the American public understandably fears Osama bin Laden and cheers Aladdin.

Little's argument builds upon that of Edward Said in his 1978 book *Orientalism*, where the author pointed to the relationship between representations and practice. Said's point was that the academic discourse of Orientalism (defined as 'a style of thought based upon an ontological and epistemological distinction made between "the Orient" and [most of the time] "the Occident"' [Said 1995a: 2]) had not only helped to make the Middle East what it has become but also made it difficult to become something else:

> a book on how to handle a fierce lion might . . . cause a series of books to be produced on such subjects as the fierceness of lions, the origins of fierceness, and so forth. Similarly, as the focus of the text centers more narrowly on the subject – no longer lions but their fierceness – we might expect that the ways by which it is recommended that a lion's fierceness be handled will actually *increase* its *fierceness*, force it to be fierce since that is what it is, and that is what in essence what we know or can *only* know about it.
>
> (Said 1995a: 94)

This is because the Orientalist discourse does not merely represent the 'Orient' but also lays down the rules that enable one to 'write, speak and act meaningfully' (Agnew and Corbridge 1995: 45). In his later works (see Said 1994b, 1995b, 1997, 2001) Said went on to show how contemporary representations of the Middle East (and Islam) in the media (as well as academia) have reduced it to terrorism and very little else. Said's argument is in line with E.P. Thompson's observation on the impact British historical representations of India have had on Indian politics (Said 2001: 44–5). According to Thompson, writings on India in English 'simply left out the Indian side of things' thereby deepening the irreconcilability between Indians and the British. Thompson wrote:

> Our misrepresentation of Indian history and character is one of the things that have so alienated the educated classes of India that even their moderate elements have refused to help the Reforms [of colonial policy]. Those measures, because of this sullenness, have failed, when they deserved a better fate.
>
> (quoted in Said 2001: 45)

Reading Thompson, one is reminded of the numerous attempts made by US policy-makers during the Cold War to generate reform and modernisation movements in the Middle East; some of which attempts have backfired (as with Iraq, Libya and Iran) (Little 2002: 193–227). What Little, Thompson and Said are pointing to are the different impact representations have on those who produce the representations and those who are represented. What all share is the damaging effect representations have had on both groups of actors.

According to Said, the Middle East as a spatial representation has been repressive in that it has had 'the kind of authority ... [that] doesn't permit or make room for interventions on the part of those represented' (Said 2001: 42). The Middle Eastern security discourse, which is informed by this representation, has reflected the Cold War security concerns of the great powers while neglecting that of regional states and peoples. Hence the argument that the current state of regional insecurity in the Middle East has its roots in practices that have been informed by its dominant representation: the 'Middle East'. By way of adopting this spatial representation, the Middle East has been categorised in terms of its politics (as the region that 'best fits the realist theory of international politics' [Nye 2000: 163]) and the type of foreign policy its 'nature' demands. In the immediate aftermath of the US-led war on Iraq, one newspaper columnist warned: 'Middle East is not Europe' (Zaharna 2003). Indeed. Yet, this should not be taken to suggest that the Middle East is destined to relive its insecure past. Such representations that emphasised Middle Eastern insecurities without reflecting upon their roots have had the effect of privileging certain security practices (such as the 1998–99 bombing campaign directed at obtaining Iraqi cooperation with the UN team inspecting the Iraqi weapons of mass destruction programme) whilst marginalising others (such as the adoption of a more comprehensive long-term policy of creating a nuclear-free zone in the Middle East).

Becoming aware of the 'politics of the geographical specification of politics' (Dalby 1991: 274) and exploring the mutually constitutive relationship between (inventing) regions, and (conceptions and practices of) security is not mere intellectual exercise; it helps reveal the role human agency has played in the past and could play in the future. Such awareness, in turn, would enable one to begin thinking differently about regional security to help constitute an alternative future whilst remaining sensitive to regional actors' multiple and contending conceptions of security, what they view as referent object(s), and how they think security should be sought in this part of the world.

Whilst admitting that the 'Middle East' is a contested term, it will still be employed throughout the study. Following Kären Wigen and Martin Lewis, it is assumed that problems of language are inescapable in a project involving the deconstruction of existing representations of world politics. In the words of Wigen and Lewis (1997: 17), 'in order to continue talking about the world, we must have the cake of metageography while deconstructing it too'. As with the use of 'women' in some feminist writing (see, for example, Sylvester 1994: esp. pp. 1–19; Zalewski 1994), the purpose behind continuing to use the 'Middle East' is to highlight the multiplicity of meanings attached to the concept, its fluidity and indeterminacy, whilst searching for the roots of its multiple representations. The goal, then, is not to present a 'brand new' alternative representation to replace that of the 'Middle East', but to draw attention to the relationship between geopolitical inventions and practices of security.

1 Pasts, presents and futures of security

Chapter 1 seeks to present an overview of the (Cold War) pasts, (post-Cold War) presents and possible futures of thinking about security. The chapter opens by historicising and contextualising the growth of Security Studies as a discipline. The argument here is that 'Security Studies', as we came to know it, was a product of the Cold War. The chapter further argues that Cold War Security Studies focused on the security of states, emphasised the military dimension and privileged the status quo. This section of the chapter also presents an overview of Cold War critiques of Security Studies in the attempt to show that alternative ways of thinking about security existed throughout the Cold War era.

The following section of Chapter 1 looks at security thinking in the post-Cold War period and traces its development in the attempt to see its differences from, as well as similarities to, Cold War approaches. This section focuses on two key debates in the attempt to present an overview of issues that have been raised by post-Cold War critics of Cold War Security Studies. These are: 'broadening security' and 'appropriate referent(s) for security'. Next, the contributions made by the students of Third World[1] security are discussed. It is argued that notwithstanding the introduction of 'new' approaches to security, much of the old thinking has remained in the post-Cold War era.

The final section of the chapter introduces critical security thinking. The aim of this section is not to provide an exhaustive overview of the origins and development of critical thinking. Rather, this section seeks to clarify the key analytical moves of critical approaches to security, namely, 'broadening security' and 'deepening security'. In the following sections, I seek to develop critical security thinking by focusing on three main themes that I identify as the silences of post-Cold War debates on security, namely, 'constitutive theory', 'agency' and 'practice'. The aim here is to show how critical approaches allow one to think and act differently.

Cold War thinking on security

What is referred to here as Cold War Security Studies was mostly called 'National Security Studies' in the United States and 'Strategic Studies' in Britain.[2] Notwithstanding the difference in titles, the focus on states as the primary referent (to whom security refers), the emphasis put on the military dimension of security, and the privilege accorded to the status quo united the two traditions (Booth 1991b: 318). This, of course, is not to suggest that Cold War Security Studies was unified in its approach to international phenomena. After all, the security community approach of Karl Deutsch *et al.* (1957) was also a product of the Cold War. Indeed, there were significant differences among its students as witnessed in the many debates that took place throughout this period.[3] However, as Hugh Gusterson has argued, these debates served to 'reinforce the foundational precepts of strategic discourse' by

> channelling disagreements into certain frameworks within which the act of disagreement obscures actors' shared allegiance to deeper structures of thought that contain their disagreements. Thus, in the act of debating, members of a discourse reproduce the categories, taken for granted, that make disagreement possible.
>
> (Gusterson 1999: 326–7)

Then, notwithstanding the differences, two common characteristics shared by its students justify treating their otherwise diverse contributions as a body of thought under the label Cold War Security Studies. These are their embrace of realism and the Cold War context in which they were produced.

The first characteristic students of this otherwise rich and diverse body of thought shared was the realist outlook. The realist theory of International Relations emphasised a state-centred outlook, a military focus, and a scientific-objectivist understanding of theory and the theory/practice relationship in the study of security (Krause and Williams 1997b: 36–43; Wyn Jones 1999: 95). John Garnett expressed the realist position as follows:

> Realists tend to be conservative in their views ... [they] tend to accept a world subdivided into independent sovereign states as being the normal, if not permanent, condition of international society, and they consider realpolitik an inescapable feature of the international environment. ... The realists also emphasise the ubiquity of the power struggle, and their literature is dominated by the concepts of national power and interest. Conflict is regarded as an inescapable condition of international life. This simple assumption is the starting point of realism.
>
> (Garnett 1987: 9–10)

Contemporary critics of realism are sometimes (rightly) criticised for caricaturing an old and sophisticated body of thought. Such a fallacy is partly in the nature of the task of summarising a rich and diverse tradition; crucial details and nuances inevitably get lost in the process. But, as will be argued below, sometimes realists themselves presented such simplistic pictures of their own thinking. Furthermore, from the mid-1950s onwards, students of realism moved away from the more sociological approaches of classical realism. Indeed, as the Cold War waxed and waned, classical realism was obscured by its more simplified and purportedly 'scientific' variant. Within the context of Security Studies this shift manifested itself in the discipline becoming increasingly state-centric and non-military dimensions of security being marginalised in favour of a military-focused security agenda (Baldwin 1995: 117–23; also see McSweeney 1999: 31–2; Tickner 1997: 618).

State-centrism could be defined as treating the state as the central actor in world politics and concentrating on states' practices when studying international phenomena. Realism's state-centred outlook introduced a degree of neatness and clarity to the study of the complexity of international phenomena. However, as with all simplifications, many crucial aspects were lost in the process (see Enloe 1996: 186–202). During the Cold War, the state-centric character of security thinking manifested itself in the notion that security is about the state and the state is about security (Buzan *et al.* 1998: 37). Though this may come as an oversimplification to some, it is nevertheless difficult to deny the way the state was viewed as both the primary referent and agent in Security Studies. Even some students of Third World security, who were otherwise critical of the Cold War security discourse, produced state-centric analyses (see, for example, Ayoob 1986; Azar and Moon 1988). However, despite this focus on states, state building was under-theorised; states were taken to be 'black boxes', the internal components of which were not considered worth investigating. As Georg Sørensen (1996: 371) has argued, the problem with International Relations in general and Security Studies in particular has had 'less to do with an exaggerated focus on the state than a lack of analysis of the state' (also see Halliday 1987).

Over the years, then, security thinking increasingly came to privilege the state as the primary referent and agent, and emphasised the role of the military instrument in maintaining stability. The military focus of realism manifested itself in a search for militarised solutions to problems that could have been addressed through non-military means. Military factors were paid more and more attention in threat assessments and policy calculations of states as the East–West conflict intensified during the 1960s. Indeed, there came a time when it was simply common sense to think that 'deterrence *was* foreign policy' (quoted in Nye 1989: 25). The title of an article by Michael MccGwire (1986), a long-time critic of Cold War thinking and the associated practices of security, summarised it well:

'Deterrence: The Problem, not the Solution'. Cold War Security Studies embraced realism's scientific-objectivist conception of theory and the theory/practice relationship as well. Indeed, even some critics of Cold War approaches to security such as those who participated in the 'traditionalist vs. behaviouralist' debate of the 1950s and 1960s, shared realism's ontological and epistemological outlook (see Bull 1969). As Steve Smith (1996: 33) noted, this debate focused on methodology (the methods through which the subject should be studied) to the neglect of ontology (what is there to be studied) and epistemology (what constitutes knowledge about the subject of study). The scientific-objectivist understanding of theory and the theory/practice relationship, in turn, resulted in essentially (but not always openly) normative theories of Cold War Security Studies masquerading as 'objective' approaches to international phenomena and being viewed as 'knowledge', whilst the explicitly normative approaches of their critics were presented as 'propaganda'.

In addition to this particular set of ontological and epistemological assumptions imported from realism, Cold War Security Studies shared a second characteristic: it was a product of the Cold War. The significance of this apparent truism is that the growth of the discipline should be understood with reference to the historical context in which it emerged, developed and helped to sustain.[4] This is especially necessary in order to understand why a rich and diverse body of thought such as classical realism was obscured during this period by its rather simplified variant. Accordingly, the development of International Relations in general and Security Studies in particular should be understood within the context of the Cold War fears and policy incentives in the West in general and the United States in particular (see Krippendorf 1987: 207–14; Smith 1987: 189–206; Baldwin 1995; Booth 1996; Krause and Williams 1997b; Hoffman 1995). The adoption of a state-centric approach to the study of security, for instance, was done in the attempt to introduce some neatness and clarity to the complexity of studying international phenomena for the purposes of building a 'scientific' discipline. This was not only because the complex task of dealing with human beings would not have produced the neat and tidy analyses a 'science' of Security Studies was thought to demand, but also because the perceived urgency of Cold War concerns made it difficult for its students to undertake the complex analyses the study of peoples (individuals and social groups) required (see Tickner 1997: 618).

Then, the choice of the term Cold War Security Studies (rather than 'traditional', 'mainstream', or '[neo-]realist' Security Studies)[5] to refer to this body of thought should be viewed as an attempt to stress the historical context in which it developed; and not necessarily a statement about it being a unified body of thought (notwithstanding some significant common characteristics identified above) or its unique approach to security matters. On the contrary, as will be argued below, there were elements of critical thinking during the Cold War; and much traditionalist thinking remains in the post-Cold War era.

Cold War critics of security thinking

The prevalence of Cold War Security Studies notwithstanding, alternative ways of thinking about security had begun to emerge from the 1960s onwards (see Bilgin 2003). This section will briefly discuss three main strands of criticism brought against the mainstream thinking by students of Alternative Security, Peace Research and Third World Security.

Alternative Security thinking

Olof Palme, in the introduction he wrote to *Common Security: A Programme for Disarmament* (1982) (prepared by the Independent Commission on Disarmament and Security Issues), outlined the main tenets of the arguments put forward by the Alternative Security thinkers. Palme wrote:

> Our alternative is common security. There can be no hope for victory in a nuclear war, the two sides would be united in suffering and destruction. They can survive only together. They must achieve security not against the adversary but together with him. International security must rest on a commitment to joint survival rather than on a threat of mutual destruction.
>
> (Independent Commission 1982: ix)

In this way, Alternative Security thinkers were rejecting zero-sum approaches to security, that is, thinking and practices based on the assumption that in an adversarial relationship one's gain is the other's loss.[6] Most of Cold War security thinking, particularly nuclear strategic theorising, was based on this zero-sum conception of security.[7]

Criticising the fashioning of defence policies on zero-sum conceptions of security, Alternative Security thinkers argued that, since both sides stand to lose in the event of a nuclear war, it was in the interest of both sides to work together to prevent it from happening. They further argued that the security dilemma could be mitigated through confidence building, adopting NOD (non-offensive defence) postures and stabilising interstate relations through strengthening interdependence (see Møller 1992). By way of showing how security practices need not be zero-sum in order to further security, students of Alternative Security attempted to address one of the issues central to critical approaches to security.[8]

However, it should be noted that much of the thinking done on Alternative Security and especially non-offensive defence during this period was in reference to European security. As was the case with the rest of Cold War security thinking, little research was undertaken on the applicability of

ideas, originally conceived for the Western European context, to other par
of the world (Møller and Wiberg 1994: 4–7). Indeed, in order to make the
adoption in the Third World of the principles of common security and in
particular the NOD postures possible, a major re-thinking would be
required as to how to make them compatible with sustainable development
in the Third World (Mosjov 1985: 77–9; Møller and Wiberg 1994: 6–7).

Peace Research

Although it was Gorbachev's adoption of the precepts of Alternative
Security thinking that made the headlines in the late 1980s, such critical
thinking had also begun to manifest itself in the practices of non-state
actors such as the US 'Freeze' movement that attempted to halt the
nuclear arms race, the UK-based Campaign for Nuclear Disarmament,
and END (European Nuclear Disarmament) which prompted a debate
centred on the nature of peace and security in Europe after détente
(Dunn 1991: 57).[9] According to the 'maximal' approach introduced by
Peace Researchers, peace did not just mean the absence of war; it was also
related to the establishment of the conditions for social justice. The distinction Johan Galtung (1969, 1996) drew between 'personal' and 'structural' violence pointed to the futility of the task of trying to achieve peace
without tackling the structural causes of insecurity. Kenneth Boulding's
(1978) conception of 'stable peace', in turn, was invaluable in emphasising that peace maintained through the threat and use of war cannot be
stable.

Although students of Alternative Security had introduced concepts
such as individual security and human rights to the security agenda, students of academic Peace Research focused with vigour on individuals and
social groups as well as a potential global society as referents for security.
They also suggested alternative (non-military, non-zero-sum, non-violent)
security practices putting special emphasis on peace education and the
role of the intellectuals (Dunn 1991; Smoker *et al.* 1995).

Where many Peace Researchers were less successful was when they
failed to challenge the claim to knowledge heretofore commanded by
Cold War Security Studies. Although many valuable works were produced
during this period on the causes of war, disarmament, conflict theory, violence and social transformation, the empiricist epistemology adopted by
many Peace Researchers did not enable them to credibly contest Cold
War Security Studies' claim to knowledge. Academic Peace Research has
been a rich tradition and has had students that adopted empiricist episte-
mologies as well as those with an explicit commitment to normative
approaches. However, since neither of these two groups contested the
objectivist conception of theory and the theory/practice relationship
adopted by Cold War Security Studies, they failed to mount a credible
challenge to Cold War Security Studies on this epistemological ground

J).[10] By failing to adequately lay bare the normative charac-
ar security thinking, students of Peace Research were them-
J to the margins whilst their research was labelled as
.'.

d Security thinking

Whereas Cold War security thinking in the United States and Western
Europe was under challenge by the likes of Alternative Security thinkers,
there was relatively little evidence of interest in concepts such as common
security or practices such as non-offensive defence in the Third World.
This is not to suggest that there were no attempts to adopt non-violent
resistance techniques. Mahatma Gandhi remains a noteworthy example of
the successful employment of non-violent resistance techniques in a Third
World context (Ambler 1995). Indeed, many Third World actors, including some from the Middle East, conducted non-violent political struggles
against former colonial powers or their own governments (Bennett 1990;
Zunes 1998). It is also worth noting that the *Intifada*, Palestinian peoples'
uprising against the Israeli regime in the occupied territories, began as
non-violent resistance in the late 1980s (Grant 1990; Dajani 1998).
However, as Third World states gained their independence, they also
embraced more conventional methods of defence – a process dubbed as
the 'internationalisation of the National Security state' by A.W. Singham
(1993: 7).

Where the Third World Security discourse differed was the emphasis
put on development. The writings of academic Peace Research, especially
Galtung's stress on the structural causes of insecurity, struck a chord in
the Third World in an era marked by the formation of the non-aligned
movement, the Group of 77 and the calls for a New International Economic Order in the United Nations (Mosjov 1985). The non-aligned
movement was composed of a group of states which proclaimed their
refusal to ally themselves with either one of the superpowers during the
Cold War – though some were closely aligned in practice (such as Egypt
and Syria). Although the ideology of the movement constituted a challenge to mainstream thinking at the time (Al-Mashat 1985: 11), its effectiveness remained.

During the 1980s, some Third World security experts took up these
issues once again. Caroline Thomas, for instance, noted that

> a great gulf exists over the basic issue of what constitutes security, and
> therefore over what constitute the most legitimate, desirable and
> appropriate methods of pursuing the goal of creating a more secure
> international environment and more security for each individual and
> state within it.

(Thomas 1989a: 3)

Thomas differentiated between two different approaches to security. The first approach was adopted by those states in the developed world that were (relatively) satisfied with the status quo and saw security mainly in terms of its maintenance. They privileged the maintenance of stability of the existing system as a foremost security concern.

The second and more holistic approach, argued Thomas, was adopted by those states in the Third World that included economic, political and environmental issues in their security agenda. The search for security in the Third World, noted Thomas (1987: 1), was about maintaining domestic security through state building, establishing secure systems of food, health, money and trade as much as it was about military build-up. Accordingly, many Third World states saw a change in the status quo not as a threat to but as conducive to security – provided that change came in the desired direction, that is, towards the creation of an international economic structure sensitive to the needs of Third World states.

Although the distinction Thomas drew between the security needs and interests of developed and developing states is helpful to a certain extent, it should be stressed that not all developing states were against the status quo. Throughout the Cold War, the conservative regimes of oil-rich Gulf states, especially that of Saudi Arabia, remained suspicious of the anti-status quo rhetoric of Egyptian president Nasser, a leader of the non-aligned movement. Furthermore, it was not always the case, as Thomas (1989a: 4) put it, that '[Western] conception of security was basically top down, while the other [Third World] was bottom up'. Rather, there were both developed states as well as developing states among those that propagated top-down views on security. For instance, when some Third World policy-makers spoke of the need to address the non-military dimension of insecurity, they often meant the need to curb the right to exercise democratic freedoms in the attempt to strengthen the state. The practical implication of this statist approach to security was the state's domination over society where, 'society's sacrifices are perceived as obligations, but the state's privileges justified as necessary to survival' (Al-Mashat 1985: 33). Accordingly, those who dared to challenge the security practices of their states were marginalised at best, and accused of treachery and imprisoned at worst.

Bottom-up views of security, in turn, were voiced by Western European peace movements. The views of non-state actors in the Third World did not get heard unless they adopted violent practices in the attempt to form a state (as in the case of the Palestine Liberation Organisation) or capture state power in their own countries (as with the Muslim Brotherhood and the Hizbullah). Academic Peace Research provided some – albeit limited – forum for non-state actors' views to be voiced (Galtung 1989; A. Said 1994).

In criticising Cold War Security Studies, students of Third World Security mainly focused on its Western origins. In particular, they drew attention to the fact that it was realism with its black-box conception of states that shaped Cold War conceptions and practices of security. Their argument was that in the developed West, threats to security were (and to an extent still are) conceived to stem from outside the state whereas in most parts of the Third World threats to security emanated from inside, thereby rendering Western conceptions of security of limited analytical utility within the Third World context (Al-Mashat 1985: 33; Ayoob 1986; Azar and Moon 1988).

They further argued that Cold War Security Studies focused on East–West stability and its maintenance through nuclear deterrence and nuclear power balancing, whereas some Third World states had been trying to reject the automatic categorisation of their problems into an East–West framework – as was the case with the non-aligned movement. Some Third World states, such as Iran and Syria, were all-too-happy to accept the nuclear umbrella provided by the two superpowers. In other words, not all Third World states were either able or willing to escape the Cold War template. Moreover, as noted above, the economic and military aid provided by the superpowers to their respective allies provided enough incentive for some (such as Iran [until 1979] and Turkey) to jump on the bandwagon.

Third World Security thinking, then, was critical of the Western origins of Cold War Security Studies, which, they argued, rendered its produce less useful in other contexts. Their criticisms emphasised the need to look at the domestic sources and non-military dimensions of insecurity in the Third World. Al-Mashat criticised the almost exclusive focus in Cold War Security Studies on crises and conflicts often to the neglect of 'longitudinal security processes' so that

> only indicators of power such as military expenditures, weapons systems, types of defence strategies, nuclear capabilities, and deterrence of adversaries have been on the priority list of security studies.
>
> (Al-Mashat 1985: 33)

This was a concern Al-Mashat shared with Western European peace movements as well as Peace Researchers, who maintained that Cold War Security thinking had become less and less relevant for the security concerns of individuals and social groups in the West as well.

Much of the critical thinking surveyed above remained on the margins throughout the Cold War. Critics of Cold War Security thinking were themselves criticised for their 'normative' or 'political' approaches to international phenomena. The essentially normative approaches of students of Cold War Security Studies, in turn, were presented as 'objective' or 'apolitical'. Such reasoning was substantiated by the commonly held assumptions as to who had relevant 'expertise' to talk about issues related to security. The assumption was that policy-makers, military elite and

Security Studies' academics knew best when it came to security issues. Feminists, Peace Researchers, Alternative Security thinkers and Third World Security experts as well as participants to myriad peace movements around Europe challenged such assumptions. But their views were marginalised by Cold War Security experts whose claim to knowledge was licensed by an objectivist conception of theory and the theory/practice relationship (Booth 1991c).

By the end of the 1980s Cold War Security thinking could no longer account for the developments taking place in Eastern Europe let alone other parts of the world. This was because the students of Cold War Security Studies expected the future to be more of the same: a ceaseless power struggle, balancing and bandwagoning of sovereign states. As Hugh Gusterson (1999: 324) argued, the 'telling failure' of Cold War Security Studies was not that 'it did not predict what actually happened, but that [it was] to a striking degree unable to even entertain the possibility of its happening' (also see Lebow and Risse-Kappen 1995). The 1989 revolutions in Eastern Europe caught Cold War Security Studies unaware, laying bare not only its limitations but also the lack of grounds for its claim to 'knowledge'.

Post-Cold War thinking on security

Critical approaches to security

Post-Cold War thinking on security focused on two major issues, namely the merits of broadening security and appropriate referents for security. These two issues, around which post-Cold War debates (see, for example, Ayoob 1995; Baldwin 1995, 1997; Bigo 2002; Bobrow 1996; Booth 1991b, 1997, 1998b, 1999a, 1999b; Buzan 1991a; Buzan *et al.* 1998; Der Derian 1995; Deudney 1990; Haftendorn 1991; Huysmans 1995, 2002; Job 1992a, 1992b; Kolodziej 1992; Krause 1998; Krause and Williams 1996, 1997a, 1997b; Lipschutz 1995; Mathews 1990; McSweeney 1996, 1999; Pasha 1996; Shaw 1993; Smith 1991, 1999; Sørensen 1996; Thomas 1991; Tickner 1992, 1995; Wæver 1994, 1995; Walker 1990a, 1997; Walt 1991; Weldes *et al.* 1999; Williams 1998; Wyn Jones 1995a, 1995b, 1999) were structured will now be examined in detail.

Broadening security

The post-Cold War witnessed a proliferation of works that sought to re-think, re-define, and re-conceptualise security.[11] Barry Buzan's *People, States and Fear* is a seminal work that brought together the ideas of Cold War critics of Security Studies in a sustained analysis that questioned the core concept of the field: security. Maintaining that those conceptions and practices of security 'bound to the level of individual states and military issues' were 'inherently inadequate', Buzan (1991a: 6) called for broadening the concept beyond its purely military focus and looking below and beyond the state for other referents. The issue of proper referent(s) for security will be addressed in the following section. What follows is an overview of the debate on broadening security.

In *People, States and Fear*, Buzan proposed to broaden security in order to come to grips with its multidimensional character by taking into consideration four other dimensions, namely the political, economic, societal and environmental in additional to that of the military. The military dimension, maintained Buzan, had so far been paid 'disproportionate' attention. This has had two consequences. First, other dimensions were paid inadequate attention. Second, by concentrating primarily on the military dimension of security, analysts had become too preoccupied with 'national' security perspectives 'where competitive self-interest dominates perceptions, and consequently discourages analyses of security interdependence and the systemic aspects of the concept' (Buzan 1991b: 36). Cold War approaches to security, with their zero-sum conceptions and practices, offered little insight into issues such as environmental threats let alone enable cooperative action to be taken to address them.

It should be noted here that Cold War Security Studies was never totally ignorant of the non-military dimensions of security. Indeed, as David Baldwin (1997) noted, the multidimensionality of security is 'not a discovery'; Arnold Wolfers (1962: 147–65) dwelt upon similar issues. However, as the Cold War waxed and waned, broader security agendas of the early years were replaced by more narrow and military-focused ones. Furthermore, although some of the ideas Buzan put forward had been around for a long time, the difference was that his was a voice from within the discipline (that is, Security Studies) as opposed to that of 'outsiders' (Peace Researchers, Third World experts) whose ideas were not taken as seriously.

Building upon Peace Researchers' broadening of the concepts violence and peace that took human beings as the referent, Ken Booth (1991b: 40) proposed broadening security to include 'all those physical and human constraints which stop them from carrying out what they would freely choose to do'. Such constraints may include human rights abuses, water shortage, illiteracy, lack of access to health care and birth control, militarisation of society, environmental degradation and economic deprivation as well as armed conflict at the state and sub-state level. Accordingly, to adopt a broader conception of security is to become aware of threats to security faced by myriad referents in all walks of life and approach them within a comprehensive and dynamic framework cognisant of the interrelationships in between.

The arguments developed by Buzan and Booth calling for broadening security have been criticised on various grounds. One major criticism from within the ranks of Security Studies came from Stephen Walt (1991) as presented in his much-cited 1991 article, 'The Renaissance of Security Studies'. Walt opposed broadening security on two grounds. First, he seemed to worry that a broader security agenda will result in less attention being paid to military threats, which he was keen to stress have not yet been eliminated despite the end of the superpower conflict. Second, argued Walt, a broader conception of security will undermine the coherence of Security Studies as a field of academic study. He believed that broadening the concept would 'destroy [the field's] intellectual coherence and make it more difficult to devise solutions to any of these important problems' (Walt 1991: 213). In short, Walt's argument was that although non-military issues deserved attention, Security Studies was not the place to address them.

Leaving aside the inconsistency of Walt's own position of arguing against broadening but nevertheless drawing up his own broad research agenda (for a critique of Walt's position, see Booth and Herring 1994: 126–7), it should be noted that his arguments are representative of Cold War Security Studies in the way the need to have a clear (that is, military) focus and intellectual coherence is emphasised. These issues were also at the core of attempts during the early 1950s to create a 'scientific' field of Security Studies. Faced with the perceived Soviet threat and the memories of the inter-war era still fresh in people's minds, having a 'scientific' field of Security Studies to produce cumulative knowledge on security issues was deemed vital at the time, and the setting up of Cold War Security Studies in the way it was done should be understood within this context. However, it does not follow that those statist, military-focused and zero-sum thinking and practices that characterised most (but not all) of Cold War Security Studies should be maintained, as Walt seems to suggest.

Moreover, Walt is indeed correct to point out that military threats have not been eliminated. But the proponents of broadening security have never claimed this to be the case. Contra-Walt, those who are in favour of broadening security do not start with the assumption, as he seems to suggest, that the end of the superpower conflict has eliminated most military threats. Rather they maintain that broadening security would enable analysts to view an array of threats in a comprehensive fashion cognisant of the dynamic interrelationships in between. Accordingly, by way of putting non-military threats on the security agenda, it would be possible to prioritise and address them before they become militarised. Then, from a critical perspective, one purpose behind broadening security is to be able to find non-military solutions to a broader range of issues. In other words, Walt's worry regarding a diminution of the attention paid to military issues is misplaced.

It should also be noted that given post-Cold War state practices, Walt's apprehension that broadening security would cause the discipline to lose its theoretical rigour is not grounded. Be it the Central Intelligence Agency that broadened its agenda in the 1990s or governments that opted for 'comprehensive security' from the 1980s onwards, numerous actors have practically been broadening security. A case at hand is Third World policy-makers who have been calling for broader conceptions of security since the 1960s. Indeed, not even governmental practices sustain Walt's arguments.

On the other side of the spectrum of critics of broadening security were Ole Wæver (1995) and Daniel Deudney (1990; see also Huysmans 1995, 2002). Their argument was mainly against the 'securitization' of non-military issues, which, they worried, would become intractable if put on governmental security agendas. Wæver argued that once issues get labelled as 'security' issues, not only a sense of urgency, but also conflictual, zero-sum, militarised mind-sets are invoked thereby rendering intractable the issue at hand. The point here is that Wæver's worries stem from his conflation of broadening security and 'securitization', which, from a critical perspective, need not be the same thing. Let me clarify this point.

In his 1995 essay, 'Securitization and Desecuritization', Wæver presented a trenchant critique of the broadening move whilst seeking to maintain a distance from those such as Walt who were also in favour of a military-focused security agenda, but for a different reason. Wæver built his argument by identifying a 'traditional progressive' approach to security against which he positioned himself. This 'traditional progressive' approach, according to Wæver, is

> (1) to accept two basic premises of the established discourse, first that security is a reality prior to language, is out there (irrespective of whether the conception is 'objective' or 'subjective', is measured in terms of threat or fear), and second the more security, the better; and (2) to argue why security should be *more* than is currently the case, including not only 'xx' but also 'yy', where the latter is environment, welfare, immigration and refugees, etc.
>
> (Wæver 1995: 46–7)

Stated as such, Wæver's argument constituted a crucial corrective to those who actually belonged to the camp of 'traditional progressive' scholars. Exactly who these people are is not clear; Wæver does not name names. What seems to be common to the proponents of the 'traditional progressive' approach is an unquestioning adoption of the nation-state as the referent and an acceptance of threats to security as pre-given and existing 'out there'. Although identifying the problems with the 'traditional progressive' approach does enable Wæver to clarify his own position, it at the same time obscures the differences between multiple voices who called for broadening security, some of whom would not fit comfortably into the 'traditional progressive' straitjacket.

For instance, feminist critics of Security Studies such as Cynthia Enloe (1990) and Ann Tickner (1992, 1995, 1997) have both criticised the military focus of Cold War Security Studies and emphasised the ways in which statist and militarised thinking and practices constituted a threat to women's security. However, neither of the two would fit Wæver's category in that both would reject the notion of security being a 'reality' prior to language. Neither would Booth's approach fit into Wæver's category. For, he views security as a derivative concept rooted in the philosophical world-view of those who define it (Booth 1997). In sum, not all of those who call for broadening security fit Wæver's classification. For, he fails to note that not all those who make a case for adopting a broader conception of security are as unreflective as is Jessica Tuchman Mathews (1990), who argued for a broader security agenda for purposes of 'national security'. By way of setting up a 'straw person' that has significant exceptions, Wæver has weakened his otherwise rather convincing case for 'desecuritization'.

To go back a couple of steps, Wæver (1995: 55) argues that security is a 'speech act'; that is, threats to security do not exist outside discourse, and that a particular issue is constituted as a threat to security via the agency of state elites who 'utter' security in reference to that issue. Presented as such, Wæver's speech act theory may not sit so uneasily with the deepening move of critical approaches, whereby the prevailing conception of security is recognised as deriving from Cold War Security Studies, which embraced realism and sought to serve those in power. In other words, the 'contrast' Wæver seeks to establish between his 'speech act' approach and students of some (but clearly not all) critical approaches who seek to broaden security, need not exist.

However, although Wæver and students of critical approaches to security start from a similar point, they build different arguments and arrive at radically different conclusions. Wæver (1995: 54–5) defines 'securitization' as a process through which state elites '[claim] a special right to use whatever means are necessary to block it' or 'to gain control over it'. Securitization is a 'conservative mechanism' for Wæver. This is different from what students of critical approaches mean by broadening security. From a critical perspective, the security agenda could indeed be broadened by state elites for the purposes mentioned by Wæver. But it could also be broadened by non-state actors who challenge the statist concerns that shape governmental security agendas and seek to address their own and others' concerns that have been marginalised (if not perpetuated) by states. In other words, critical approaches take seriously the agency of non-state actors – whose activities have been labelled as 'grassroots statecraft' (Marsh 1995) – who may seek to broaden security to include non-military issues regardless of states' preferences. Wæver, on the other hand, maintains that securitization is a 'conservative mechanism' operated by state elites, and that it would remain as such. His conclusion is that in the long run security analysts should be seeking to desecuritize issues, by bringing them into the realm of 'ordinary' politics.

Viewed as a critique of Cold War approaches to security, Wæver's essay is an immensely valuable contribution. For, securitization has indeed been used by state elites to keep issues outside the realm of 'ordinary' politics, to justify the mobilisation of resources into addressing military and non-military issues. Middle Eastern oil, for instance, was securitized in the United States in the immediate aftermath of the Second World War. This enabled the Arab-American Oil Company (ARAMCO) to play up the 'communist threat' faced by the Saudi regime in the attempt to ensure the US government's financial support in meeting Saudi demand for a 50 per cent share of the oil royalties. This act (which amounted on the part of the US government to channelling funds to a private firm from the national budget to help maintain its share in Middle Eastern oil markets) was made possible by the prior 'securitization' of oil (Philip 1994: 23, 108; Little 2002: 53–6). The point here is that by helping reveal such examples of securitization as a 'conservative mechanism' whereby state elites use it to move issues outside the realm of 'ordinary' politics, or to justify the allo-cation of meagre resources into one area, Wæver has made a significant contribution to post-Cold War debates on security.

However, the move Wæver makes to associate all proponents of broad-ening security with state elites and their practices of securitization may not be equally welcome, because it is misleading. There arguably is a dif-ference between merely broadening governmental security agendas but relying on traditional practices in addressing them (what Wæver labels as the 'traditional progressive' approach) and broadening security from a critical perspective. The latter also deepens security and seeks to re-conceptualise agency and practice.

Indeed, feminists as well as students of other critical approaches do not only broaden but also deepen security cognisant of the political and con-stitutive character of thinking and writing about security. Furthermore, both have sought to re-conceptualise security in the attempt to move away from statist, military-focused and zero-sum thinking as well as practices. Two cases pointed to by Christine Sylvester (1994) in her work on feminist approaches to security and cooperation are the Greenham Common Peace Camp and women's cooperatives in Harare, Zimbabwe. Students of critical approaches to security have also emphasised theory as a form of practice. In other words, both feminists and students of critical security are aware of the ways in which security has functioned as a 'conservative mechanism'. They nevertheless favour broadening security whilst at the same time seeking to find ways to avoid falling back on traditional mind-sets and practices. This, I submit, amounts to taking broadening more seriously than the 'traditional progressive' approach would allow. To recap, the argument here is that, by way of failing to recognise other responses to securitization, Wæver weakens the case he makes for desecu-ritization (taking issues outside the realm of security to address them through 'ordinary' politics) as an effective way of dealing with issues heretofore not considered as threats to security.

What is also significant to note here is that Wæver (1995: 76; see also Buzan *et al.* 1998) does see some value in adopting a broader conception of security depending on time and place. Nevertheless, his overall argument is that problems should be solved within the realm of 'normal' politics without revoking emergency measures. This, Wæver argues, is what has smoothened the process of European integration and enabled the formation of a 'security community' in Western Europe in the post-War era. Western Europe evolved into a security community 'primarily through a process of "desecuritization"', argues Wæver (1998: 69) – through a process of 'progressive marginalisation of mutual security concerns in favour of other issues'.

When defined by policy-makers, the definition of 'national security' could indeed include anything and everything depending on the policies they wish to pursue. However, when defined by non-state actors such as environmental NGOs 'security' is relatively more likely to be conceived globally and practised locally with a view on the future implications of current policies. Then, although governmental actors have a privileged position in defining 'security', there nevertheless remain opportunities for non-state actors to contest these definitions thereby creating room for debate on governments' security policies (as did the Common Security thinkers during the Cold War) (see Marsh 1995).

Wæver's understanding of 'security' as a 'speech act' puts emphasis on the agency of elites in securitizing issues. 'By definition, something is a security problem when the elites declare it to be so', writes Wæver (1995: 54). Students of constructivist approaches to International Relations, on the other hand, view the process of securitization as contested. Accordingly, they look also at how the speech act is received by its audience (be it other policy-makers or the public) and the extent to which it is 'successful' in remoulding identities and interests (see Milliken 1999; Weldes *et al.* 1999). As Weldes *et al.* (1999: 28) argue, 'the production of insecurity . . . occurs at a variety of sites in world politics. Diverse communities – of states and of both local and regional subjects – reproduce or transform themselves in representations of their insecurities'.

To recap, Wæver's 'speech act' theory provides us with an account of how threats to security are not 'objective' or 'external' to what it is to be secured. In the works of Jutta Weldes *et al.* (1999: 10), we find additional analytical tools that enable one to understand the processes through which 'insecurities and the objects that suffer from insecurity are mutually constituted'. Then, rather than taking for granted pre-existing entities and analysing the 'threats' faced by them, Weldes *et al.* focus on 'representations of danger' (Campbell 1992) and ask 'what do they do?' (Weldes *et al.* 1999: 10). This approach, in turn, is in contrast to the traditional approaches to security that assume the subject(s) of security to be pre-given and fixed and define security as 'securing those fixed entities against objective and external threats' (Weldes *et al.* 1999: 9).

Daniel Deudney's argument against broadening security is based on concerns similar to that of Wæver. Deudney's worry is that the securitization of issues evokes an 'us versus them' mentality whereas in the environmental sphere 'we' not 'they' are the enemy. This is because, as Ulrich Beck (1992) argues, human agency has been complicit in perpetuating if not creating environmental threats. Viewed as such, Deudney's response to the broadening move is rooted in his worry that the Cold War security discourse, which remains prevalent to this day, would be used to address a broader security agenda thereby perpetuating existing threats. As noted above, the Cold War security discourse was characterised by militarised, zero-sum conceptions and practices of security whereby security was sought *against* an adversary.

However, during the 1980s Alternative Security thinkers pointed to the problems involved in such approaches and called for the adoption of common security practices whereby security is sought *with* the adversary not *against* him/her, the point being that security maintained through the threat and use of war has not proven to be stable. Then, if the problem Deudney identifies with adopting a broader conception of security stems from a particular approach to security in theory and practice, an alternative approach that embraces common security would enable environmental issues to be tackled within a security framework but without rendering their solution intractable.

This is not to deny that Wæver's preferred strategy of 'desecuritization' may constitute a solution in the attempt to avoid meeting environmental threats through traditional statist, military-focused and zero-sum practices. However, this would amount to leaving a useful tool (in terms of its mobilisation capacity) such as security to the monopoly of state elites who have not, so far, proven to be sensitive towards the security concerns of peoples (individuals and social groups) (Wyn Jones 1999: 108–12). It would also mean remaining uncritical of the ways in which military threats have traditionally been dealt with by state elites. As noted above, Alternative Security thinkers as well as feminists have presented valuable critiques of, as well as alternatives to, such traditional practices. Taking up from where they have left, the students of critical approaches to security sought to re-conceptualise agency and practice.

To summarise, from the perspective of critical approaches to security, broadening security does not simply mean putting more issues on governmental agendas but re-thinking what security is (or may be) all about. The prior is an offshoot of the latter, but not its main purpose. Security may mean different things to different peoples depending on where they come from, where they are and what they want to do with their lives. This brings us to the question of what the appropriate referent(s) for a broadened security agenda should be.

Referent(s) for security

A plethora of works produced in the post-Cold War era critical of Cold War Security Studies have argued that security should be about referents other than the state, such as individuals, social groups, or a potential global society. Ken Booth (1991b: 319) submitted that, following Kant, 'we should treat people as ends and not means. States, however, should be treated as means and not ends'. Martin Shaw called for a 'sociologically adequate' approach to the study of security when he wrote that

> individual and collective human security do not depend overwhelm-
> ingly on the state and/or ethnic-national context. . . . Security issues
> are faced at all levels of social life.
>
> (Shaw 1993: 110; also see McSweeney 1999)

On the relatively conservative end of this critical spectrum was Barry Buzan (1991a) who called for looking upwards to the systemic level and downwards to the individual level in order to move beyond statist Cold War conceptions of security. Buzan's position is a curious one, for he, whilst critical of statism in Security Studies, nevertheless argued for state-centric analyses thereby ending up reinforcing statism (albeit unintentionally). The argument here needs further clarification.

In *People, States and Fear*, Buzan presented a broader framework for studying security, a framework that covered its economic, societal, environmental and political as well as military dimensions. As regards the referent for security, Buzan maintained that

> security has many potential referent objects. These objects of security
> multiply not only as the membership of the society of states increases,
> but also as one moves down through the state to the level of indi-
> viduals, and up beyond it to the level of the international system as a
> whole.
>
> (Buzan 1991a: 26)

Buzan's study (first published in 1983) marked a crucial corrective to statist Cold War conceptions of security prevalent at the time. However, Buzan, whilst mentioning other potential referents at the sub- and supra-state levels, nevertheless made a case for focusing on the security of states. He built his argument in two moves. First, argued Buzan, the anarchic structure of the international system rendered the units the 'natural focus of security concerns'. Since states were the 'dominant' units, reasoned Buzan (1991a: 19), 'national security' was 'the central issue'.

Buzan's (1991a: 328) second move was to look at the state's agency ('at the end of the day security policy still has to be made by states', he wrote) and infer from its privileged position as a security agent that its security should be prioritised over other potential referents. 'Because policy-making is very largely an activity of states', argued Buzan (1991a: 328), 'there is an important political sense in which national security subsumes all of the other security considerations found at the individual and systemic levels'. This argument, in turn, hints at a confusion between agents and referents. I will come back to this point later. Let us now look more closely at these two moves Buzan made to build up his argument.

Buzan's first move could be criticised first, for its depiction of the international system as anarchical (and therefore the realm of insecurity) and second, for identifying individuals' security with citizenship and the state (the realm of security). This (neo-realist) stance adopted by Buzan has been criticised forcefully by Alexander Wendt (1992) among others (see, for example, Tickner 1995; Wyn Jones 1995b; Krause and Williams 1997b) and will not be dealt with here in detail. Suffice it to note that the anarchical conception of the international system derives from assumptions made by neo-realists about subjectivity and sovereignty, and the reasoning that the absence from the international arena of what makes order possible at the domestic arena (i.e., a central government) is what renders the latter anarchical (Krause and Williams 1997b: 41). There is indeed no world government; but it does not necessarily follow that this makes international security impossible.

Furthermore, the anarchy/order, inside/outside divides introduced by this argument are problematic for, as Keith Krause and Michael Williams (1997b: 43) maintained, both are built upon the assumption that 'security comes from being a citizen, and insecurity from citizens of other states' and that 'threats are directed towards individuals qua citizens (that is, toward their states)'. However, although states are there, in theory, to provide security for their citizens, there remain the practices of many states, which are constant reminders of the fact that some are worse than others in fulfilling their side of the bargain. Added to this is the case of 'gangster' states that constitute a major threat to the security of their own citizens (see Wheeler 1996).

Moreover, as Ann Tickner (1992: 57) reminds us, the international arena is not the only realm characterised by the absence of mechanisms of order and there may be construed yet another anarchy/order divide – that of the 'boundary between a public domestic space protected, at least theoretically, by the rule of law and the private space of the family' which is not always as well protected, particularly concerning the case of domestic violence. In sum, the first move Buzan makes to justify the privileged position of the security of states is contested in both theory and practice.

Buzan's second move, that of underlining the dominant agency of the state to fortify the case for state-centred analyses of security, has been the less contested of the two. This is partly because states have had the licence to legitimate use of violence and therefore are better endowed than any other agent to provide for (certain aspects of) security. But, perhaps more significant is the fact that students of International Relations have not been oriented to look at the agency of actors other than the state concerning security issues (Turner 1998: 25–42; Bleiker 2000). The prominence of the state's agency in the economic and financial sectors has for long been challenged, but it is yet to be de-throned in (military-focused) security issues. Hence the prevalent focus on states as central actors in world politics, i.e. state-centrism.

A broader security agenda, such as the one propounded by Buzan, on the other hand, requires the analyst to look at agents other than the state, such as transnational corporations, grassroots movements, and individuals, instead of restricting his/her analysis to the state's agency. This is essential not only because states, as noted above, are not always able (or willing) to fulfil their side of the bargain in providing for their citizens' security, but also because there already are agents other than states – be it social movements or intellectuals – who are striving to provide for the differing security needs of peoples (themselves and others). In other words, a broadened conception of security such as that of Buzan should be coupled with moving away from state-centrism and paying attention to the agency of non-state actors. This is necessarily because broadening security without attempting a re-conceptualisation of agency would result in falling back on the agency of the state in meeting non-military threats to security. The problem with resorting to the agency of the state in meeting such threats is that states may not be the most suitable actors to cope with them. The state being the most equipped actor in coping with some kinds of threats does not necessarily mean that it is competent (or willing) enough to cope with all.

Related to Buzan's argument regarding the state's dominant agency in security matters is Mohammed Ayoob's interjection into the debate. He has been prominent amongst critics of Cold War Security Studies with his submission that in the case of Third World states, what is needed is more not less state-centrism. In *The Third World Security Predicament*, Ayoob emphasised the need for adopting an 'explicitly state-centric' definition when studying security in the Third World on the grounds that the state is *the* provider of security. It should be pointed out that Ayoob does not neglect other dimensions of security such as the economic or environmental. He rather thinks these other dimensions should be taken into consideration only if they 'become acute enough to acquire political dimensions and threaten state boundaries, state institutions, or regime survival' (Ayoob 1995: 9). This is necessarily because, argues Ayoob, the Third World states, as opposed to states in the developed world, are still busy with state-building and therefore in need of being given the time and space to construct 'credible and legitimate political apparatuses with the capacity to provide order – in many respects, the foremost social value – within the territories under their juridical control' (Ayoob 1997: 131).[12]

Ayoob's analysis constitutes a crucial corrective to the outward-directed Cold War conceptions of security, and a reminder of the often neglected domestic political dimension of the (in)security problem in the Third World. Nevertheless, criticisms made above regarding the problematic character of Buzan's assumption about the state being the provider of security in the domestic arena are valid for Ayoob's stance as well and need not be repeated here. Moreover, as noted above, by way of taking the Western developed state as a finished project, Ayoob fails to push his argument to its logical conclusion and call for a more comprehensive conception of security that is cognisant of the character of the state as an 'unfinished project' (Devetak 1995). After all, state building is an ongoing process; its identity in need of re-inscription, its sovereignty in need of reaffirmation by the recognition of other states and the symbolic acts of diplomacy (Campbell 1992, 1993). Furthermore, as Georg Sørensen (1996: 371) has argued, the problem with realist-dominated International Relations theory in general and Security Studies in particular, has had 'less to do with an exaggerated focus on the state than a lack of analysis of the state'.

To put it in a nutshell, Ayoob's (1995: 4) argument is that if Third World states were given the time to grow up to become 'adequate' states, the problem of security at the international as well as domestic levels could be better addressed (see also Ayoob 2002). This argument, in turn, echoes Buzan's (1991b) call for the establishment of 'mature anarchy' through creating 'strong states'.[13] One crucial problem with the logic of this type of argument is that it is rooted in a statist conception of security that privileges the security of states over that of other referents. Viewed through such statist lenses, the security concerns of individuals and social groups are marginalised if not rendered invisible. The argument here is not to suggest that 'weak' states of the world need not strengthen their infrastructures or try and boost their legitimacy. Rather, the argument here is that a conception of security that privileges the security of the state to the extent suggested by Ayoob may not be helpful in understanding the problem of (in)security in the Third World. The practical implication of Ayoob's (and Buzan's) argument is that security at the domestic and international level should be sought through strengthening the infrastructure and boosting the legitimacy as well as coercive power of the state, which, in turn, would have detrimental effects on the security of other potential referents at the sub-state level (see Al-Mashat 1985: 33–4). Hence Barnett's (2002a: 57) point that Ayoob's approach 'elevates the perspective and interests of the Third World regime and marginalises the knowledge claims of the society that the regime now constructs as a threat'.

Moreover, Ayoob's position not only neglects the security of other potential referents, but also fails to establish crucial connections between the problem of security in the Third World and those individuals and social groups in the world as a whole, whose security is threatened directly or indirectly by the policies of states. After all, as noted in the previous section, those states that provide security for their citizens are able to do so largely due to their privileged position in the international economic system, which further deepens the security predicament of some others who live in the peripheries of the world. As Tickner (1995: 186) has argued,

> Buzan's claim that strong states can successfully provide security might be challenged by marginalised groups, such as women and minorities, whose economic security is often compromised when military security takes priority.... even strong states implement dubious policies that are not always formulated democratically.

Some invaluable insight into these processes is provided in Cynthia Enloe's works (1990, 1993) where she has laid bare how the United States – a strong state which is supposed to provide for its citizens' security – has built its security on the insecurities of some women at home and abroad. In other words, the record of strong states does not always back Buzan's and Ayoob's arguments.

Added to these is the fact that the process of building strong states defies underestimation or being viewed with rose-tinted spectacles; for, it is a long, brutal and often violent process. In this sense, remembering how state building in Western Europe 'cost tremendously in death, suffering, loss of rights, and unwilling surrender of land, goods, or labour', should serve as a reminder that there is very little in the Western European state building experience to be idealised (quoted in Sørensen 1996: 376).[14] Furthermore, there is no guarantee that building strong states in the Third World would lead to 'stable, liberal democratic governance', as Ayoob (1997: 135) seems to expect. There is also the impact made by the forces of globalisation and fragmentation that often mitigate against the creation of strong states (Sørensen 1996: 376). And lastly, but perhaps most importantly, these statist approaches foreclose alternative non-statist conceptions of security at the international level thereby making it more difficult to imagine alternative futures that are not built around states as the primary focus of loyalty, decision-making power and practice. This is necessarily because the attempts to achieve security via establishing strong states at the domestic level are often detrimental to community building at the global level for it diminishes peoples' respect for difference. This brings us back to the point made earlier about the continuing reign of statism in Security Studies.

As mentioned above, statism in Security Studies has taken many guises. Some, such as Ayoob, are self-conscious and open about their statist credentials (see Ayoob 2002). Some, such as Buzan, on the other hand, argue against statism but nevertheless end up reinforcing it. As noted above, Buzan's argument (that since it is states that act for security, their security should be given primacy in our analyses) is a clear indication of his confusion of agents and referents. By way of this rather uncritical acceptance of the state's agency as being central, the agency of non-state actors is at best marginalised and at worst rendered invisible.

In a recent work co-authored with Ole Wæver and Jaap de Wilde, Buzan tried to address this problem of the confusion between referents and agents that obfuscated his analysis in his previous work (Buzan *et al.* 1998). Pointing to the difference between adopting a 'state-centric approach' and operating in a 'state-dominated field', Buzan *et al.* (1998: 37) clarified their position as that of the latter. Consider the following quotation:

> We do not say security is only about the state (although there is much truth to the argument that the state is the ideal security actor) nor that security is equally available to all – states and other social movements. Security is an area of competing actors, but it is a biased one in which the state is generally privileged as the actor historically endowed with security tasks and most adequately structured for the purpose.

To be fair, this explanation does indeed acknowledge 'the difference between a state-centric approach and a state-dominated field' (Buzan *et al.* 1998: 37). Furthermore, there is no denying that the state has for long been the agent best endowed to meet (certain types of) challenges to security (as it remains to be the sole agent that has the licence to legitimate use of violence). However, I still find contestable Buzan *et al.*'s argument that their analysis is not state-centric.

Since Buzan *et al.* do not look at the agency of actors other than the state when it comes to decision-making and especially taking action, it could be inferred that they assume states to be the agents of peace and security. Non-state actors do crop up in their analysis to try and force an issue onto the security agenda (such as the environmental groups lobbying for action to be taken against a pollutant factory), to defend themselves when charged for constituting a threat to security (such as the company that owns the pollutant factory) or as referents whose security is under threat (as with individuals and social groups that are affected by this pollution), but no actor other than the state is considered to have the potential to act towards actually meeting this threat (whereas nowadays it is often the case that environmental groups would take action themselves or try and reach out for support from international environmental groups like Greenpeace or Friends of the Earth before trying to invoke the agency of the state that may or may not choose to step in afterwards). Then, it is by way of looking solely at the agency of the state that Buzan *et al.* end up moving only partially away from presenting a state-centric analysis.

Furthermore, if Security Studies is dominated by states – as Buzan *et al.* suggest – it is partly because security analysts got it that way, not because there are no other potential referents and agents that challenge the state's dominance. In other words, the difference between these two positions which Buzan *et al.* try to establish – the difference between state-centrism and operating in a state-dominated field – dissolves when the theory/practice relationship is conceived as mutually constitutive. State-centric approaches to security do not simply reflect a state-dominated field, but also help constitute it. The argument here is not meant to deny the salience of the roles states play in the realm of security; on the contrary, they remain to be significant actors with crucial roles to play. Rather it is to argue that the state's dominant position as the actor best endowed to provide (certain dimensions of) security does not justify privileging its security; nor does it warrant adopting a state-centred conception of security in our studies. Accordingly, Buzan *et al.*'s approach, by way of failing to recognise the important role that is already being played by non-state actors, ends up giving the state's agency more credit than it deserves. This is also why the distinction between state-centrism and statism blurs in that an analytical choice made by the analyst (i.e. choosing to focus at state's agency) has had normative implications (according primacy to the state). To accord primacy in our security analyses to the state (i.e., state-centrism) does not simply reflect a 'reality' out there, but helps reinforce statism in Security Studies by way of making it harder to imagine non-statist futures.

Third World security thinking

'Southern Instability, Security and Western Concepts: On an Unhappy Marriage and the Need for a Divorce', the title of an article by Caroline Thomas (1989b) summed the main argument put forward by most of the post-Cold War writings on security in the Third World. Thomas, along with other students of Third World security such as Mohammed Ayoob, Brian Job and Yezid Sayigh, maintained that the concepts of Cold War Security Studies were far from being able to provide a full account of (in)security in the Third World (Thomas 1987, 1989b, 1991; Ayoob 1994, 1997, 2002; Job 1992a; Sayigh 1990). This, she argued, was because the character of the security problems faced by the Third World states were different from those faced by their developed counterparts. This led her to call for an alternative approach to study security in the Third World, an approach that puts more emphasis on the domestic political and developmental dimensions of security.

Yezid Sayigh (1990) maintained that it was the 'crisis of the state' that was the major source of insecurity for developing states. Cold War Security Studies, despite all its state-centrism, had been surprisingly silent when it came to conceptualising states, state formation and consolidation. This neglect of the domestic dimension of insecurity, in turn, failed to provide fuller accounts of security in the Third World, concluded Sayigh.

Brian Job (1992b) took up this issue and pushed it further when he argued that the concepts of Cold War Security Studies, such as the security dilemma, were not helpful in accounting for the security problems faced by developing states; for threats to their security emanated from inside, not necessarily outside the state. The conception of security adopted by the students of Cold War Security Studies, argued Job, needed to be turned on its head within the Third World context. Job's conclusion was that the concept of 'insecurity dilemma' would be more helpful in understanding security in the developing world.

However, notwithstanding the strength of Job's argument regarding the limits of the security dilemma in accounting for the security predicament of the Third World, his assumption of a certain degree of external security entertained by Third World states is contestable. Put in other words, Job's assumption holds only when security is conceived in purely military terms. As Thomas (1987) has maintained, Third World states are very vulnerable *vis-à-vis* their external environment when economic or environmental dimensions of security are concerned. Furthermore, it would be misleading to suggest that it is developing states alone that are concerned with the domestic dimension of security. Ethnic conflicts that have haunted developed states of the West indicate that the security dilemma has limited analytical utility anywhere in the world when accounting for the domestic dimension of security.[15] Lastly, it should also be noted that 'states are never finished as entities'. As David Campbell (1992: 11) argued:

> The tension between the demands of identity and the practices that constitute it can never be fully resolved, because the performative nature of identity can never be fully revealed. This paradox inherent to being renders states in permanent need of reproduction: with no ontological status apart from the many and varied practices that constitute their reality, states are (and have to be) always in a process of becoming.

As Campbell showed in his study on US identity, it is through the making of foreign policy that the United States has re-inscribed its identity. Seen in this light, it is not only developing states but also developed states (such as the United States) that constantly busy themselves with state building (see also Devetak 1995). In sum, deepening our insight into state building and consolidation, as called for by Sayigh, would help enhance our understanding of security not only in the developing world, but also in the world as a whole.

On the relatively conservative end of this critical spectrum was Mohammed Ayoob (1995, 2002) who emphasised the ways in which the predicament of Third World states are different from the West, and made a case for prioritising the security of states. In a deliberate echo of the distinction Barry Buzan (1991a: 96–107) drew between weak and strong states, Ayoob (1995: 115) maintained that Third World states are 'junior' states; they are at an early stage of state-making, and 'as the European experience has shown, violence and conflict are inevitable at this stage'. States in the West had centuries to reach their current stage, argued Ayoob, and if Third World states are going to grow up and become 'proper' states, they should be allowed to prioritise state security for a while. Accordingly, Ayoob defined security

> in relation to vulnerabilities that threaten to, or have the potential to, bring down or significantly weaken state structures, both territorial and institutional, and regimes which preside over these structures and profess to represent them internationally.
>
> (Ayoob 1995: 15)

Note here that Ayoob's definition does not include a reference to the security of other potential referents such as individuals or social groups. He maintained that the security of state is of prime importance within the Third World context and that individuals and groups might have to endure some insecurity if the ultimate purpose is the enhancement of the security of the state. By arguing that state security should be prioritised on the way to becoming a 'proper' state, Ayoob not only presented a state-centric analysis, but also called for more, not less, statism.

If one is to follow Ayoob's logic, the security of other referents is deemed of significance so far as this has an impact upon the legitimacy and stability of the state/regime, and the policy-making and implementation capacity of the government. This is why, argued Ayoob (1994: 16), those approaches that focus on individuals' security are 'far removed from Third World realities', for in the Third World it is the security of the state that is the priority. In reply to Booth's call for conceptualising security as emancipation, Ayoob wrote:

> It may be . . . possible to equate emancipation with security in Western Europe (although grave reservations are in order even on that score). But it would be extremely far-fetched and intellectually disingenuous to do the same in the case of the Third World, where basic problems of state legitimacy, political order, capital accumulation are far from being solved and may even be getting worse.
>
> (Ayoob 1995: 11)

The statist assumptions that underpin Ayoob's argument will be discussed in greater detail in the final section of this chapter. Suffice it to make three brief points here. First, from Booth's critical perspective, emancipation is not an added extra, something to be aspired to after all other aspects of security are achieved, as Ayoob seems to suggest. Defining security as emancipation, according to Booth, means adopting an alternative conceptualisation of security that incorporates the environmental, societal, economic as well as political and military dimensions of security faced by multiple referents (see Booth 1991b, 1994a, 1997). Indeed, Ayoob's preference for focusing on the political and economic dimensions of state security is challenged by some other students of Third World security such as Abdel-Monem Al-Mashat (1985: 33), who maintained that the practical implication of such statist approaches is the state's domination over society at the expense of individuals and social groups' concerns. Second, the problems identified by Ayoob, such as state legitimacy, political order and capital accumulation are not isolated to Third World states. All states have had to cope with similar problems, albeit with varying degrees. The third and related point is that, following Thomas (1991; also see Pasha 1996), it is not possible to account for (let alone address) such problems faced by developing states without searching for some of its roots in the practices of developed states.[16] Hence the call of critical approaches for a comprehensive approach that takes into account multiple dimensions of threats to the security of myriad referents in different parts of the world.

The overall point here is that although the critiques of students of Third World security are helpful in pointing to the limited analytical utility of the concepts of Cold War Security Studies in understanding the security predicament of developing states, their conclusion that security in the Third World should be looked at through different analytical lenses is not helpful. This is not to deny the differences between security problems faced by developing states and their more developed counterparts. The argument here, to take up Thomas's (1989b) analogy, is that if the marriage between Third World states and Western concepts has been an unhappy one, the solution may be found in counselling for both sides rather than a divorce.

Indeed, students of Third World security often underestimate the degree to which their critiques of Cold War Security Studies have contributed to a re-thinking of security by helping to reveal its limitations in accounting for the domestic political and developmental dimensions of security and the need for broader agenda, as well as emphasising the linkages between security needs of myriad actors in different parts of the world. Failing to realise the contributions they have made in the past and could potentially make in the future, most students of Third World security have so far tended to restrict their conclusions to developing states, refraining from commenting on the implications of their analyses on the bigger picture of Security Studies. However, as Amitav Acharya maintained

> the security predicament of Third World states provides a helpful point of departure for appreciating the limitations of the dominant

understanding and moving it toward a broader and more inclusive notion of security. This redefinition is crucial to understanding the problems of conflict and order in the post-Cold War period.

(Acharya 1997: 301)

Notwithstanding Acharya's call, the mainstream tendency has been one of focusing on the different character of Third World states and their security needs. As a result, the critiques presented by students of Third World security regarding the underdeveloped state of core concepts such as state and security have yet to be fully incorporated into Security Studies.

Critical Security Studies

In 1998 Critical Security Studies was presented by some of its students as a candidate for 'the Next Stage' in security thinking and practices (Bilgin *et al.* 1998). Critical Security Studies has yet to fulfil this promise of becoming the next stage in security thinking. The September 11 attacks have only added to the already existing pessimism in Security Studies (that draws partly from its roots in realism) in that it has become more and more difficult to make a case for the adoption of critical approaches to security. Yet, a crucial point to be made is that adopting critical approaches to study security does not mean adopting an 'optimistic' attitude regarding the future of world politics. On the contrary, many students turn to critical approaches because of their dissatisfaction with what the existing approaches promise regarding the future – that is, not because they think the future would be better than the past, but because they think the future might be even worse than the past unless the necessary precautions are taken here and now. Nor does it mean to forego thinking about what needs to be done 'here and now' in favour of presenting long-term perspectives that neglect policy needs. Although critical approaches adopt long-term perspectives to show how we have come to be the way we are, they are necessarily interested in shaping the future. Notwithstanding the differences among students of critical approaches as to their normative commitments, they all share the basic assumption that insecurities are constructed by human beings themselves (see Farrell 2002 for a review of the constructivist security studies literature).

The aim of this section of Chapter 1 is to introduce a critical security perspective, which will then be utilised to analyse the Middle Eastern case in the rest of the study. My purpose here is not to provide an exhaustive overview of the origins and growth of critical approaches to security. Rather, this section seeks to clarify the key concepts and analytical moves central to critical thinking on security and most relevant to this study. Here I will look at 'Broadening security', 'Deepening security', 'Constitutive theory', 'Agency', and 'Practice'.

Broadening security

As an analytical move, broadening security entails questioning the military-focused security agendas of Cold War Security Studies and calling for opening up the agenda to include other non-military threats. In making this move, students of critical approaches to security have followed in the footsteps of Peace Researchers who, from the 1960s onwards, had gradually widened their conceptions of peace and violence. Distinguishing between 'negative' and 'positive' peace, John Galtung argued that peace defined as here by the absence of armed conflict is 'negative peace'. 'Positive peace', maintained Galtung, means the absence of not only direct physical violence but also indirect (and sometimes unintentional) 'structural violence' – that is, those socio-economic institutions and relations that oppress human beings by preventing them from realising their potential. Galtung (1969, 1996) also emphasised that to attain 'positive peace', it is not enough to seek to eliminate violence; existing institutions and relations should be geared towards the enhancement of dialogue, cooperation and solidarity among peoples coupled with a respect for the environment. It is also worth noting here that for Galtung (1996: 265) peace is not a static concept; it is rather a process (as with security and emancipation for students of critical approaches to security; see Booth 1991b; Wyn Jones 1999).

Building upon Peace Researchers' broadening of the concepts of violence and peace that took human beings as the referent, students of critical approaches to security broadened security to include – in Ken Booth's words – 'all those physical and human constraints which stop them from carrying out what they would freely choose to do' (Booth 1991b: 319; Booth 1999b: 40). Such constraints may include human rights abuses, water shortage, illiteracy, lack of access to health care and birth control, militarisation of society, environmental degradation and economic deprivation as well as armed conflict at the state- and sub-state level. Accordingly, the purpose behind broadening security, from a critical perspective, is to become aware of threats to security faced by referents in all walks of life and approach them within a comprehensive and dynamic framework cognisant of the interrelationships in between.

Understood as such, broadening security does not simply mean putting more issues on governments' security agendas, but opening up security to provide a richer picture that includes all issues that engender insecurity. In other words, although the broadening of governmental security agendas is an offshoot of broadening security, it is not its main purpose. After all, the US Central Intelligence Agency also broadened its agenda in the 1990s (Johnson 1993), but sought to address them through its traditional practices.

Moreover, presenting the broadening move simply as one of adding more issues to governmental security agendas would be misleading in that those who drew up Cold War security agendas were never totally ignorant of non-military dimensions of security (see Baldwin 1997; McSweeney 1999). Although broader conceptualisations of the earlier years had been replaced, by the mid-1950s, by more military-focused approaches, economic, political and even environmental issues were never totally excluded from national security agendas as noted above. For instance, water scarcity has always been considered a security issue in the Middle East. Likewise, the issue of unhindered flow of oil at reasonable prices was successfully securitized by US policy-makers in the post-Second World War period. As Bill McSweeney (1999: 35; also see Walker 1997: 75–6) has argued, the problem with Cold War Security Studies was not only that it emphasised the military dimension of security to the neglect of other dimensions, but also that it focused on military and non-military issues from a statist perspective.

Therefore, it was the narrow conception of security adopted by Cold War Security Studies, compounded by its statist outlook and zero-sum thinking and practices that was the problem. Singling out one of these dimensions (i.e. narrow security agendas) and identifying it as the problem whilst neglecting others betrays an underestimation of the problems involved in Cold War approaches to security – some of which are still apparent in post-Cold War thinking and practices. Such an underestimation is also apparent in the 'new security' approaches of Bassam Tibi (1998a) and Lenore Martin (1998), who have sought to adopt a broadened security agenda when analysing Middle Eastern dynamics, while remaining within a state-centric framework that privileges states as the referents of security.

It could further be argued that the debate about broadening security and especially the calls for 'desecuritization' are all rooted in such an underestimation (see the discussion above). It should suffice to say here that conceptualising security in a narrow, military-focused manner has so far helped gloss over other structurally based (economic, political, societal or environmental) security concerns. Dealing with the military security agenda is always necessary, but the adoption of military-focused and determined security agendas (coupled with zero-sum conceptions and practices of security) have so far caused a diversion of valuable resources into the military sector in the Middle East. The ensuing militarisation of the region not only made it difficult to meet traditional (i.e. military) challenges, but also undermined regional states' capacity to provide welfare to their citizens thereby exacerbating non-military threats to security as voiced by various actors.[17]

Deepening security

From a Critical Security Studies perspective, re-thinking security also requires deepening one's conception of security to be able to see the links between security discourses and the worldviews from which they derive (Booth 1997: 111; 1996: 337). Concepts such as 'national security', 'security policy', and 'Security Studies' are all inter-subjectively constituted. As Booth (1997: 110–12) has maintained, different worldviews and political philosophies deliver different discourses about what 'security' is or may be. Or, as R.B.J. Walker (1997: 63) has argued, 'questions about security cannot be separated from the most basic questions of political theory'. For example, if the conception of Arab national security adopted by Middle Eastern actors is different from the US conception of regional security in the Middle East, this is because the two are rooted in different worldviews. Becoming able to grasp the ways in which the two are different, rather than explaining away the differences solely with reference to the promises of Arab nationalism (or with reference to the 'Arab mind' in true 'Orientalist' fashion) requires students of Security Studies to embrace the deepening move and understand security as a derivative concept.

By way of deepening security, students of critical approaches to security take inspiration from two main sources. The first is Robert Cox's (1981: 182) maxim, 'theory is always *for* someone and *for* some purpose', and the second is the feminist motto, 'the personal is political' (Enloe 1990). These formulations seek to reveal the linkages between theorist and theory, and thinking about security and acting for security. From a critical perspective, whether they are self-conscious and open about it or not, all approaches to security have normative concerns embedded within them. Such concerns may include the maintenance of the status quo in the international system or the promotion of state sovereignty, at times to the detriment of individual and group rights. Critical approaches, on the other hand, favour an explicitly normative security agenda based on human emancipation. This is in contrast to Cold War approaches to security, which, under the guise of objectivism, privileged the security of the state (or certain states), and, in Walker's (1997: 63) words, 'allowed questions of political theory to curdle into caricature'.

Furthermore, viewing alternative conceptions of security as rooted in alternative understandings of 'what politics is and can be all about' (Booth 1997: 111) serves as a reminder that having a better grasp of security requires students of security to question – in Walker's words – 'how the modern subject is being reconstituted and then ask what security could possibly mean in relation to it' (Walker 1997: 78). The point here is that conceiving security in a narrow manner merely with reference to military issues and the state betrays a statist approach (embedded in realism) that could only help produce more of the same. Embracing statism affirms the centrality of the state as the primary referent of and agent for security, thereby challenging the 'possibility of referring to humanity in general – and by extension, to world politics or world security – in any meaningful way' (Walker 1997: 73). Deepening security, on the other hand, leaves open the possibility of the transformation of political community.

Lastly, deepening security enables students of security to further broaden the security agenda. A broader conception of security was defined above as inclusive of 'those physical and human constraints which stop people [as individuals and groups] from carrying out what they would freely choose to do' (Booth 1998b: 319). The key phrase here is 'what they would freely choose to do'; for, it suggests an element of choice. People, however, may not be presented with choices. Or, to put it differently, their choices may not be apparent to them because of the way security discourses are set up. The deepening move, however, enables students of critical approaches to security to investigate how security discourses are constructed. Depending on the theory or theories employed, security discourses close off certain possibilities whilst opening others; they lay the groundwork for the practices of politicians, soldiers and 'ordinary people' by providing the assumptions on which they operate and the norms with which they judge (see Dalby 1990: esp. pp. 4–29). Realism, for example, helped to produce the Cold War discourse in the United States. Its statist norms helped to legitimise certain security practices whilst marginalising calls for 'common', 'cooperative' or 'global security'. Critical approaches to security, in turn, seek to present peoples with a different reading of their situation, taking into account issues that were marginalised if not rendered invisible by Cold War security discourses; they point to choices that were made in the past and unfulfilled potential that could have been tapped.

The task of presenting peoples with choices that have been obscured by prevailing discourses should not be interpreted as a claim to know about peoples' 'real interests'. The argument here is *not* that students of critical security can point to what peoples' 'real interests' are. Rather the argument is that, given the ways in which dominant discourses shape security agendas, one could reasonably assume that regional security agendas could have been set up differently, had other discourses come to prevail. For example, during the Cold War 'female illiteracy' was not treated as a threat to security in the Middle East although it was (and still is) at the root of problems such as population rise, unemployment, lack of awareness of health issues, and women's low life expectancy.[18] This, however, could not be taken as evidence that women in the Middle East chose not to define illiteracy as a threat to their security. It cannot be assumed that Middle Eastern women made such a choice, especially if they were not aware of the choices available to them. As Fatima Mernissi (1996) has argued, many Arab women were discouraged from making any 'radical' demands from their governments; such 'radical' demands included the right to basic education. Thus, by way of continual invocation of the need to divert resources into the military sector in order to eradicate the last remnants of colonialism and/or address the threat posed by Israel, policy-makers made women feel unpatriotic if they asked for more resources to be put into their own well-being. The point is that prevailing

security discourses that emphasised state security and privileged the channelling of meagre resources into the military obscured women's choices.

By presenting female illiteracy as a security issue that was kept off
regional security agendas, I do not claim to know what Middle Eastern
women's 'real interests' were/are (although one could reasonably argue
that many would prefer not to remain illiterate if given the choice).[19]
Rather, by pointing to feminist thinking about security that embraced
broader conceptions of security, I argue that had Cold War security discourses not prevailed, the issue of 'female illiteracy' could have been
raised as a security issue. Critical approaches to security, by way of deepening security and pointing to the links between theory and theorist, security
thinking and practices, aims to raise peoples' awareness of their choices –
those that were made in the past and those that are available at present.

Constitutive theory

Critical approaches reject the scientific-objectivist conception of theory
and theory/practice relationship adopted by students of Cold War Security Studies. This is because the adoption of an objectivist conception of
theory and the theory/practice relationship resulted in essentially normative theories of Cold War Security Studies masquerading as 'objective'
approaches to international phenomena and being viewed as 'knowledge'
whilst the writings of their critics were presented as propaganda. The
following quotation by John Garnett illustrates how Cold War approaches
to security failed to reflect upon the normative character of strategic theorising. Garnett (1987: 13) maintained that the moral dimension of military power is

> a quite separate subject from strategic studies in that it requires a
> quite different expertise, and it is therefore unfair to blame specialists
> in the latter for their lack of competence in it.

Though research in a subject does not necessarily imply approval of it,
it would nevertheless be wrong to overlook the normative baggage strategists bring to their subject. For, issues of morality are not optional extras
to be left, as Garnett (1987: 13) suggested, to 'theologians, philosophers,
and political scientists' only. By choosing to privilege the security of states,
often to the detriment of individuals and groups whose security the state,
in theory, is there to provide for, state-centric approaches already have
intrinsic (if not always explicit) normative commitments. In Garnett's case
this commitment manifests itself as statism. In other words, the moral
choice is not in choosing to study nuclear strategy or not, but in deciding
what to say about it; and decisions always have moral choices embedded in
them (see Green 1973).

The objectivist conception of the theory/practice relationship adopted by students of Cold War Security Studies not only helped to gloss over the normative character of strategic theorising but also proved crucial in that it did not reveal the mutually constitutive relationship between the two.[20] Perhaps the best example of the constitutive relationship between security conceptions and practices is the symbiotic relationship between Security Studies and the Cold War. As argued above, Security Studies is a product of the Cold War. The academic field not only originated in but also thrived upon the Cold War environment. The concepts, assumptions and findings of Cold War Security Studies, in turn, helped sustain the Cold War.

Mary Kaldor's *The Imaginary War* (1990) is an excellent illustration of how Cold War security discourses expressed and legitimised power relationships worldwide, and helped to maintain social cohesion within the two blocs thereby sustaining the conflictual relationship between them. Throughout her analysis, Kaldor stresses the role played by strategic theories, explaining how they became representations of politics instead of playing the objective or neutral role of explanation assigned to them by realist Strategic Studies, and maintains that 'evolving strategies did not necessarily bear much relation to actual military capabilities' (Kaldor 1990: 192).

Kaldor's argument is that 'the very unreality of strategic discussions contributed to the imaginary nature of the East–West confrontation, allowing it to become a deep, ongoing, unrealisable fear' (Kaldor 1990: 192–3). The role theories play, however, should not be over-emphasised. The growth of actual military capabilities was also influenced 'by institutional factors such as inter-service rivalry, technological innovation or industrial pressure' (Kaldor 1990: 192) that fed into strategic theorising via institutions such as the RAND Corporation, which was a major scene of strategic theorising in the United States especially during the 1950s and 1960s (see Kaplan 1983).

Not all authors re-considering Cold War history would reach the same conclusions as Kaldor. Colin Gray (1992: 612), for instance, blames the propagation of 'erroneous' or 'shoddy' ideas, such as stable deterrence, collective security and arms control, for what he termed Cold War policy 'errors'. In contrast to Kaldor's (1990: 7) starting point, that 'any explanation of natural and social phenomena ... is partial', Gray views the theory/practice relationship as one of the prior informing the latter, but very little else. He accordingly sees the academic study of strategy as an objective enterprise that 'can and should provide knowledge useful for official practitioners of strategy' (Gray 1992: 611). Consider the following statement by Garnett: 'We need more, not less, objectivity if we are to survive' (Garnett 1987: 22–3). Gray (1992: 626) concurs: 'Strategic study (unlike the strategist) is value-neutral and topic-indifferent'.

The positions of Gray and Garnett regarding the theory/practice relationship are similar to that of their conception of theory. Both authors are in favour of and open about the role theories play in informing practice. However, their conception of practice is restricted in that they understand practice as policy-making and implementation at governmental level. In this sense, those who do not engage in issues directly relevant for policy-making are not considered to be engaging with practice. This position hints at a narrow view of politics where it is considered only to do with governance at the state level. This, in turn, flows from the objectivist position adopted by the authors where the study of strategy in particular and academic enterprise in general is viewed as a politics-free zone. This is a powerful move, for once an approach is regarded as 'objective', others that are critical of it are immediately labelled at best 'subjective' or 'political' in a derogatory sense, and at worst 'propaganda'.

It is not only the conception of practice adopted by Gray and Garnett but also that of theory that is restricted in that both conceive theory as 'problem-solving theory', in Robert Cox's (1981) terms; it is there to assist policy-makers in solving problems (Gray 1992: 626–31). Security Studies, in this sense, is supposed to deal with issues that are deemed problematic by policy-makers,[21] leaving untouched other issues that do not make it to governmental agendas. This, in turn, creates a vicious circle where issues to be put on the security agenda are decided by policy-makers and analysed by those who they consider as 'experts'. Those who propound alternative views are dismissed as mere propagandists and the issues they identified, such as 'structural violence', are not allowed on security agendas. This position is still prevalent in certain strands of security thinking in the post-Cold War era (see, for example, Walt 1991).

Moreover, Garnett argues that strategists, even if they adopted a critical stance (and were allowed to get their voices heard) would not make much difference. He maintains that:

> if a conflict-oriented view of international politics has caught the public imagination ... this is not because it is propagated by strategists but because it offers the man in the street a more plausible interpretation of international reality than any of the alternatives to which he has been exposed.
>
> (Garnett 1987: 22)

This statement is yet another manifestation of Garnett's restricted notion of theory (which, in turn, is representative of Cold War thinking on security). After all, what the 'man in the street' views as 'a more plausible interpretation of international reality' (Garnett 1987: 22) is shaped by theories and discourses that were/are dominant at the time.[22]

Garnett's statement also hints at an underestimation of the power of theories in informing not only governmental policies, but also individuals' conceptions of the world. These conceptions that individuals absorb, accept and live uncritically constitute what Gramsci calls 'common sense' which helps sustain the status quo by 'making situations of inequality and oppression appear to them as natural and unchangeable' (Forgacs 1988). To go back to Kaldor's argument regarding the Cold War, it was the 'imaginary war' discourse of realist Security Studies that informed men and women in North America and Western Europe of the relevance, legitimacy and inescapability of power politics, tough responses and brinkmanship.

In sum, it was these objectivist conceptions of theory and the theory/practice relationship, a restricted notion of theory as 'problem-solving theory' and practice as governmental policy-making that have, for long, sustained an underestimation of the role theories play in helping constitute 'reality' and narrowed the ethical and political horizons of security thinking and practice. Contra Garnett, the role of theories is not to take these conceptions as given but to try and enter into people's 'common sense' and to present them a critical understanding of their own situation.

Accordingly, theory is viewed as constitutive of the 'reality' it seeks to explain. As Steve Smith has argued:

> Theories do not simply explain or predict. They tell us what possibilities exist for human action and intervention; they define not merely our explanatory possibilities but also our ethical and political horizons.
>
> (Smith 1996: 13)

The argument here is not that theories 'create' the world in a philosophical idealist sense of the term, but that theories help organise knowledge, which, in turn, informs, enables, privileges or legitimises certain practices whilst inhibiting or marginalising others (as with the relationship between Middle Eastern security discourse and the 'invention' of the 'Middle East').

Given this self-constitutive potential of security thinking, critical self-reflection becomes crucial for students of critical approaches to security. The role of the students of security, in this sense, is to try and be self-conscious about the normative and mutually constitutive relationship between theory and practice in their thinking and writing rather than feeding 'common sense' back into the system hiding behind a notion of 'objectivity'.

It should be noted that one advantage of feeding 'common sense' into the system is that it is readily accepted by those who are in a position of power. Indeed, as Steve Smith maintains,

> once established as common sense, theories become incredibly powerful since they delineate not simply what can be known but also what it is sensible to talk about or suggest. Those who swim outside these safe

waters risk more than simply the judgement that their theories are wrong; their entire ethical or moral stance may be ridiculed or seen as dangerous just because their theoretical assumptions are deemed unrealistic. Defining common sense is therefore the ultimate act of political power.

(Smith 1996: 13; see also Smith 1997)

In other words, although theory/practice relationship is one of mutual constitution, not all theories get to shape practices. Then, the answer to the question why theorising may become self-constitutive in some cases (such as the Cold War security discourse) but not in others (as with Peace Research) is rooted in the power/knowledge relationship. More often than not, it is theories that are picked up by those in positions of power that get to shape what men and women in the street view as 'a more plausible interpretation of international reality' – as John Garnett (1987: 22) wrote when explaining the way realism has prevailed over the years.

Furthermore, 'dominant discourses, especially those of the state, become and remain dominant because of the power relations sustaining them' (Weldes *et al.* 1999: 18). In this sense, it is difficult to underestimate the power of theories in informing not only governmental policies, but also individuals' conceptions of the world. Here, Kaldor's (1990) argument regarding the Cold War is again instructive in accounting for the ways in which Cold War security discourse informed men and women in North America and Western Europe of the relevance, legitimacy and inescapability of power politics, tough responses and brinkmanship.

The competition between theories over shaping practices and therefore the future never takes place on a level playing field. To understand theory as constitutive of 'reality' is not to suggest that once we get our theories right the rest would follow. What shape the future might take would depend on whose theories get to shape practices. For example (as Chapter 2 will argue), the reason why the lands to the southwest of Asia and north of Africa were lumped together in the mind's eye and labelled the 'Middle East', but not something else, has had its roots in the dominance of British and US security discourses. The sources of their dominance could, in turn, be found in the material (military and economic) as well as representational power of these actors.

Here I distinguish between the representational and material dimensions of power for analytical reasons in an attempt to stress that the workings of the power/knowledge relationship cannot be accounted for by adopting a narrow or purely material conception of power. Rather, one's conception of power should account for its representational dimension as well; that is, the power to shape ideas. One potential problem involved in trying to account for the representational dimension of power is that it cannot be observed in the same way as the material dimension can be; the latter is often utilised to keep issues outside security agendas, thereby averting conflict. In the absence of overt (or latent) conflict, no observable behaviour change takes place. However, the absence of an observable power relationship does not necessarily mean there is not one.

To be able to account for such instances of power relationships, I adopt, following Steven Lukes (1974: 24), a 'three-dimensional view of power' that 'allows for consideration of the many ways in which *potential issues* are kept out of politics, whether through the operation of social forces and institutional practices or through individuals' decisions'. Adopting a conception of power that stresses both its material and representational dimensions enables me to account for the ways in which some discourses come to dominate others, shaping 'reality' by informing certain practices whilst marginalising others. 'Our liberation will come through a rereading of our past', wrote Fatima Mernissi (1993: 160) when discussing the future of women in the Arab world and the need for writing alternative accounts of the Islamic and pre-Islamic past to point to instances of women's struggle and triumph. Indeed, one task of students of critical security is to present alternative readings of the past and to account for choices that were made – or were obscured due to the way security agendas were set up by keeping certain issues out (as was the case with female illiteracy as argued above) (also see Booth 1998a: 29–55).

It should also be stressed that neither material nor representational dimensions of power could be monopolised by one actor only. This is more so in the case of the latter. For, although it is true that it is a combination of ideas and material resources that has enabled some discourses to dominate others, history is replete with examples of the ideas of the weak coming to power (by being taken up by those who are in power, or directly through revolutions). One example of this phenomenon is the 1989 revolutions in Eastern Europe and the role played by Polish Pope Jean Paul II and the Catholic Church.[23] It is perhaps ironic that the current Pope, whose predecessor Stalin famously ridiculed for not having enough material power when he quipped, 'how many divisions has the Pope?', played a major role in the 1989 revolutions that eventually culminated in the dissolution of the Soviet Union (Garrison and Phipps with Shivpuri 1989: 76–84).

Another example of the ideas of the weak coming to power was observed when Gorbachev reinterpreted the Soviet domestic situation and external relations and decided to change the course of Soviet foreign policy in the 1980s and adopted the ideas of Peace Researchers, Alternative Security thinkers and peace movements who have been propounding ideas about common security and non-offensive defence since the 1960s (Risse-Kappen 1995b). As Ken Booth (1998b: 353) has noted,

> the Berlin Wall did not fall: it was pushed. It was thought up, unthought and pulled down. This most symbolic material structure of the Cold War was demolished by people changing their minds.

Without such ideas being floated by some (in the Soviet Union and else-where) Gorbachev would not have had the intellectual resources to tap into when he decided to change course. Those who floated such ideas, on the other hand, needed Gorbachev for their ideas to be put into practice. The end of the Cold War, in this sense, evolved as a symbiosis of top-down and bottom-up approaches to security, neither of which would have been successful without the other (Galtung 1995; Kaldor 1997).

In sum, critical approaches to security suggest putting into use the con-stitutive role played by theories by presenting a fundamentally different approach to security in theory and practice in the attempt to open up space for political action to take place and to help shape alternative futures. The roles students of security could play as agents of security will be further developed in the following section. Suffice it to say that there should be some self-reflection on their part as to the fact that their theories do not leave the world untouched. In other words, students of security should reflect upon the constitutive implications of their own thinking and writing – to the extent that they can be aware of them.

Agency

The state, as noted above, has traditionally been viewed as both the primary referent of and agent for security in Cold War Security Studies. Students of critical approaches, by posing the question 'whose security are we concerned with?', have challenged the primacy accorded to the state as the primary referent for security. However, although the privi-leged status of the state as the primary referent has been challenged, Security Studies continues to accord the state a central position largely due to its status as the dominant agent for security. This is partly because states have had the licence to legitimate use of violence and are therefore better endowed than any other agent to provide for certain dimensions of security (such as military defence).[24] But perhaps more significant is the fact that students of International Relations in general and Security Studies in particular have not been oriented to look at the agency of actors other than the state concerning security issues (Turner 1998). The prominence of the state's agency in the economic and financial sectors has for long been challenged, but it is yet to be de-throned in (certain types of) security matters.

The point is that a broader security agenda requires students of security to look at agents other than the state, such as social movements, non-governmental organisations (NGOs) and individuals, instead of restricting their analysis to the state's agency. This is essential not only because states are not always able (or willing) to fulfil their side of the bargain in provid-ing for their citizens' security, as noted above, but also because there already are agents other than states – be it social movements or intellectuals – who are striving to provide for the differing needs of peoples (themselves and others). This is not meant to deny the salience of the roles states play in the realm of security; on the contrary, they remain significant actors with crucial roles to play.[25] Rather, the argument is that the state's dominant position as an actor well endowed to provide (certain dimensions of) security does not justify privileging its agency.

Furthermore, broadening the security agenda without attempting a reconceptualisation of agency would result in falling back upon the agency of the state in meeting non-military threats. The problem with resorting to the agency of the state in meeting non-military threats is that states may not be the most suitable actors to cope with them. In other words, the state being the most qualified actor in coping with some kinds of threats does not necessarily mean it is competent (or willing) enough to cope with all. This is why students of critical approaches aim to re-conceptualise agency and practice.

Critical approaches view non-state actors, in particular, social movements and intellectuals, as potential agents for change (Cox 1981, 1999; Walker 1990b; Hoffman 1993; Wyn Jones 1995a, 1999). This echoes feminist approaches that have emphasised the role of women's agency and maintained that 'women must act in the provision of their own security' if they are to make a change in a world where their security needs and concerns are marginalised (Tickner 1997; also see Sylvester 1994). This is not necessarily wishful thinking on the part of a few academics; on the contrary, practice indicates that peoples (as individuals and social groups) have taken certain aspects of their own and others' security into their own hands (Marsh 1995: 130–5; Turner 1998). Three successful examples from the Cold War era – the Nestlé boycott, the anti-apartheid campaign for South Africa and the campaign against nuclear missile deployments in Europe – are often viewed as having inspired the social movements of the post-Cold War era (Lopez *et al.* 1997: 230–1; Marsh 1995). Christine Sylvester (1994) has also pointed to the examples of the Greenham Common Peace Camp in Britain (1980–89) and women's producer co-operatives in Harare, Zimbabwe (1988–90) to show how women have intervened to enhance their own and others' security. These are excellent examples of how a broader conception of security needs to be coupled with a broader conception of agency.

It should be noted here that the call of critical approaches for looking at the agency of non-state actors should not be viewed as allocating tasks to preconceived agents. Rather, critical approaches aim to empower non-state actors (who may or may not be aware of their own potential to make a change) to constitute themselves as agents of security to meet this broadened agenda. Nor should it be taken to suggest that all non-state actors' practices are emancipatory.

Then, paying more attention to the agency of non-state actors will enable students of security to see how, in the absence of interest at the governmental level (as is the case with the Middle East), non-state actors could imagine, create and nurture community-building projects and could help in getting state-level actors interested in the formation of a security community. It should, however, be noted that not all non-state actors are community-minded – just as not all governments are sceptical of the virtues of community building. Indeed, looking at the agency of non-state actors is also useful because it enables one to see how non-state actors could stall community-building projects.

In the Middle East, women's movements and networks have been co-operating across borders from the beginning of the *Intifada* onwards. Women's agency, however, is often left unnoticed, because, as Simona Sharoni (1996) has argued, the eyes of security analysts are often focused on the state as the primary security agent. However, the *Intifada* was marked by Palestinian and Israeli-Jewish women's adoption of non-zero-sum, non-military practices that questioned and challenged the boundaries of their political communities as they dared to explore new forms of political communities (Mikhail-Ashrawi 1995; Sharoni 1995). Such activities included organising a conference entitled 'Give Peace a Chance – Women Speak Out' in Brussels in May 1989. The first of its kind, the conference brought together about 50 Israeli and Palestinian women from the West Bank and Gaza Strip together with PLO representatives to discuss the Israeli–Palestinian conflict. The follow-up event took place in Jerusalem in December 1989 where representatives of the Palestinian Women's Working Committees and the Israeli Women and Peace Coalition organised a women's day for peace which, Sharoni noted, 'culminated in a march of 6,000 women from West to East Jerusalem under the banner "Women Go For Peace"' (Sharoni 1996: 107). Aside from such events that were designed to alert public opinion of the unacceptability of the Israel/Palestine impasse as well as finding alternative ways of peace-making, women also undertook direct action to alleviate the condition of Palestinians whose predicament had been worsening since the beginning of the *Intifada* (Mikhail-Ashrawi 1995). In this process, they were aided by their Western European counterparts who provided financial, institutional as well as moral support. In sum, women's agency helped make the *Intifada* possible on the part of the Palestinian women, whilst their Israeli-Jewish counterparts helped enhance its impact by way of questioning the moral boundaries of the Israeli state.

The *Intifada* is also exemplary of how non-state actors could initiate processes of resistance that might later be taken up by policy-makers. The *Intifada* began in 1987 as a spontaneous grassroots reaction to the Israeli occupation and took the PLO leadership (along with others) by surprise. It was only some weeks into the *Intifada* that the PLO leadership embraced it and put its material resources into furthering the cause, which was making occupation as difficult as possible for the Israeli government. Although not much came out of the *Intifada* in terms of an agreement with Israel on issues of concern for the people living in the occupied territories, the process generated a momentum that culminated in 1988 with the PLO's denouncement of terrorism. The change in the PLO's policies, in turn, enabled the 1993 Oslo Accords, which was also initiated by non-state actors, in this case intellectuals (Sharoni 1996). The point here is that it has been a combination of top-down and bottom-up politics that has been at the heart of political change, be it the 1989 revolutions in Eastern Europe, or *Intifada* in Israel/Palestine.

Emphasising the roles some non-state actors, notably women's networks, have played as agents of security is not to suggest that all non-state agents' practices are non-zero-sum and/or non-violent. For instance, there are the cases of Islamist movements such as FIS (the Islamic Salvation Front) in Algeria and Hamas in the Occupied Territories that have resorted, over the years, to violent practices as a part of their strategies that were designed to capture the state mechanism. However, although they may constitute threats to security in the Middle East in view of their violent practices, what needs to be remembered is that both FIS and Hamas function as providers for security for some peoples in the Middle East – those who are often neglected by their own states (Esposito 1995: 162–83). In other words, some Islamist movements do not only offer a sense of identity, but also propose alternative practices and provide tangible economic, social and moral support to their members. However, the treatment women receive under the mastery of such Islamist movements serves to remind us that there clearly are problems involved in an unthinking reliance on non-governmental actors as agents for peace and security or an uncritical adoption of their agendas.

Middle Eastern history is replete with examples of non-state actors resorting to violence and/or adopting zero-sum practices in the attempt to capture state power. In fact, it is often such violent practices of non-state actors (that is, terrorism or assassination of political leaders) that are mentioned in security analyses. Nevertheless, the fact that not all non-state actors are fit to take up the role of serving as agents of emancipatory change should not lead one to downplay the significant work some have done in the past, and could do in the future. After all, not all states serve as providers of security; yet Security Studies continues to rely on their agency.

Then, in order to be able to fulfil the role allocated to them by critical approaches, non-state actors should be encouraged to move away from traditional forms of resistance that are based on exclusionist identities, that solely aim to capture state power or that adopt zero-sum thinking and practices. Arguably, this is a task for intellectuals to fulfil. This is not to suggest that intellectuals should direct or instruct non-state actors. As Wyn Jones (1999: 162) has noted, the relationship between intellectuals and social movements is based on reciprocity. The 1980s' peace movements, for instance, are good examples of intellectuals getting involved with social movements in bringing about change – in this case, the end of the Cold War (Galtung 1995; Kaldor 1997). The relationship between intellectuals and peace movements in Europe was a mutually interactive one in that the intellectuals encouraged and led whilst drawing strength from these movements.

Emphasising the mutually interactive relationship between intellectuals and social movements should not be taken to suggest that to make a change, intellectuals should get directly involved in political action. They could also intervene to provide a critique of the existing situation, what future outcomes may result if necessary action is not taken at present, and by pointing to potential for change immanent in world politics. Students of security could help create the political space that would enable the emergence of a Gorbachev, by presenting such critique. It should, however, be emphasised that such thinking should be anchored in the potential immanent in world politics. In other words, intellectuals should be informed by the practices of social movements themselves (as was the case in Europe in the 1980s). The hope is that non-state actors such as social movements and intellectuals (who may or may not be aware of their potential to make a change) may constitute themselves as agents when presented with an alternative reading of their situation.

Lastly, intellectuals could make a change even if they limit their practices to thinking, writing and self-reflection. During the Cold War very few security analysts were conscious and open about the impact their thinking and writing could make. Richard Wyn Jones cites the example of Edward N. Luttwak as one such exception who admitted that 'strategy is not a neutral pursuit and its only purpose is to strengthen one's own side in the contention of nations' (cited in Wyn Jones 1999: 150). Still, such explicit acknowledgement of the political dimension of strategic thinking was rare during the Cold War. On the contrary, students of International Relations in general and Security Studies in particular have been characterised by limited or no self-reflection as to the potential impact their research could make on the subject of research (Wyn Jones 1999: 148–50).

To go back to the argument made above about the role of the intellectual as an agent of security and the mutually constitutive relationship between theory and practice, students of critical approaches to security could function as agents of security by way of reflecting upon the practical implications of their own thinking and writing. Self-reflection becomes crucial when the relationship between theory and practice is conceptualised as one of mutual constitution. State-centric approaches to security do not simply reflect a reality 'out there' but help reinforce statism. Although it may be true that the consequences of these scholarly activities are sometimes 'unintended', there nevertheless should be a sense of self-reflection on the part of scholars upon the potential consequences of their research and teaching. The point here is that critical approaches that show an awareness of the socially constructed character of 'reality' need not stop short of reflecting upon the constitutive relationship between theory and practice when they themselves are theorising about security. Otherwise, they run the risk of constituting 'threats to the future' (Kubálková 1998: 193–201).

Practice

The issue of re-conceptualising practice has been central to critical approaches to security. Given the emphasis put on the theory/practice relationship by its students, they are expected to suggest alternative or emancipatory practices. However, in fulfilling this task, they have not received much help from Critical International Theory. As Richard Wyn Jones (1999: 151) maintains, the absence of 'systematic considerations of how a Critical Theory of international relations could help generate, support or sustain emancipatory politics' has meant that Critical International Theory has yet to fulfil its promise of becoming a 'force for change' (Hoffman 1987: 233) in world politics. Despite the limited nature of guidance provided by Critical International Theory, students of critical approaches to security have chosen not to remain silent on the issue of re-conceptualising practice. In the attempt to find and suggest ways in which critical approaches can 'orient toward political practice in a manner that encourages and supports emancipatory transformation' (Wyn Jones 1999: 153), its students have so far put emphasis on theory as a form of practice, the point being that by informing actors' practices, theories help shape the world in line with their tenets. This is in contrast with Cold War Security Studies' conception of theory as an explanatory tool. From a critical perspective, theories do not just explain; they are constitutive of what we may choose to call 'reality'. Different theories produce different security discourses by way of laying down the rules that enable one to 'write, speak, listen and act meaningfully' (Agnew and Corbridge 1995: 45). Depending on the theory or theories employed, discourses close off certain possibilities whilst opening others, and lay the groundwork for the practices of various agents.

Perhaps the best example of the mutually constitutive relationship between theory and practice is the relationship between Security Studies and the Cold War. As argued above, Security Studies is a product of the Cold War. It developed as a specific answer to the problems of that era and attempts to understand its evolution require an awareness of the context in which it originated and, in turn, shaped. For, Security Studies not only originated in but also thrived upon the Cold War environment. The concepts, assumptions and findings of Cold War Security Studies helped sustain the Cold War.

Revealing the mutually constitutive relationship between security theories and security practices, in this sense, is more than an 'intellectual' exercise; it is a form of practice in itself. Thus, the purpose of critical approaches in pointing to the normative character of theory and the theory/practice relationship is to undermine Cold War Security Studies, its claim to knowledge and its hold over practice. Furthermore, the task of critical approaches is not only to uncover the workings of the theory/ practice relationship of days gone but also be self-conscious and open about the mutually constitutive relationship between theory and practice when thinking and writing about security at present. As argued above, those students of Security Studies who produce state-centric analyses do not just explain a world where states are the main referents of and agents for security; but they also help perpetuate statism in world politics by feeding 'common sense' back into the system thereby marginalising other potential referents and agents and making it difficult to invent alternative futures.

One implication of conceiving theory as a form of practice is that theorising itself is recognised as a political act. As Richard Devetak (1999: 72) has argued: 'Theory-as-practice ... defines a task that is simultaneously theoretical and practical, philosophical and political'. Once theorising is recognised as a political act, then the role of the theorist could no longer be viewed as that of an 'objective' or 'neutral' observer but an actor with his/her own normative agenda to pursue. As opposed to most (but not all) of their Cold War counterparts, students of critical approaches to security recognise and are open about the normative character of the relationship between theory and practice, theorist and what is being theorised.

Admittedly, providing a critique of existing approaches to security, revealing those hidden assumptions and normative projects embedded in Cold War Security Studies, is only a first step. In other words, from a critical security perspective, self-reflection, thinking and writing are not enough in themselves. They should be compounded by other forms of practice (that is, action taken on the ground). It is indeed crucial for students of critical approaches to re-think security in both theory and practice by pointing to possibilities for change immanent in world politics and suggesting emancipatory practices if it is going to fulfil the promise of becoming a 'force of change' in world politics. Cognisant of the need to find and suggest alternative practices to meet a broadened security agenda without adopting militarised or zero-sum thinking and practices, students of critical approaches to security have suggested the imagining, creation and nurturing of security communities as emancipatory practices (Booth 1994a; Booth and Vale 1997).

Although Devetak's approach to the theory/practice relationship echoes critical approaches' conception of theory as a form of practice, the latter seeks to go further in shaping global practices. The distinction Booth makes between 'thinking about thinking' and 'thinking about doing' grasps the difference between the two. Booth (1997: 114) writes:

Thinking about thinking is important, but, more urgently, so is think-ing about doing.... Abstract ideas about emancipation will not suffice: it is important for Critical Security Studies to engage with the real by suggesting policies, agents, and sites of change, to help humankind, in whole and in part, to move away from its structural wrongs.

In this sense, providing a critique of existing approaches to security, revealing those hidden assumptions and normative projects embedded in Cold War Security Studies, is only a first (albeit crucial) step. It is vital for the students of critical approaches to re-think security in both theory and practice.

Karl Deutsch and his colleagues developed the concept of security community in the 1950s. What Deutsch *et al.* (1957) were interested in was finding ways of creating a community characterised by the cessation of inter-state violence and the creation of dependable expectations of peace-ful change by way of strengthening relationships among a group of states. Accordingly, Deutsch *et al.* defined a (pluralistic) security community as 'one in which there is real assurance that the members of that community will not fight each other physically, but will settle their disputes in some other way' (1957: 5). Their conviction was that once the conditions and processes that give rise to security communities were identified, it would be possible to replicate them in different parts of the world so that (prepa-rations for and the idea of) war would not enter into calculations of those states (Deutsch *et al.* 1957: vii, 3, 20–1). Although Deutsch *et al.* were posit-ive regarding the potential for security communities to travel to different parts of the world, their ideas remained largely on paper for four decades until Emanuel Adler and Michael Barnett (1998a) revived them in the late 1990s. What follows is an account as to why the process of imagining, cre-ating and nurturing security communities constitutes emancipatory prac-tices from a critical security perspective.

The preference of students of critical security for the security commun-ity approach builds upon the emphasis the proponents of Critical Theory in International Relations have put on the transformation of political community. Common to both Mark Hoffman (1993) and Robert Cox (1999) is the stress they put on the agency of social forces towards creating a future world order where the boundaries of political community extend beyond that of sovereign states. In a series of studies, Andrew Linklater (1990a, 1990b, 1995, 1998) has sought to fortify the case for the creation of more inclusive communities cognisant of peoples' multiple identities.

Linklater's argument is that the twin processes of globalisation and fragmentation are already transforming political communities around the world, thereby constituting a potential for creating more inclusive communities. The creation of more inclusive communities has been con-sidered desirable but not attainable for a long time. As Linklater has noted, this had to do with the perceived need to organise within states for economic and military purposes. His argument is that although the West-phalian state system and its cornerstone, the sovereign state have served these purposes for a long time, the reasons for persisting with the system of sovereign states as an organising principle of world politics have been gradually eroding in that, given the impact made by the forces of globali-sation and fragmentation, the state is no longer able to fulfil these roles. The realisation of these developments, maintains Linklater (1995, 1998), constitutes an immanent potential for the transformation of political community.

The case Linklater makes for the transformation of political community echoes the call Booth and Vale make for

> moving away from simple patterns of statism to complex structures and processes characterised by shifting power away from the state level (upwards to regional community institutions and downwards to local community bodies) and moving away from nineteenth century notions of identity towards more complex answers to the question 'who am I?'.
>
> (Booth and Vale 1997: 352)

From a critical security perspective, transformation of political community is desirable not only because the twin processes of globalisation and fragmentation have made it more difficult for existing forms of political community (that is, states) to fulfil their roles; or that there already exist some potential for this transformation to take place; but also that the cre-ation of security communities would help directly address the problem of regional security. Indeed, the security community approach emphasises the need to organise at the regional level by way of forming an inclusive community – a community that takes security issues seriously.

One point of strength for the security community approach is that it directly addresses the problem of achieving security, rather than treating it as a side effect of increasing globalisation or regionalisation. It also puts emphasis on the political project behind the construction of a community. Furthermore, the security community approach provides an explicit account of the potentialities of human agency. Lastly, it might provide (however imperfect) the start of a path from an insecure past to a more secure future. This, in turn, might provide a good starting point for re-conceptualising regional security in theory and practice and investigating the potential for the creation of security communities in different parts of the world.

Conclusion

The aim of this chapter was ground-clearing. It sought to introduce a critical security perspective, which will then be utilised to critique Cold War and post-Cold War conceptions and practices of security in Parts I and II. Such ground-clearing is considered crucial given the novelty of critical approaches to security and their somewhat contested character. Indeed, the perspective introduced here is only one of a variety of critical approaches to security. Keith Krause and Michael Williams (1996, 1997a, 1997b), for instance, view Critical Security Studies as an umbrella term covering a number of approaches that are critical of Cold War Security Studies in one way or another. Krause's definition in particular embraces work produced by, among others, James Der Derian (1995), who stresses the impossibility of being 'secure', and calls for a strategy to 'celebrate' the anxiety and insecurity of the contemporary world; Ole Wæver (1995), who questions the usefulness of a broader security agenda and makes a case for 'desecuritization' instead; and Mohammed Ayoob (1995, 1997) who has adopted a 'subaltern realist perspective' to study security in the Third World. The specific approach adopted here – following Ken Booth (1991b, 1994a, 1997, 1999a, 1999b) and Richard Wyn Jones (1995a, 1995b, 1999) – favours broadening and deepening our conceptions of security to have fuller agendas as part of an attempt to achieve security conceived as a process of emancipation. What will be referred to as Critical Security Studies in the rest of the thesis is the perspective introduced here.

The chapter discussed key concepts and analytical moves central to critical approaches and most relevant for study. It was argued that re-thinking security entails re-conceptualising security in both theory and practice by broadening and deepening; looking below and beyond states for other referents and agents; and suggesting emancipatory practices towards shaping alternative futures. The critical security perspective on thinking about the future will be presented in Chapter 6.

Part I
Pasts

2 Representations of the Middle East during the Cold War

One of the central arguments put forward in this study is that when re-thinking regional security from a critical perspective, both concepts – 'region' and 'security' – should be opened up to investigate the relationship between (inventing) regions and (conceptions and practices of) security. Part I is devoted to investigating the workings of this relationship during the Cold War. Chapter 2 opens the discussion by tracing the trajectory of the Middle East from its origins in Britain's security policies during the late nineteenth century into the Cold War era when reference to this part of the world as the Middle East became 'common sense'. This is intended as a further illustration of the point (also reinforced in Chapter 4) that regions are geopolitical inventions that have their roots in the security discourses of their inventors. The Middle East was invented to help British and later US policy-makers to think about and organise action in this part of the world. It is sometimes argued that researching into the invention and/or inventors of regions is a futile exercise in that once a region is 'invented' it becomes an object of security. Yet, such arguments underestimate the role geopolitical discourse and spatial representations play in shaping 'how we see the world and how we decide to act' (Ó Tuathail and Agnew 1992: 190). To quote Gearóid Ó Tuathail and John Agnew,

> It is only through discourse that the building up of a navy or the decision to invade a foreign country is made meaningful and justified. It is through discourse that leaders act, through the mobilisation of certain simple geographical understandings that foreign-policy actions are explained and through ready-made geographically-infused reasoning that wars are rendered meaningful.
>
> (1992: 191)

Choosing to represent a part of the world as the 'Middle East' is by no means an innocent act; it involves the 'construction of a special kind of geographical "Other"' (Sidaway 1994: 366). This, in turn, 'reflects and supports the kind of Western military intervention (such as the raids on Libya and the Gulf War) that ultimately does very little to deal with the persistent and underlying causes of conflict in the region' (Sidaway 1994: 366). This is not to suggest that regions as spatial representations are fixed and unchanging. On the contrary, defining and redefining regions are political processes that are continually being resisted and contested (as with Arab actors' representations of this part of the world as the 'Arab Regional System'). What is more, prevailing representations are continually being redefined in line with the changing security interests and concerns of the major actors (as with Britain and the United States in the nineteenth and twentieth century). Viewed as such, researching into the processes through which regions are (re)defined becomes central to studying regional security, for such (re)definitions give away the changing security concerns of various actors as well as the conceptions of security they are rooted in.

Chapter 2 also presents critiques of the Middle East as the dominant representation, and an alternative that was offered by Arab actors, that of the 'Arab Regional System'. This is intended to show that notwithstanding the prevalence of the 'Middle East' as the representation of this part of the world, there existed alternative representations rooted in the alternative security concerns of myriad actors. The chapter will conclude by teasing out the conceptions of security in which these alternative spatial representations are rooted.

The 'cartographic slipperiness'[1] of the Middle East

There is an agreement in the literature on the Middle East (see, for example, Davison 1960; Buheiry 1989; Tibi 1993; Sidaway 1994; Adelson 1995; Khalidi 1998b) to ascribe the invention of the Middle East as a geopolitical concept to Captain Alfred Thayer Mahan, US naval officer and author of key works on naval strategy.[2] In an article published in *The National Review* in 1902, Mahan suggested that Britain should take up the responsibility of maintaining security in the (Persian) Gulf and its coasts – an area he labelled as the 'Middle East' – so that the route to India would be secured and Russia kept in check (Mahan 1902). However, despite this seemingly unanimous agreement in the literature to ascribe the coinage of the term to Captain Mahan, the first reference to the Middle East could be found in an article entitled 'The Problems of the Middle East' by General Sir Thomas Edward Gordon published in *The Nineteenth Century* (1900). General Gordon was an officer of the British Army who was assigned to India for over four decades and his article was written from the perspective of a person who had spent most of his life thinking about India's defence. It is not known whether General Gordon himself coined the term or merely adopted it; he does not offer a definition let alone some explanation. Assuming that he would have included a definition had he been the inventor, it could be argued that the term's origins go further back. However, no earlier reference has yet been found (Koppes 1976).

What is beyond doubt is that the geopolitical concept Middle East was invented when thinking about and organising action for India's security. Then, the Middle East has its origins, via Gordon and Mahan's descriptions, in British policy-makers' security concerns and practices in the late nineteenth and early twentieth century.

Notwithstanding its origins in the British India Office, the term Middle East seems to have entered public discourse via Mahan's use in 1902 (Sidaway 1994: 357). The term took off from then onwards but as time progressed, the area so designated shifted westwards. During the inter-war period, the discovery of considerable quantities of oil in the Arabian peninsula and the increasing pace of Jewish migration into Palestine linked these chunks of territory to Mahan's Middle East. During the Second World War, British policy-makers began to use the term with reference to all Asian and north African lands to the west of India. No definite boundaries were set to the region during this period. In line with changes in British wartime policies 'Iran was added in 1942; Eritrea was dropped in September 1941 and welcomed back again five months later' (Davison 1960: 669). Towards the end of the Second World War the United States got involved in the Middle East adopting the British wartime definition. These switches from one definition to another took place so swiftly that it prompted a well-known historian of the region, Roderic Davison (1960) to ask in the pages of *Foreign Affairs*: 'Where is the Middle East?'

Writing in 1960, Davison's concern was with the 'cartographic slipperiness' (Wigen and Lewis 1997: 71) of the Middle East. For, he thought that this lack of a precise definition of the region resulted in an ambiguity in US foreign relations in that US policy-makers, by way of changing their definition of the region to suit different policy purposes, were giving contradictory signals as to where they were prepared to act if needed. For instance, in 1957, when the Eisenhower Doctrine was declared, Secretary of State John Foster Dulles defined the Middle East as 'the area lying between and including Libya on the west and Pakistan on the east and Turkey on the north and the Arabian peninsula to the south' plus the Sudan and Ethiopia (Davison 1960: 665). Davison noted that Dulles was hesitant to provide a more precise definition lest the Soviet policy-makers considered drawing a 'defence perimeter' as issuing an invitation to seize anything outside that line. One year later, in 1958 when Eisenhower addressed the United Nations General Assembly (following the crisis in and intervention into Lebanon and the revolution in Iraq), the region had shrunk considerably; now its definition covered Egypt, Syria, Israel, Jordan, Lebanon, Saudi Arabia and the Gulf sheikhdoms only. Considering the fact that the Eisenhower Doctrine of 1957 was still in practice, this change in the definition of the Middle East further complicated the matter. In criticism, Davison (1960: 675) argued that although a degree of ambiguity could be considered useful for deterrence purposes, it was also 'important to know where the United States ... [was] prepared to do something and presumably to let other governments to know'. Concerned with the confusion caused by the multiple definitions of the 'Middle East', Davison suggested that the term should either be properly defined or abandoned altogether.

Without wishing to underplay the significance of Davison's apprehension regarding the pitfalls of ambiguity in policy-making, it should nevertheless be noted that such 'cartographic slipperiness' is not isolated to the Middle East. There exist contending definitions of Central Europe as well, as Timothy Garton Ash explained in an aptly titled article: 'The Puzzle of Central Europe' (1999). The point here is that the presence of multiple definitions of regions such as the Middle East and Central Europe stem from the fact that they are geopolitical inventions rooted in the security thinking and practices of their inventors. As these concerns and practices change, the definitions of these regions also change. For instance, during the first half of the twentieth century, the area represented as the Middle East shifted in tandem with the changes in British security conceptions and practices (see below). In other words, there is nothing unique about the 'cartographic slipperiness' of the Middle East.

It could further be argued that coming to an agreement on a more precise definition of the Middle East, although useful for policy purposes, would bring a premature end to a potentially fruitful discussion on the reasons behind the coinage of the Middle East as a term and its adoption as the representation of the landmass to the south-west of Asia and the north of Africa as a 'region'. The key point is that questions such as 'why the lands to the south-west of Asia and north of Africa were lumped together to constitute a region?' and 'why "Middle East" but not, for instance, "Southwest Asia and North Africa" was adopted to represent this part of the world?' could be answered only by looking at the security thinking and practices of Western policy-makers in the late nineteenth and early twentieth century. Whilst accepting Davison's argument that it may be necessary for practical purposes to adopt a common and more precise definition of the Middle East, it will be argued that it is also imperative to raise one's awareness of the region's character as a geopolitical invention in order to understand how the region has developed in the past and could (potentially) change in the future.

The argument so far should not be taken to suggest that it was solely the military strategic interests of Western powers that have been the driving force behind the production of such geopolitical concepts. Throughout history, all societies have produced their own representations of the world. The term 'Maghreb' (meaning 'the West' in Arabic) has its origins in the geopolitics of an earlier era, that of the first waves of Arab invaders who came to the north of Africa in the seventh and eighth centuries (Eickelman 1989: 3). However, not all societies have been able to impose their maps onto others. This is where relative endowment of material resources comes into play in deciding whose discourse emerges as the dominant one. To put it in other words, the reason why the lands to the southwest of Asia and north of Africa were lumped together in the mind's eye and labelled the Middle East has its roots not merely in the strategic interests of Britain in the late nineteenth and early twentieth century, but also in Britain's material and representational power.

It is not only the relative endowment of material resources of rival powers but also the changes in communications and transportation technologies that have had an impact on the way geographical categories are invented and adjusted. During the nineteenth and twentieth century, as the military strategic interests and capabilities of the major geopolitical actors changed (such as the opening of the Suez Canal in 1869 and the Royal Navy's switch from coal to oil in 1912), the Middle East shifted in tandem with these changes (see the following two sections). Indeed, technological, economic as well as political changes alter the way actors 'see' the world thereby helping shape their practices. For instance, the idea of Europe began to take firmer root in the minds of people living in this part of the world with the 'discovery' of other continents in general and America in particular (see, for example, Hay 1968; Attali 1999). Likewise, it became possible for peoples to begin thinking and acting globally only after they were able to imagine the world they lived in as a globe – thanks to the developments in astronomy and geographical discoveries (see Agnew 1998).

Having noted the way spatial representations are shaped by the security concerns of their inventors, the following sections will seek to illustrate this process. The next section provides a brief history of the evolution of the dominant representation – the Middle East – until the beginning of the Cold War. The third section traces its development during the Cold War era. Finally, the chapter looks at the critiques of the Middle East and the alternative representations that emerged during this period. The concluding section will seek to tease out the security conceptions in which these spatial representations are rooted.

The Middle East as a geopolitical invention

Notwithstanding its origins in the British India Office, the term Middle East entered public discourse via Mahan's use in 1902 (Sidaway 1994: 357). Mahan had made his reputation with *The Influence of Sea Power upon History, 1660–1783*, published in 1890. He had soon become a public figure sought out by magazine editors for articles on naval affairs and strategy (Davison 1960: 667). In an article entitled 'The Persian Gulf and International Relations', Mahan called for Britain to take up the responsibility of maintaining security in the Gulf in order to secure the route to India and hold Russia in check. He wrote:

The Middle East, if I may adopt a term which I have not seen, will some day need its Malta as well as its Gibraltar; it does not follow that either be in the Gulf. Naval force has the quality of mobility which carries with it the privilege of temporary absences; but it needs to find on every scene of operation established bases of refit, of supply, and, in cases of disaster, of security. The British Navy should have the facility to concentrate in force, if occasion arise, about Aden, India, and the Gulf.

(Mahan 1902: 39)[3]

Mahan had used the term Middle East to refer to the (Persian) Gulf and its coasts. It was Valentine Chirol, who was then the head of the foreign department of *The Times* (London), who adopted and popularised the term by using it in a series of twenty articles entitled 'The Middle Eastern Question' published during 1902–03 (Davison 1960: 667–8). Chirol's Middle East represented an area larger than the one conceived by Mahan. This new definition included not only the Gulf and its coasts (Mahan's Middle East) but all land as well as sea approaches to India (Adelson 1995: 24). In this way Chirol adopted the term invented by Mahan but changed the area designated as the Middle East. Mahan's Middle East was essentially a naval concept; Chirol's definition, on the other hand, was drawn up when calling for securing all land and sea approaches to India in a context shaped by the deepening rivalries amongst the European powers. This was to become the first of the many changes in the definition of the Middle East in tandem with changing security concerns of external actors.

By the time *The Times* finished publishing Chirol's articles in 1903, it had ceased to place Middle East in quotation marks (Adelson 1995: 26). However, although the term Middle East gradually became common sense from then onwards, the definition of the region changed in tandem with the security thinking and practices of British policy-makers. One thing that remained constant throughout this period was that the Middle East as a region was tied to the defence of India.

In the aftermath of the First World War, the definition of the region changed due to the expansion of the British Empire and the incorporation of the former Ottoman territories of Palestine, Jordan and Iraq. In 1921, the Colonial Secretary Winston Churchill set up a Middle Eastern Department in the Foreign Office to supervise Palestine, Jordan and Iraq. The reasoning behind this westwards shift was that these chunks of territory had become linked, in the minds of British policy-makers, to the defence of India (see Davison 1960: 668; Adelson 1995: 26). Moreover, another factor, that of oil had also entered the picture. By 1912, oil had begun to replace coal in the British Navy, and British policy-makers were anxious to find 'dependable sources of oil' (Adelson 1995: 97–100). Although the significance of the oil reserves in this part of the world were still to be discovered, and notwithstanding the fact that the United States still supplied about 80 per cent of British demand for oil at this stage, the politics of oil was not totally absent from British policy-makers' calculations (Monroe 1981: 95–115).

However, this broad definition of the region adopted by Churchill failed to win broader approval either in Britain or in the United States for a long time. At this stage, US policy-makers' interest in the region was still peripheral (despite the increasing pace of Jewish migration into Palestine). Officially, they preferred to adhere to an earlier term, the Near East (the definition of which included former Ottoman territories in the Balkans, Africa and Asia Minor, the Arabian peninsula and most of Iran). The Mediterranean was also used to represent this part of the world in US strategic discourse well until the end of the Second World War (see, for example, Reitzel 1948: 94–101). During the inter-war period, Middle Eastern (and to a certain extent European) affairs constituted peripheral interests for an isolationist United States. Knowledge of the region as studied in the universities or disseminated in the media depended largely on travellers' accounts and the information provided by their continental counterparts (Said 1995a: 290).[4]

In Britain as in France, Germany and the Netherlands, there has been a tradition of studying the East, or the 'Orient'. The study of and accounts of the 'Orient' and imperial policy-making had a symbiotic relationship (Said 1995a)[5] in that the study of lands far away was funded by either governments or private entrepreneurs who had business interests in these lands. For instance, the University of London's School of Oriental Studies (which later became the School of Oriental and African Studies) was founded in 1917 for the study of Asian and African languages in order to meet the needs of an expanding empire. Until then, 'Oriental Studies' was offered in the universities of London, Oxford and Cambridge, among others, but these programmes mainly focused on the study of ancient texts rather than the study of contemporary languages, the knowledge of which was becoming increasingly necessary to maintain British presence in the East.[6]

Then, it was not solely British policy-makers but also students of the East (including members of the Royal Geographical Society)[7] as well as other opinion-makers (such as Mahan and Chirol) who helped to invent and establish the Middle East in the minds of the British public. The role played by Chirol (and *The Times*) has already been noted. The Royal Geographical Society, for its part, decided in the early 1920s that, 'henceforth the Near East should denote only the Balkans; the lands from the Bosphorus to the eastern frontiers of India would be named the Middle East' (Davison 1960: 668). With this definition Turkey was moved from its earlier position in the Near East into an expanding Middle East.

In the late 1920s another British institution, the Royal Air Force, created its own Middle East comprising Egypt, the Sudan and Kenya.

During the late 1930s, with the crisis in Europe looming on the horizon, it was decided that in the case of war breaking out, the Middle East Air Command should cover not only the aforementioned territories in Africa, but also Palestine, Jordan and Iraq (that were included in Churchill's Middle East) as well as Aden and Malta. The British Army followed suit in 1939 by consolidating the heretofore separate commands of Egypt, the Sudan and Palestine-Jordan, whilst adding Cyprus, Iraq, Aden, British Somaliland and the Persian Gulf. General Archibald Percival Wavell was sent to Cairo to take up the post of Commander-in-Chief, Middle East. With the outbreak of the war, especially the fall of France and Italy's entry into the war, the Middle East Command became a significant part of the war effort, thereby contributing to the Middle East as a term and as a region becoming 'common sense'. As the German expansion continued, the Middle East Command stretched to cover Ethiopia, Eritrea, Libya, Greece and Crete as well (Davison 1960: 669).

During the War, the allies established a Middle East Supply Centre based in Cairo and Britain created the post of Minister of State for the Middle East. The areas over which the Centre and the Minister had control were not the same, 'but in general they stretched from Malta to Iran and from Syria to Ethiopia' (Davison 1960: 669). This broadest yet definition of the Middle East largely corresponded with the early definitions of the Near East (with the exception of Turkey, which was not yet a party to the War).

The Second World War helped further reinforce the term Middle East as a representation of this part of the world. By the end of the 1950s, the term Middle East had replaced Near East in British official documents (Ovendale 1998: 320). At this stage, the area represented as the Middle East had changed to the extent that Mahan would not have recognised it. Notwithstanding these changes in its definition, and the shift in its centre of gravity from India to Cairo, the Middle East of the Second World War Britain, like Mahan and Chirol's Middle Easts before that, remained a geopolitical concept imposed from outside in line with external actors' thinking and practices of security.

During this period, the Middle East as a spatial representation had not yet entered peoples' consciousness within the region itself; still, the lumping together of these chunks of territory under the Middle East Command during the Second World War had made a significant material impact on regional actors. The establishment of the Middle East Supply Centre to supervise the flow of goods within the region to compensate for the break-up of the communication and transportation links with Europe during the War, helped re-institute the intra-regional trade links that had been interrupted during the colonial period (Owen 1999). These links were once again to be broken at the end of the War, but the inter-personal and inter-institutional relations that were established among Arab actors during this period were to contribute to the development of

Arabism and the spatial representation Arab Regional System (see below) in the years to come.

Middle Easts during the Cold War

Towards the end of the Second World War, the United States, alongside Great Britain, got more closely involved in the Middle East. During the War the Middle East had become a part of the public discourse in the United States, largely with the help of the US press that adopted the British wartime definition. Although the Department of State continued to operate with an Office of Near Eastern Affairs, some US policy-makers had already begun to refer to the Middle East in discussing this part of the world. In 1957, when the Eisenhower Doctrine was declared promising to provide US military and economic aid to the states in 'the general area of the Middle East', the Department of State still did not officially use the term in its organisational structure (Davison 1960: 666–9).

As noted in the previous section, during Congressional meetings on the Eisenhower Doctrine, in response to a question on the definition of the Middle East, Secretary of State Dulles provided a broad definition that stretched from Libya to Pakistan and from Turkey to the Arabian Peninsula including the Sudan and Ethiopia. One year later the definition provided by the Department of State designated a much more restricted area (covering Egypt, Syria, Israel, Jordan, Lebanon, Saudi Arabia and the Gulf sheikhdoms). This, in turn, created an ambiguity as to where the United States was prepared to act if and when the Eisenhower Doctrine was put into practice. Further complicating the matter was the definition adopted by the newly created (1958) 'Aegean and Middle East Division' of the Office of Research of the US Department of State. This definition covered Greece, Turkey, Cyprus, Iran, Afghanistan and Pakistan only (Davison 1960: 666).

These three different definitions adopted and used by actors working for the same government (who presumably functioned with similar conceptions of regional security) could be explained by the confusion of a transitory era where some still used the Near East as a representation (such as the Department of State) whereas others adopted the Middle East to designate either the same area (as did the Secretary of State Dulles) or a more narrow one (as with the Office of Research). Although the use of such significantly different definitions might have been a deliberate tactic adopted by US policy-makers to create ambiguity in the minds of their Soviet counterparts as to where they were prepared to act, the multiplicity of Middle Easts seemed to reflect more confusion than resolve.[8]

During the Second World War, oil had become a more significant factor in both US and British policy-makers' calculations regarding the Middle East, but there were considerable differences between the stress placed upon it by the policy-makers of Britain and the United States. Although the politics of oil was not totally absent from British security practices, US interest in the region surpassed that of Britain by the end of the War (Monroe 1981: 95–115; Little 2002: 43–75). In the beginning of the twentieth century US production not only met its own consumption but provided above 80 per cent of what Britain needed as well. At that stage, the United States still produced 140 times more oil than did Iran (where the first discovery of oil was made) (Fromkin 1989: 29). This was to change during the inter-war period when major quantities of oil were discovered in Iran and the Arabian peninsula, and US oil-production companies began to take over from British firms in the region. By the 1950s, Saudi Arabia's reserves alone had overtaken that of the United States (Philip 1994: 68) and ARAMCO (Arab-American Oil Company) had replaced British companies in many Arab countries. US policy-makers' interest in the region during this period had less to do with its own domestic needs than the needs of its Western European allies. For, during the 1950s it had become clear that the United States did not have enough reserves to 'oil another war' beyond a year or two, if need be (Kemp 1991: 47). As Britain began to withdraw from the region and US oil-production companies began to replace their British counterparts, US interest in this part of the world expanded.

The formation of Israel in what once was Palestine also helped increase US policy-makers' as well as peoples' interest in the Middle East (see Little 2002: 77–115). It was in such a climate of rising interest in world affairs in general and that of the Middle East in particular that Area Studies was established in the United States. In the US the study of foreign cultures and societies remained, until the 1940s, an intellectual enterprise pursued largely by 'amateur enthusiasts' (McCaughey 1984: 34).[9] During the War the US Army had set up a school of languages to meet the needs of the war effort (on the relationship between Department of Defense and International Studies in the United States, see Lambert 1989). The framework created for these schools was later adopted by the Social Sciences Research Council when founding Area Studies. In the 1950s half a dozen Area Studies associations were created with the help of government funding (on the symbiotic relationship between Area Studies and the Cold War, see Wallerstein 1997; Cumings 1998; Bilgin and Morton 2002). The Middle East Institute was founded in 1946 under the aegis of the US government (Said 1995a: 295). Out of that grew the Middle East Studies Association, established in 1966. The first academic programme was opened at Princeton in 1947 (under the title 'Near Eastern Studies') with support and encouragement from the government as well as private sources (such as the Ford Foundation) (see Johnson and Tucker 1975; Winder 1987; Ismael and Ismael 1990; Hajjar and Niva 1997).

The point here is that since US intellectual circles had little experience of direct contact with the region, when Middle East Studies began to flourish during the 1950s, students of Area Studies, with little historical legacy to draw upon, allowed their research to be shaped directly by the interests of their funding institutions and governmental agencies that had Cold War concerns at the top of their agenda (Tucker 1988: 312–21; Said 1995a: 301–2; Anderson 1990). This is not to deny the role scholars played in getting the government interested in providing the funds necessary for setting up Middle East centres. Yet, the significance of the Cold War concerns of the US government cannot be underestimated. After all, Middle East scholars had tried before (in the inter-war era) to set up Area Studies centres but with little success. At the time, scholars sought to emphasise how 'studies of ancient language and history can serve to avoid conflict by correcting the distorted perspective of a narrow nationalism, and promoting international sympathy and understanding between East and the West' (Johnson and Tucker 1975: 4). Those who lobbied for governmental funding in the early years of the Cold War were more successful in their efforts. Their success was partly to do with their familiarity with the efforts of the state after having served the US war effort during the Second World War. The links that were established between key actors during the war were maintained (Lambert 1989: 95). Once Middle East centres were set up, State Department representatives sat on the boards of selection committees that decided which projects to fund – a practice that was not common to all Area Studies (see Mitchell 2003).

The Cold War origins of Middle East Studies in the United States distinguished it from British and French approaches to the region. Although the concerns of their respective governments and business interests did shape the studies of British and French scholars to some extent, they also retained their literary, philological and religious-text oriented approaches to the study of the East. US area experts, with limited pre-Cold War experience or knowledge to draw upon, concentrated on language (that is, the use of contemporary languages) and technical knowledge as instruments of influence and control. The mid-1950s shift from the strategy of 'massive retaliation' to 'flexible response' (which required the use of the military instrument including counter-insurgency and limited warfare) brought to the surface the need for intimate knowledge of the world beyond Europe. This need only served to reinforce the instrumentalist approach to the study of the Middle East (Johnson and Tucker 1975). As a result, students of the Middle East in the United States tended to reduce the region to ' "attitudes", "trends", statistics' (Said 1995a: 291). This was true to a great extent even for the so-called 'Arabists' of the State Department, who were often criticised for their pro-Arab stance (see Kaplan 1993).

Although other disciplines such as Latin American Studies were also influenced by Cold War concerns, the presence of Israel and the influential role played by the Jewish lobby in the society in general and the US Congress in particular introduced a uniqueness to Middle Eastern

Studies in that it ended up being more policy-driven than some other disciplines in which there seemed to be relatively little public interest.[10] Soviet Studies in the United States was perhaps the only other discipline shaped mostly by policy concerns (see Wallerstein 1997). As a result, when, during the late 1960s and early 1970s, Latin American, East Asian and African Studies were undergoing a critical phase reflecting upon their Cold War origins, Middle Eastern Studies remained, to quote Judith Tucker (1988: 312–13), the 'Rip Van Winkle' of the Area Studies scene well until the publication of Edward Said's *Orientalism*.[11] This, however, is not to suggest that there was no self-reflection and criticism by students of the Middle East. Indeed, some of the challenges brought against the representation of this part of the world as the Middle East came from within the discipline itself. The next section presents critiques of Middle East as a spatial representation and the suggested alternatives.

Is there a Middle East?

The question heading this section was put by a well-known student of Iran, the anthropologist Nikki Keddie, in an article published in the *International Journal of Middle East Studies* in 1973. By asking this question, she went one step further than Davison (who had asked where the Middle East was) and challenged the existence of a region called the Middle East. Following an analysis of the factors that worked for and against making the Middle East a 'real historical entity' (1973: 257) Keddie concluded that 'what probably keeps the strange term "Middle East" (What is Morocco supposed to be in the middle of?) alive today is the cumbersomeness of any more scientific designation thought of thus far' (1973: 267). The 'cumbersome' designation Keddie had in mind was 'South West Asia and North Africa' (SWANA). One could add Marshall Hodgson's (1974: 60) 'Nile to Oxus' to the short list of such alternatives.

Keddie's critique could be summarised in two main points. First, the term Middle East is Eurocentric and has its origins in Western strategy. Second, the region is not a 'real historical entity', and there are relatively few common characteristics that could be used to view this group of states together as a region.

Without wishing to downplay Keddie's criticism regarding the Western strategic origins of the term, it should be noted that this is not a phenomenon unique to the Middle East. For, throughout history, the naming of land has often implied control of that land (Whitelam 1996: 40). Colonial powers in the Middle East and Africa as well as the settlers in the Americas and Australia mapped the areas they set foot on; invented places when naming them, engaging in acts of 'imaginative geography' (Said 1995a: 49); and then wrote histories of these lands rendering authority to the new names and constructs that were instituted often in neglect of what they replaced – what Said (2001: 252) refers to as 'epistemological conquest of territory'. Ghana, for instance, was known as the 'Gold Coast' until its independence. The people of Guinea, on the other hand, chose to retain the name, which is another colonial relic. Latin America was called 'Latin' by France (as a colonial power) to emphasise the notion of a 'Latin' character linking France with Spanish- and Portuguese-speaking south American peoples in the attempt to outdo its (non-Latin) rivals in the competition for colonies in south America (Wigen and Lewis 1997: 181). Furthermore, peoples of the Middle East have once been at the other (not receiving but giving) end of this relationship. As noted above, the term 'Maghreb' was coined by Arab invaders of the north of Africa in the seventh and eighth centuries and is therefore vulnerable to a similar set of criticisms. The Middle East, in this sense, is no exception; it is just another representation (like Maghreb) which has its origins in the security concerns and practices of external actors.

Neither should the Eurocentric character of the term Middle East constitute a sufficient reason to do away with it. It is true, as some critics have noted, that the Middle East could be viewed as being in the middle only in terms of latitude; viewed in terms of longitude, part of the region lies to the west of Greenwich. Moreover, viewed from India, for instance, the region could be regarded as in the middle west. Indeed there has been an attempt in India to adopt 'Western Asia' to replace the term Middle East (Davison 1960: 675). The problem with this alternative is that – as Bernard Lewis (1994: 4), another well-known student of the Middle East noted – 'it is no less misleading to view the region as the west of an entity called Asia than as the Middle East of another unspecified entity'. The ambiguous character of the lines dividing continental Europe from Asia reinforces Lewis' argument (on Europe as a continent, see Hay 1968: xvi; for an account questioning the categorisation of Europe as a 'continent', see Wigen and Lewis 1997: 35–8).

Thus, Keddie's first set of criticisms regarding its Eurocentric character and Western strategic origins is not unique to the Middle East. Throughout history the naming of land has always been done by some people who at the time were in a position to exercise power over the land and its peoples. In this sense, the answer to the question set in the beginning of the chapter, namely 'why "Middle East" but not, for instance, "Southwest Asia and North Africa" was adopted to refer to this part of the world?' is power – be it military, economic or representational. Edward Said's *Orientalism* (1995a) is an exceptional account of the workings of the unequal relationship between Western colonial powers and peoples of the Middle East during the nineteenth and twentieth century and how this manifested itself in the production of knowledge about this part of the world which, in turn, helped to keep the distance and further reinforced the inequality between the two. In sum, the reason why the lands to the southwest of Asia and north of Africa have been lumped together in the mind's eye and labelled as the Middle East has its roots not merely in the strategic interests of Britain in the late nineteenth and early twentieth century, but also in Britain's material and representational power.

The second set of criticisms advanced by Keddie arguing that the Middle East is not a 'real historical entity' and that there are relatively few common characteristics linking this group of states together as a 'region' is more difficult to dismiss. Leaving aside the problematic character of Keddie's use of the phrase 'real historical entity' (there are very few if any 'real historical entities' as such; what makes constructs seem 'real' is the myths created through the stories people tell themselves; on this issue, see, for example, Hobsbawm and Ranger 1983; Anderson 1991) it should be noted that her second point goes to the heart of the other question set in the beginning of the chapter that asked 'why the lands to the south-west of Asia and north of Africa were lumped together to constitute a region?' Keddie maintained that the answer could not be found in historical experience or religion. For, although the area roughly corresponds to the three largest Muslim empires – those of the Umayyads, the Abbasids and the Ottomans – as Keddie (1973: 257) noted, 'for pre-Islamic times the Middle East as defined by its current borders has no meaning'.

The point here is that the reason why the answer to this question cannot be found in historical experience or religion is necessarily because the origins of the region lie in the security thinking and practices of actors external to the region. The Middle East was invented because it served as a convenient geopolitical concept to help British (and later US) strategists think about and organise action in this part of the world – not because General Gordon or Captain Mahan thought this part of the world shared a history and culture and therefore constituted a region. If, to paraphrase Robert Cox (1981: 182),[12] all regions are for someone and for some purpose, the Middle East, for most of the nineteenth and twentieth century, has been for Western strategists and has served their purposes. When, in the late 1960s, Soviet policy-makers re-conceptualised their approach to Arab countries within the framework of 'collective security in Asia' (see Clark 1973; Booth and Dowdy 1982) it was still the military strategic interests of an external actor that were behind this representation; it was still an outward-directed conception of security that was adopted to secure 'Asia'.

In one sense, then, dwelling upon the Eurocentric character of the term Middle East, or the lack of shared characteristics that make it a region is a rather futile exercise. Such criticism misses the point. It hardly matters if the region is called the Middle East or 'Southwest Asia and North Africa'. For, the latter term also represents the same part of the world; the strategic purposes behind viewing *this* group of states together as a region is still there. Besides, if the reasoning behind viewing this group of states together and presenting them as a region called the Middle East is not indigenously generated but invented by actors outside the region, adopting a new label to represent the same area would not constitute too much of an improvement. Continents such as Asia, Africa and Europe are also constructs; they were invented by someone and for some purpose as Kären Wigen and Martin Lewis (1997) demonstrate in their aptly titled book, *The Myth of Continents*. After all, there is no way of getting away from representations – 'they are as basic as language' (Said 2001: 42). This, however, should not be taken to suggest that there is no need to question the origins of the Middle East. Rather it is to argue that while doing this, one should go beyond simply stating the 'obvious' (i.e. that the Middle East is a geopolitical invention rooted in British colonialism) and question the reasoning behind the invention of such a region.

Keddie was not alone in questioning the existence of a region called the Middle East (also see Abdel Aal 1986: 197–8; Kaplan 1994a). In 1978 Mohammed Heikal, editor of the Egyptian daily *Al-Ahram* and one-time advisor to President Nasser, raised similar concerns as voiced by Arab actors. Heikal's argument was that the representation of this part of the world as the Middle East marginalised Arab peoples living in these lands (Heikal 1978). Instead, Heikal opted for another representation, 'Arab System' which was based, he maintained, on the unity of religion, history and culture. According to Bahgat Korany (1997: 139), Heikal's words exemplified the mood of the time in the Arab world where many refused to be 'reduced' to become a part of a 'hinterland laying between Europe and Asia, a mere geographical expansion' (Heikal 1978: 719). The Arab System, submitted Heikal (1978: 319), could be better conceived as 'one nation having common interests and security priorities distinct from those of the West'.

One year later, two Egyptian authors, Ali Eddin Hillal Dessouki and Jamil Matar put the sentiments voiced by Heikal in conceptual terms when they introduced the representation 'Arab Regional System' to replace that of the Middle East, in their 'standard and widely read' Arabic work entitled *The Arab Regional System: An Examination of Inter-Arab Political Relations*. First published in 1979, the book was reprinted twice in 1980 and 1983 and has since become a 'popular' textbook in Arab universities (Gause 1999: 13).[13] The following quote represents the core of their argument:

> (1) the term Middle East does not refer to a geographical area but rather it represents a political term in its creation and usage; (2) the term is not derived from the nature of the area or its political, cultural, civilisational and demographic characteristics; for when we use the term 'Middle' we have to ask 'middle' in reference to what?; (3) the term tears up the Arab homeland as a distinct unit since it has always included non-Arab states.

> (Abdel Aal 1986: 197–8)

The first two points made by Dessouki and Matar echoed Keddie's critique, but the third point went one step further and challenged the reasoning behind the representation of the Middle East as a region.

Elaborating upon this latter point, Dessouki and Matar maintained that the reasoning behind Western usage of the term Middle East was to portray the region as an ethnic mosaic thereby weakening the cause of Arab nationalism and discrediting the calls for Arab unity. The spatial representation Arab Regional System could have served better, argued Dessouki and Matar, as a key for the analysis of 'interactions among Arab states, with their neighbours and with the international system at large'.[14] In other words, by proposing an alternative, Dessouki, Matar and others challenged not only the colonial origins or Eurocentric character of the Middle East, but the conception of security behind lumping this part of the world together and representing it as a region.

It should be noted that there existed other terms, before Dessouki and Matar coined the term Arab Regional System, to represent the lands where Arab peoples have historically lived. 'Arabian peninsula', 'Arab world' and 'Arab homeland' had been widely used to refer to these lands that stretched from the Gulf in the east to the Atlantic Ocean in the west. What distinguished the spatial representation Arab Regional System from these others was the fact that the former was rooted in a state-centric perspective whereas the latter predated the independence of Arab states and the emergence of the Arab state system, and were therefore reminiscent of an earlier era (when Arab peoples were not divided into states) or a future dream (that of Arab unification) (see Noble 1984). In short, the Arab Regional System as a representation not only emphasised the Arab character of this part of the world thereby de-legitimising the roles played by non-Arab actors (such as Britain, the United States, Iran, Israel and Turkey) but was also *state-centric*.

Adopting the Arab Regional System to replace the Middle East could be considered to have one advantage; it is an indigenously generated representation – not 'a euphemism for secure spheres of influence for any outside power', to use the words of Dessouki and Matar (see Abdel Aal 1986: 198). However it still is not much of an improvement over the Middle East. For one thing, it does to non-Arab peoples of the region what the term Middle East does (according to Heikal, Dessouki and Matar) to Arab peoples: it downplays their existence. Although all representations are misrepresentations to an extent, some systems of representation are more repressive because they either do not permit, or 'make room for interventions on the part of those represented' (Said 2001: 42). As conceived by Dessouki and Matar, Arab Regional System has the potential to be repressive by way of denying the existence of non-Arab peoples in this part of the world. It also neglects the roles played by Iran, Israel and Turkey. Lastly, the portrayal of the region as an Arab Regional System overemphasises its Arab character. Non-Arab peoples (including Berbers and Kurds) make up nearly half of the population in this part of the world. Moreover, the definition of who is and is not Arab is highly contested among Arab peoples themselves (see Tibi 1999).

The fact that the Arab Regional System is no less ambiguous a representation and that it does not necessarily constitute an improvement over that of the Middle East should not be taken to suggest that it should be neglected. On the contrary, as noted above, the arguments Heikal, Dessouki and Matar made in justifying their choice of term go to the very heart of the argument of this study. For, by way of criticising the spatial representation Middle East, Dessouki and Matar laid bare the (Western) conception of security at the root of this representation and presented an alternative, that of Arab Regional System, which has been shaped by the Arab national security discourse (see below).

The juxtaposition of these two spatial representations Middle East and Arab Regional System in this chapter should not be taken to mean that no other alternatives existed. There emerged at least two more alternatives, namely, the 'Euro–Med Region' and the 'Muslim Middle East'. From the late 1960s onwards, particularly following the 1967 war and the ensuing decline of pan-Arabism, these other representations came to the fore (Selim 1997). For instance, although Egypt's Mediterranean identity had been mentioned in debates, following the 1967 defeat, voices were raised suggesting that 'Egypt should stop fighting the wars of the Arabs and turn to its Mediterranean roots' (Selim 1997). The decline of pan-Arabism coincided with the efforts of the European Community (later the European Union) to distance itself from US policy towards the Middle East and adopt a more equivocal attitude by way of initiating a Mediterranean policy. Although some progress was made in creating a Euro–Mediterranean framework that would bring together EC-member states and Mediterranean-rim countries towards strengthening economic and cultural relations, the onset of the Cold War meant reverting back to the domination of the superpower agenda and the shelving of the Mediterranean policy to be revived once again in the post-Cold War era. Then, despite its origins being in the Cold War era, the Euro–Med Region will be discussed in further detail in Chapter 4 in view of the fact that it was then that it came to prominence.

Another alternative that emerged during this period was that of the 'Muslim Middle East', which was shaped by the Islamist security discourse. Its proponents consider the Middle East a representation designed to downplay the region's Muslim character and legitimise Israel's presence. As is the case with the Euro–Med Region, the spatial representation Muslim Middle East came to prominence in the post-Cold War era and will be discussed in Chapter 4.

Conclusion

This chapter sought to trace the development of the spatial representation 'Middle East' and presented an overview of the criticisms to it and the alternatives that emerged during the Cold War. It tried to answer the two questions set in the beginning, namely: 'why the lands to the south-west of Asia and north of Africa were lumped together to constitute a region?' and 'why "Middle East" but not some other label was adopted to refer to this part of the world?' Answers to both questions were found in the security concerns and practices of Britain and later the United States.

British policy-makers adopted the term Middle East to designate an area (then under Ottoman control) that was viewed as crucial in maintaining the security of British interests in India. The term Middle East became common sense afterwards, but the definition of the region changed as the security concerns and practices of its inventors changed. Changes in communications and transportation technologies also had an impact on the way this particular representation was invented and adjusted. As the military strategic interests and capabilities of the major geopolitical actors of the time changed, the 'Middle East' shifted in tandem with these changes. When US policy-makers got more closely involved in regional affairs this group of states had already become linked in the minds of many people in the West. In many Western languages, terms similar to the English – Middle East – are used: *El Medio Oriente* (Spanish) and *Le Moyen-Orient* (French). In German, the older terms, *Vorderasien* (Anterior Asia) or *Naher Osten* (Near East) are used (see Wigen and Lewis 1997: 235). In time, regional peoples themselves have also adopted the spatial representation Middle East. *Al-sharq al-awsat, khavare mirayeh, orta doğu* and *ha mizrakh a tikhan* represent its Arabic, Persian, Turkish and Hebrew equivalents, respectively (see E. Boulding 1995: 12). *Al-Sharq al-Awsat* (Middle East in Arabic) is the name of a newspaper with international circulation published in London.

However, the fact that it has become 'common sense' to represent this part of the world as the Middle East should not hide its Western strategic origins. As this chapter tried to argue, emerging alternatives such as the Arab Regional System challenged not only the Middle East's colonial origins or its Eurocentrism, but also uncovered its character as a geopolitical invention. By examining these alternative representations, and in particular that of Arab Regional System, the chapter tried to lay bare the way representations of regions are rooted in the security concerns and practices of their inventors.

It is also worth emphasising the point that not all societies have been able to impose their maps onto others. This is where relative endowment of material resources come into play in deciding whose discourse emerges as the dominant one. To put it in other words, the reason why the lands to the south-west of Asia and north of Africa have been lumped together in the mind's eye and labelled as the 'Middle East' has its roots not merely in the military strategic interests of Great Britain of the late nineteenth century, but also in Britain's material and representational power.

As Chapter 1 argued, Cold War security thinking had its origins in the security concerns and interests of Western states, mainly the United States.

This Western bias was reflected in regional security thinking as well in that regional security issues acquired relevance 'insofar as they can be slotted into the overall pattern of major power geopolitical global conflict' (Klein 1994: 14). Even when regional security issues were addressed, 'the dominant intellectual framework has been a regionalised version of the global security/strategy paradigm, so that the dilemmas facing "small" or "less powerful" states are analogised to that of the states system of the major powers' (Klein 1994: 14).

The implication of this Western bias in Cold War security thinking within the Middle Eastern context has been that much of the thinking done on regional security was based on Western conceptions of 'security' and 'region'. Indeed, the Middle East is a geopolitical invention rooted in the security concerns of Britain as an imperial power in that it was invented when thinking about and organising action for India's security. What Mahan meant by security in the Middle East was maintaining security in the Gulf in order to secure the route to India and hold Russia in check. This policy advice rested on a top-down conception of security that was directed outwards and prioritised military threats.

Even before the intensification of the Cold War in the Middle East, there was agreement amongst British and US policy-makers as to what 'security in the Middle East' meant. Notwithstanding the differences (as with the British stress on maintaining ties with the former colonies as long as possible and growing US emphasis on Israel's well-being)[15] by the early 1950s US and British policy-makers agreed that maintaining 'security in the Middle East' meant its defence against Soviet expansionism and interventionism. At the root of this approach was a top-down conception of security (regional actors' threat perceptions were not considered as relevant) that was directed outwards (threats were assumed to stem from outside) and privileged the maintenance of stability (for fear of unleashing forces that might invite Soviet interventionism). As discussed in Chapter 1, this conception of security is rooted in a realist outlook that shaped the security thinking and practices of Western actors during the Cold War.

The alternative spatial representation that emerged during this period, that of 'Arab Regional System' was developed in criticising the strategic rationale behind the representation of this part of the world as the Middle East, for it was considered as a 'euphemism for secure spheres of influence' for either Moscow or Washington (Abdel Aal 1986: 198). The spatial representation Arab Regional System rested on an alternative conception of security, namely 'Arab national security', which rested on two assumptions: the security concerns and interests of Arab states could be better understood when viewed in relation to one another; these concerns are different from if not opposed to those of non-Arab states. These two assumptions, in turn, were rooted in the precepts of the pan-Arabist movement of the late nineteenth and early twentieth century that shaped Arab peoples' conceptions of 'nationhood'. During this period of incessant struggle against Ottoman and later British and French domination, Arab policy-makers shaped their policies in line with the assumption that their 'shared Arab identity generated a common definition of what threatened their interests' (Barnett 1998: 223; also see Nasser 1955).

The argument above should not be taken to suggest that a pre-existing Arab identity preceded and shaped Arab actors' interests. Although the peoples living on the lands that have historically been called the 'Arabian peninsula' have shared a common language, culture and traditions, the myth of a shared Arab identity was invented in the struggle against colonialism and for political independence during the late nineteenth and early twentieth century.[16] While this notion of a shared Arab identity helped organise resistance at the state as well as sub-state level against external actors, it, at the same time, restrained their actions in that demands made in line with the precepts of Arab national security often clashed with that of state security. Indeed, as Abdel Monem Said Aly (1996: 26) argued, 'it is very difficult to find any conceptualisation of security perceptions that is not coloured by a pan-Arab perspective'. It is worth quoting him at length:

> Most of the Arab literature on security perceptions is based on the notion that Arabs have common security needs, even when the much narrower security perceptions of one or another Arab state are being represented. Major research centres in the Arab world take it as a point of departure and analysis. The annual *Arab Strategic Report* of the Al-Ahram Center for Political and Strategic Studies in Cairo takes the Arab world as a point of departure for analysis of Arab relations with neighbours and the world; *The States of the Arab Nation,* annual report of the Center for Arab Unity Studies in Beirut, takes a similar approach, the studies of the Arab Though Forum in Amman do not deviate from the same tradition.
>
> (Said Aly 1996: 27; see also Korany 1994; Korany *et al.* 1993)

It should be noted that early conceptualisations of Arab national security referred to the security of the society of Arab peoples, i.e. the transstate entity of the Arab nation. However, as more and more Arab states became independent, there emerged a tension between the demands of 'state security' and 'societal security'. Practical manifestations of this interplay between state security and societal security will be explored in Chapter 3. Suffice it to say that during the 1950s and 1960s, when Nasser was at the peak of his popularity, he adopted the early, more societal-focused understanding of Arab national security and used the Arab national security discourse as a tool in the attempt to nudge his fellow Arab policy-makers into line. In other words, Nasser's adoption of a societal-focused approach to Arab national security stemmed not necessarily from his concern with the security of Arab peoples, but from his leader-ship aspirations. In the long run, Nasser's interventionism led to the decline of his understanding of Arab national security; conservative Arab regimes of the Gulf felt threatened by his moves and in reaction adopted more and more statist approaches. As more Arab states became indepen-dent, the early and more societal-focused conceptualisation of Arab national security was replaced with a state-centric understanding. When they put forward the Arab Regional System as an alternative representa-tion, Ali Eddin Hillal Dessouki and Jamil Matar sought to conceptualise this more state-centric understanding of Arab national security (see also Toukan 1997). The early societal-focused understanding of Arab national security, however, remained alive at the societal level, constituting a con-straint upon the increasingly statist practices shaped by the later under-standing.

The concept of Arab national security constituted a development over Cold War conceptions of regional security in two ways. First, it was gener-ated by peoples in this part of the world and reflected (some, if not all of) their security concerns that did not make the agendas set by the Western-originated conceptions of regional security. Issues such as food, economic and water security were invariably presented as Arab national security issues. However, as will be discussed in Chapter 3, these issues were almost always viewed from a statist perspective.

Second, the concept of Arab national security partially did away with the top-down perspective of the Cold War approaches – only partially because it substituted the top-down perspective of the United States with the statist and top-down perspectives of the Arab states that often acted in defiance of the concerns of peoples and social groups. Indeed this state-centric conceptualisation of Arab national security left little room for the concerns of individuals and social groups that chose to define themselves with reference to other dimensions of their identity such as gender or (in the case of non-Muslims) religion. This thinking stemmed from an outward-directed conception of security that assumed threats to Arab national security to stem from outside the Arab Regional System, that is, from non-Arabs. Inside was assumed to be a realm of peace and security (see also Toukan 1997). In this sense, the criticisms the proponents of Arab national security voiced against Western-originated approaches to Middle Eastern security stemmed not so much from their state-centric or outward-directed character, but from their referent, the Middle East.

In sum, albeit cognisant of non-military dimensions of security, stu-dents of Arab national security embraced the state-centric and zero-sum approach of the Cold War approaches to security. Students of Arab national security called for a broader conception of security to study the security needs and concerns of Arab *states*. This amounted, on the one hand, to the privileging of (military and non-military) threats to the security of Arab *states* thereby marginalising the concerns of individuals and social groups. On the other hand, this meant that the relations between Arab states and their non-Arab counterparts (the Arab–Israeli relationship, for instance) were understood as being governed by the outward-directed, zero-sum and military-focused conceptions and practices of security, which characterised the Cold War security discourse – an approach of which they were otherwise highly critical.[17]

3   Practices of security during the Cold War

Chapter 3 concludes Part I by bringing together the arguments made in Chapters 1 and 2 in the attempt to illustrate further the relationship between (inventing) regions and (conceptions and practices of) security during the Cold War. Here I look at the practical manifestations of adopting particular spatial representations and the security conceptions in which they are rooted. The purpose here is not to present a comprehensive account of Middle Eastern history, but only to direct attention to those practices that were designed to achieve regional security. As a result, not all practices will be covered. Rather, the chapter will focus on those attempts to address the problem of regional security. The aim is to show how representations of the region helped to shape practice; how they enabled some practices whilst marginalising others; how they addressed some insecurities while constituting others.

The chapter will first look at those practices of security designed to secure the 'Middle East'. These practices were informed by Cold War approaches to regional security. Next, the chapter will turn to look at the practices of regional actors that were adopted to achieve security in the Arab Regional System in line with the precepts of 'Arab national security'. The final section of the chapter will provide an account of the practical implications of the rivalry between these two contending approaches to security.

Security in the Middle East

Britain in the Middle East until the Cold War

Due to the significance of India for British interests, Britain had been concerned with the security of land and sea routes that led to the south of Asia since the very early days of its engagement. Indeed, as Elizabeth Monroe (1981: 11) noted, it is difficult to exaggerate how significant India was for Britain until the Indian Independence Act of 1947. Britain's interest in security of the Gulf increased gradually from the sixteenth century onwards in tandem with the intensification of its involvement in India.

The opening of the Suez Canal in 1869 added to the strategic importance of Egypt as well as the Gulf. The practices British policy-makers adopted during this period to secure the Middle East included signing a 'General Treaty of Peace' with Arab tribes of the Gulf to suppress piracy and slave traffic, the capture of Aden (1837) and assuming the responsibility for Bahrain's external affairs in return for the Sheikh of Bahrain's pledge not to prosecute war, piracy and slavery by sea (1880) (Ovendale 1998: 3–4). In the years to come, Aden and Bahrain (together with Cyprus) were to become significant staging posts to carry out air operations in the Middle East (Monroe 1981: 183–4). Then, from the late nineteenth century onwards, Britain's grip over the Gulf began to strengthen with the rulers of the emirates and sheikhdoms along the Gulf coast beginning to follow Bahrain's example and choosing to conduct their foreign relations through the British government. In 1899 a treaty was concluded with the Sheikh of Kuwait recognising it as an independent state under British protection.

Britain's search for bases in the region culminated in its occupation of Egypt in 1882, symbolising a shift in British practices from 'security by influence to security by occupation' (Monroe 1981: 18). Following Germany's acquisition of a concession from the Ottoman Empire to build a Berlin–İstanbul–Baghdad railway (1903), British policy-makers came to an understanding with their French counterparts that Britain would exchange a 'free hand' in Egypt with a 'free hand' for France in Morocco (1907). This constituted a further shift in British security practices in that British policy-makers had, until then, avoided partitioning Middle Eastern interests with their rivals, preferring to maintain a weak but nevertheless intact Ottoman Empire (Ortaylı 1983; Palmer 1992). The agreement with France was followed by a deal with Russia to divide Iran (Persia) into spheres of influence (Ovendale 1998: 6; Monroe 1981: 19). By the time the First World War broke out, Britain had firmly established its control over the Middle East. The strengthening of British control over the Gulf and Egypt was followed by the construction of railways and roads in the region strengthening the links between the Mediterranean and the Gulf coasts (Smith 1968: 5). These developments not only helped lump these chunks of territory in the minds of British policy-makers but also led to an increase in its strategic significance.

The main reason for Britain's interest in securing the Middle East remained India's defence throughout this period. It should also be noted that by 1914 oil discoveries had been made in Iran as well as the Arabian Peninsula, which further increased the significance of the area in the eyes of British policy-makers. The Royal Navy had switched from coal to oil in 1912 and although it was the United States that supplied 80 per cent of British demand at this stage, and notwithstanding the fact that it still was not known how rich the Middle Eastern reserves were, British policy-makers were nevertheless determined to keep a check on the region's oil reserves (Adelson 1995: 95–100). In 1914, the British government became the majority shareholder in the Anglo-Persian Oil Company.[1] The Anglo-Turkish Oil Company, which exploited the (then) 'hypothetical' oil fields of Iraq, was also controlled by Britain. The Iraqi oil fields were hypothetical because there had yet to be discovered commercial quantities of oil. Still, this did not prevent British policy-makers from keeping Mosul (where some of these hypothetical oil wells were located) in Iraq when drawing the Iraqi–Turkish border (1926) (Lenczowski 1980: 123; Monroe 1981: 103–4; Akşin 1991: 126–31).

With the outbreak of the First World War, British and French policy-makers sought to support the war effort against the Ottoman Empire by encouraging Arab peoples in the region to revolt against the *Sublime Porte* (the imperial centre). At the same time, Britain and France signed the Sykes–Picot agreement (1916), partitioning the Arabian Peninsula into zones of influence, with France assuming control in the north and Britain in the south (Monroe 1981: 32–7). The terms of the agreement were not disclosed to Arab peoples who had agreed to incite the revolt in return for the promise of independence.

It is difficult to exaggerate the disappointment Arab peoples who joined the revolt felt when they found out about the terms of the Sykes–Picot agreement (which were disclosed by the Bolsheviks after they took power in Russia in 1917). The creation of separate states – Iraq, Jordan (under British mandate), Syria and Lebanon (under French mandate) – further deepened the disappointment of those Arab nationalists who seemed to assume that Arab peoples would become independent as a unified entity after the war (Gomaa 1977: 3; Fromkin 1989). Needless to say, neither British nor French policy-makers were in favour of Arab unification. This was not necessarily because they opposed it in principle, but rather because each feared the other might enhance its influence if Arab peoples were to unite. Moreover, the partitioning of Arab peoples into separate states and the creation and consolidation of local nationalisms served the purposes of the mandate powers by making it easier to maintain stability (Gomaa 1977: 26–9).

The inter-war period in the Middle East was characterised by two inter-related themes, namely, the struggle for Arab independence and the emerging deadlock over Palestine. Following the consolidation of the mandate system, the struggle for independence had become the main purpose of Arab nationalists, resulting in the marginalisation of the calls for Arab unity (Gomaa 1977: 5). The aim of the Jewish movement at this stage was to ensure unlimited immigration and settlement in Palestine. National independence within Palestine was also the aim of Palestinian Arabs. The point here is that although the urge to independent statehood took precedence over unification among Arab actors, the latter was never kept off the agendas for reasons to do with the salience of the Palestine issue. In the words of one author, the Palestinians were viewed 'symbolically as the conscience of the Arab world' (Sirriyeh 2000: 56). Indeed, it was not only the fear of an emergent Jewish state, but also the plight of the Palestinian peoples that reinforced the arguments of the proponents of Arab national security. As will be seen in the following section, the strength of Arab peoples' feelings on the Palestinian issue made it impossible for regional policy-makers (even those who were rather sceptical of pan-Arabism such as the Saudi leadership) to ignore it.

In order to cope with Arab actors' increasingly vociferous calls for independence and a solution to be found to the Palestinian conflict, British policy-makers followed a two-pronged strategy. On the one hand, they granted nominal independence to Egypt, Iraq and Jordan and encouraged their leaders to consolidate their own regimes, the assumption being that the region would be easier to control if it remained divided into smaller units. In 1921, when setting up Jordan and Iraq as separate states, Colonial Secretary Winston Churchill had reached an understanding with their leaders that they would contain the Arab nationalist movement and help to maintain the status quo in the region (Gomaa 1977: 26). On the other hand Britain also sought to ensure the co-existence of two separate communities in Palestine by perpetuating existing divisions and appearing to favour both sides. In other words, British efforts to stall Arab unification efforts were also designed to prevent the formation of a unified Arab front in Palestine (Heikal 1996: 50–85).

Although the policy of divide-and-rule seems to have worked for a while, as the pace of Jewish migration into Palestine quickened in the mid-1930s, Arab disgruntlement over the existing situation reached its peak, which culminated in the Palestine Arab revolt of 1936 that lasted intermittently until 1939. By the time the Second World War broke out, an 'uneasy truce' (Gomaa 1977: 16) prevailed in Palestine. Outlining the situation in the region at the outbreak of the War, Ritchie Ovendale wrote the following:

> On outbreak of war against Germany, Iraq breaks off relations with Germany. Turkey is neutral. Those areas of the former Ottoman Empire under British or French control are non-belligerent but within the war zone. The Suez Canal and retention of India is of strategic and political importance to Britain. Protection of oil supplies from Iraq is also important. Egypt is Britain's Mediterranean base. The Allies regard the Middle East as *secure.*
>
> (Ovendale 1998: 15)[2]

Judging by the top-down, military-focused and outward-directed conception of regional security adopted by British (and other allied) policy-makers, the Middle East could indeed have been considered 'secure'; regional stability was not threatened by any local or external actor.

At the end of the Second World War, the significance of the Middle East further increased in the eyes of Western policy-makers. For Britain, following the India Independence Act of 1947 the Middle East had ceased to be important for where it was, that is, on the route to India, but what it was – a region housing a significant portion of the world's known oil reserves. Following the declaration of the Marshall Plan (1947), the stable flow of oil from the Middle East rose higher on the US security agenda as well. By now, the Middle East's contribution to world oil production had increased considerably. In 1938, one year before the start of the Second World War, the region's production amounted to less than one-twentieth of the world oil output. By 1948, the ratio had become one-eighth (Monroe 1981: 95). The security of the stable flow of oil, together with checking Soviet expansionism and the well-being of the state of Israel, were to become the pillars of the US approach to regional security in the Middle East.

This period of increasing US interest in Middle Eastern oil coincided with the advances the Soviet government made to Iran and Turkey in the immediate aftermath of the Second World War. Although it could be (and has indeed been) argued that there was sparse evidence of Soviet expansionism in the Middle East until well after Khrushchev's ascent to power (Dawisha 1982: 8–23), security assessments of British and US policy-makers suggested otherwise. Indeed, the demands the Soviets made from Iran and Turkey in the immediate aftermath of the Second World War were considered as instances that signalled the emerging tension between the Soviet Union and the United States – a tension that culminated in the Cold War (Kuniholm 1980; also see Yapp 1982: 25–6; Little 2002: 117–55).

Securing the Middle East during the Cold War

The demands Soviet policy-makers made from Turkey in the aftermath of the Second World War included making the renewal of its 1925 Treaty of Friendship and Neutrality with Turkey conditional on the latter's surrendering of Kars and Ardahan, two eastern provinces, and the revision of the Montreaux convention governing the Turkish Straits (Bosphorus and Dardanelles) so that they would gain a say in their control. Although Soviet policy-makers retreated from their demands, and denied any breach of Iranian sovereignty or attempts to change its regime during its occupation of the north of Iran towards the end of the War, both Iran and Turkey soon joined anti-Soviet alliances with the West (Ramazani 1976: 324–5; Kuniholm 1980). This is not to suggest that it was purely Stalin's threats and demands that caused these two states to ally with the West. On the contrary, the Soviet threat seems to have been used by both Iranian and Turkish policy-makers for domestic security purposes, to curb the 'extreme' left and re-inscribe Iranian and Turkish state identities as staunch Western allies thereby strengthening their economic as well as military relations with the United States (on Turkey, see Kürkçüoğlu 1972: 36–7; on Iran, see Ramazani 1976).

Although both Iran and Turkey had their own reasons for joining anti-Soviet alliances, the same could not be said about the Arab states of the region. Nor did Soviet policy-makers pursue a consistent policy towards Arab states until the mid-1950s. It should also be noted that the Soviets had little direct economic interest in the region other than disrupting that of the West (Dawisha 1982: 10; Chubin 1984: 125–74) and complicating the US strategic position thereby drawing Western capability away from the Soviet Union (MacGwire 1987: 222).

Even during the mid-1950s when Egypt turned to the Soviet Union, or the late 1960s when Soviet policy-makers adopted the policy of 'Collective Security in Asia' (see Clark 1973: 473–82; Booth and Dowdy 1982: 342), it was more the pressure US and British policy-makers put on regional states to join anti-Soviet alliances or to grant military bases, rather than mere Soviet inducement, that enabled it to become a force in Arab politics (Dawisha 1982: 8). For, the policy-makers of the newly independent Arab states in the Middle East had already made it clear that they did not wish to enter into an alliance with any Western power. With the exception of Iraq, most Arab states did not perceive the Soviet Union or communist infiltration to be the most significant threat to their security. Indeed, many assumed that sheer geographical distance would deter the Soviet Union from undertaking any military attack (see Heikal 1978: 720).

Even in Iraq (which was geographically closer to the Soviet Union) the anti-colonial and anti-Western mood of the public made it difficult to enter into an alliance with the West. The experience of the 1948 Treaty of Portsmouth signed between Iraq and Britain, which had to be repudiated within a week because of public outcry in Iraq, had showed how strong Arab public opinion was on the issue of any concessions given to former colonial powers. The event also showed how security needs and interests of people in Iraq differed from their regime, which was in favour of the sustenance of close military links with Britain due to concerns about domestic and regime security. It is also worth noting here that the 1948 protest by Iraqi people was one of the few instances of the successful employment of non-violent action in this part of the world (Bennett 1990: 47–8).

When it became clear that regional states would no longer be as subservient to British security interests as they were in the past, British policy-makers decided to adopt an alternative approach. Instead of seeking to maintain military bases by conducting bilateral agreements, they sought to create a regional security organisation to which Britain would be a party. It was hoped that this would not only enable Britain to maintain access to military bases in the Middle East, but also do this in a cost-effective manner whilst avoiding the animosity of an increasingly bitter Arab public opinion. They also hoped that creating a region-wide defence organisation would be more attractive to Arab policy-makers than the maintenance of purely British military bases and bilateral alliances. The idea of forming a Middle East Command (MEC) modelled after NATO emerged when thinking along these lines (Campbell 1958: 40; Monroe 1981: 155–6; Little 2002: 125–9).

The original idea foresaw the formation of two rings. The 'inner ring' would consist of Egypt and other Arab states and would be led by a British commander. The 'outer ring' would stretch from Greece in the West to Iran in the East. As Little (2002: 126) noted,

> Convinced that this U.K. initiative would serve 'to build up the will of the area to resist communism' by working 'to strengthen the whole Near Eastern will to defend itself and to join with the West', the Truman administration agreed to provide modest amounts of U.S. military assistance to key Arab states under the auspices of America's new Mutual Security Program.

Yet, from the outset Egyptian policy-makers made clear that they were not interested in participating in a Middle Eastern Command, which would enable Britain, the colonial power, to maintain its grip over Egypt.

US policy-makers took this as a sign of 'the decline of the U.K. as a world power' (Little 2002: 126) and moved in with their own proposal for the formation of a Middle East Defense Organisation (MEDO) in 1952. The semantic change was intended to prevent the revoking of colonial memories by the word 'command'. However, since MEDO was also designed to defend this part of the world against Soviet expansionism and involved British participation, it was not too different from MEC in the eyes of many in the Arab World. Besides, given such indifference to regional actors' different conceptions of security, US policy-makers had proved not much different from their British colleagues. Theirs, too, was a top-down approach to regional security that prioritised the concerns of external powers at the expense of those of the regional actors.

Still, the MEDO proposal did not fall on deaf ears so far as some regional actors were concerned. As British policy-makers expected, the pro-Western Iraqi government of Nuri Said embraced the idea of re-packaging its treaty with Britain by putting it into a multilateral format as opposed to its current form (a bilateral treaty with a former colonial power) (Lenczowski 1980: 284). Turkish policy-makers were also keen in participating in the formation of MEDO not so much because they believed such an organisation would help maintain regional security, but rather because they wished to strengthen their relations with the West (the United States in particular). As a part of the deal British and Turkish policy-makers struck in the aftermath of the Second World War, the former was to help Turkey become a NATO member in exchange for the latter helping to set up a regional security organisation in the Middle East. During this period, Turkish policy-makers also sought to present Turkey as a 'bridge' between the West and Middle East, an actor that could persuade half-hearted Arab policy-makers to join an alliance with the West. In other words, for Turkish policy-makers the proposed Middle East regional security schemes constituted means to an end – that is, becoming a NATO member (Kürkçüoğlu 1972: 36–7, 71–2; also see Karpat *et al.* 1975; Tamkoç 1976; Karaosmanoğlu and Taşhan 1987; Bölükbaşı 1992).

It is significant to note here that in Spring 1951 Turkey was invited by the Egyptian government to join an alternative regional security scheme that would have brought together Turkey with the members of the Arab League to create a professedly non-aligned bloc in the region. The proposal failed to generate any interest among Turkish policy-makers who did not consider non-alignment a feasible policy option. Besides, they had already set their eyes on NATO membership (Lenczowksi 1980: 520). Later in 1951, soon after its refusal of the Egyptian proposal, Turkey joined Britain, France and the United States to formulate a proposal for the creation of MEDO. The aim was initially to establish MEDO with five members (Britain, Egypt, France, Turkey and the United States) and gradually increase the number of members. Egypt's participation in the scheme was crucial for its success, but this never occurred. The Egyptian government rejected the proposal within two days of receiving it, making it clear that it was not given much consideration (Campbell 1958: 43).

Notwithstanding the Egyptian refusal, both Britain and Turkey were still in favour of setting up the Organisation basing it in Cyprus instead of Egypt. The United States, on the other hand, was sceptical as to whether a Middle East Defence Organisation without Arab participation would serve the purpose of making the Middle East inviolable to Soviet intervention (McGhee 1990: 153–4). At this stage US policy-makers had become aware of the hesitance on the part of Arab states of entering into an alliance with their former colonial powers, France and Britain. However, they were still oblivious to the degree to which Arab governments did not accord the same significance to the Soviet threat as they did.

The argument here is that behind Egypt's rejection of the MEDO proposal lay the discrepancy between contending approaches to regional security: 'Arab national security' and 'Middle Eastern security'. The MEDO initiative helped to crystallise the differences between these two contending approaches in a way that had not become clear before; solidifying the Arab/non-Arab distinction was to become central to Arab national security thinking. The regional actors' practices (which were shaped by the Arab national security discourse) will be looked at in the next section. It should suffice to note here that Nasser's invitation to Turkey, in early 1951, to join a non-aligned pact with the Arab League members may have been political expediency on the route to Arab leadership. Alternatively, he might have intended to construct a more inclusive regional security scheme with the inclusion of some non-Arab states (Sanjian 1997: 238). What is more clear is that at this stage, Nasser's Arab national security discourse was defined against former colonial powers, and not against all non-Arab states. It took two more episodes, namely, the Northern Tier and the Baghdad Pact, for the Arab/non-Arab distinction to become more central to his understanding of Arab national security.

The proposal for the creation of a Northern Tier scheme was put forward by US Secretary of State John Foster Dulles, who came to conclude that those states that had the Soviet Union as their northern neighbour were more 'conscious' of the Soviet threat and were therefore more ready to enter into bilateral or multilateral military assistance agreements, if not to join a regional security scheme with the West (Lenczowksi 1980: 283). The assumption behind Dulles' thinking, an assumption which was also shared by Turkish Prime Minister Adnan Menderes, was that those Arab states (such as Egypt) that did not prioritise the Soviet threat were not aware of what the 'real' threats to their security were and therefore not ready for cooperation with the West (Campbell 1958: 70; McGhee 1990; Sanjian 1997: 231). Dulles hoped that Turkey, Iraq, Syria and Pakistan could be convinced to enter into an anti-Soviet alliance, thereby creating the Northern Tier – a regional security scheme made up of an association of local forces under an indigenous command (Sanjian 1997: 227; Little 2002: 128). The provision of US military assistance was hoped to constitute enough of a reason for these states to join the scheme.

US policy-makers were encouraged in their thinking by their Turkish and Iraqi counterparts who were keen to receive US military and economic aid (Sanjian 1997).[3] Indeed, following Dulles' tour in 1953 of the Northern Tier, Turkish and Iraqi policy-makers took the initiative and began to look for ways of cooperation. In April 1954 Turkey and Pakistan signed a defence cooperation agreement. In February 1955 Turkey and Iraq signed a separate text agreeing to 'cooperate for their security and defence'. Later in the year, the Turco-Iraqi agreement became the Baghdad Pact, with Pakistan, Britain and Iran's adherence. In short, initiatives made for the creation of a low-profile Northern Tier scheme led to the formation of the more ambitious Baghdad Pact. Hesitant to further alienate the Egyptian government the United States declined to join the Pact, but maintained 'full cooperation', which meant that it provided economic and military aid (Ashton 1993: 123–37; see also Little 2002: 126–30). With US membership to the Baghdad Pact not forthcoming, Britain's membership put the Iraqi government in a very difficult position; for it became vulnerable to the criticism that the Pact allowed Britain to 'leave by the door but come back by the window' (Lenczowksi 1980: 286). The disgruntlement among the Iraqi population culminated in the Iraqi coup of 1958 and the fall of the Hashemite dynasty that had been installed in power by Britain in 1921.

Following the Iraqi revolution, the Baghdad Pact headquarters was moved from Baghdad to Ankara. The name was changed from the 'Baghdad Pact' into the 'Central Treaty Organisation' (CENTO). It is difficult to know whether the Baghdad Pact/CENTO ever served as a deterrent against potential Soviet attack. It is highly likely that its main contribution remained in the field of development, by providing economic as well as technological aid transfer to member-states (Hadley 1971: 36–8). It supported member states in their state building efforts thereby helping to raise the standard of living as well as maintaining regime security.

Although the Baghdad Pact/CENTO had little practical impact from 1959 onwards, it remained a symbol of the discrepancy between the two contending approaches to regional security in the years to come. Indeed, the Iraqi coup and the demise of the Baghdad Pact were decisive moments of conflict between these two security discourses. In the following three decades, the Arab national security discourse failed to prevail over that of the Middle East or put the aims behind the formation of the Arab League Collective Security Pact into practice (see the following section). US policy-makers made no more attempts to create an all-encompassing regional security scheme, but concentrated on key states, namely Iran, Saudi Arabia, Turkey and Israel (increasingly on the latter after the 1967 war) whilst trying to prevent the prevalence of Nasser's approach to regional security.

The argument so far should not be taken to suggest that the practices of British and later US policy-makers were designed purely to divide-and-rule and to maintain regional stability. On the contrary, British practices during the colonial period included building up an infrastructure as well as enhancing transportation and communication links between different parts of the region. Although these were done partly to make the control of the region easier, enhanced communication and transportation facilities also helped strengthen the pan-Arab movement by enabling peoples to become more aware of their shared characteristics and cooperate and collaborate at the grassroots level (Hourani 1947: 127). Later, during the 1950s, successive US governments poured military as well as economic aid into the region in the attempt to win hearts and minds. The economic development of Turkey, for instance, owed a lot to US aid. However, notwithstanding such constructive attempts to enhance Western influence in the region, other practices such as the maintenance of the mandate system, covert operations undertaken to prevent the downfall of pro-Western leaders/regimes, or attempts to block Arab unity efforts alienated many Arab actors who ranked de-colonisation through closer cooperation and collaboration among Arab actors high on their security agenda. The next section will look at the practices of regional actors who located themselves in the Arab Regional System, before presenting, in the third section, an overview of the practical manifestations of the competition between two contending approaches to security.

Security in the Arab Regional System

It has so far been argued that the security practices adopted by the United States and its allies during the Cold War were shaped by and, in turn, shaped the Cold War approach to (regional) security. It was further argued that some, such as Iraqi, Iranian and Turkish policy-makers, also shaped their practices in line with this approach, albeit for reasons of their own – be it rapid development with the help of US economic and military aid and/or regime security – concerns shared by other developing countries. Arab policy-makers, on the other hand, with the exception of their Iraqi counterparts, were rather hesitant to enter into anti-Soviet alliances with the West. There were three main reasons for this. First, they did not consider the threat posed by the Soviet Union so significant as to be ranked above all other security concerns. In response to Dulles' invitation to join the Northern Tier scheme, Nasser is reported to have said:

> How can I go to my people and tell them I am disregarding a killer with a pistol sixty miles from me at the Suez Canal to worry about someone who is holding a knife 5000 miles away?
>
> (Brands 1991: 277)

Nasser clearly saw the cessation of the British presence in Egypt as the priority so far as the stability of his regime was concerned. This ties into the second reason why Arab policy-makers were hesitant to join anti-Soviet alliances in that they were more concerned with issues of de-colonisation and achieving political and economic sovereignty (also see Niva 1999). Saudi Arabia and Yemen did not have a colonial history, but were also interested in issues of de-colonisation, particularly because of their interest in the Palestinian peoples' predicament, which constituted the third reason why the Soviet threat did not dominate regional security agendas. The Palestine issue occupied many Arab peoples' minds making it very difficult for even conservative regimes not known for their pan-Arab credentials (such as that of Saudi Arabia) to keep it off their own security agendas.

Indeed, as Edward Said noted, the issue of Israel/Palestine has been 'a symbol for struggle against social injustice' in the Arab world. During the Egyptian student demonstrations of the early 1970s a frequent slogan was: 'We are all Palestinians' (Said 1992: 125). The Israel/Palestine issue and the very inability of Arab regimes to find a solution to the plight of the Palestinian peoples proved instrumental in voicing a number of other issues such as development, economic and social justice, and democratisation. Given the linkages Arab peoples established between the question of Israel/Palestine and that of Arab national security, it is no wonder that schemes such as MEC, MEDO or the Baghdad Pact (which were not only initiated by the former colonial powers and their allies but also threatened to marginalise issues that were on top of regional peoples' security agendas) were deemed unacceptable. So much so that, even those more conservative states, which practically distanced themselves from the Arab national security discourse from the late 1950s onwards, found it difficult to publicly denounce its precepts. The Iraqi regime, which did denounce the main principle of Arab national security by joining the Baghdad Pact, was toppled by its own people in 1958.

During their struggle against former colonial powers, many Arab actors assumed that their 'shared Arab identity generated a common definition of what threatened their interests' (Barnett 1998: 223). The leaders of the pan-Arab movement, when they joined the rebellion against the Ottoman Empire during the First World War, believed that Arab peoples would become independent as a unified entity in exchange for their efforts. The partitioning of the Arabian peninsula into separate (but not yet sovereign or independent) states and their allocation to Britain and France as the mandatory powers, and the reluctance of British policy-makers to prevent the inflow of Jewish immigrants into Palestine or purchase land away from the Palestinians, only added to the disillusionment of Arab peoples and strengthened the calls for a unified Arab front to be formed to address these issues.

However, although the appeal of Arab unification for Arab peoples made it difficult for regional regimes to openly oppose it, they made little effort to think of ways of achieving Arab unity. On the contrary, Arab leaders were busy minimising the threats posed to their regimes by their fellow Arab leaders. In 1936, to minimise such interference in each other's internal affairs, Saudi Arabia and Iraq concluded the 'Treaty of Arab Brotherhood and Alliance', which Yemen acceded to one year later. Although the treaty was presented as comprising 'collective security arrangements', it did not amount to more than an affirmation of respect for each other's territorial integrity and sovereignty and a declaration of intention to cooperate closely on all fields, including security (understood as defence).[4] The formation of the Arab League was to constitute a firmer step taken in the same direction.

As noted above, the accelerating pace of Jewish immigration into Palestine during the 1930s had further increased the calls for Arab unity and hastened Arab actors' efforts to come up with ideas as to what shape Arab unification should take. The 1936 Arab revolt in Palestine was one manifestation of the struggle on the part of Arab actors to come up with ways of countering the increasing pace of Jewish immigration and land purchases which signalled the establishment of a Jewish state. Conferences organised by Britain during the 1930s and 1940s to discuss the Palestine issue increased Arab representatives' awareness of inter-Arab differences whilst helping them realise the need to create an Arab body to represent their views (Seabury 1949: 636; Gomaa 1977: 8–10).

The Alexandria Protocol marked the beginning of the road that led to the establishment of such a body, the League of Arab States (LAS). The Protocol was signed on 7 October 1944 at a meeting of a preparatory committee; Egypt, Iraq, Jordan, Lebanon, Saudi Arabia, Syria and Yemen were represented in this committee (for a detailed account of the negotiations, see Gomaa 1977: 153–234). It was declared that the signatories to the Protocol were

> anxious to strengthen and consolidate the ties which bind all Arab countries and to direct them toward the welfare of the Arab world, to improve its conditions, insure its future, and realize its hopes and aspirations.[5]

As Ahmed Gomaa (1977: 226) noted, the document, agreed after long deliberations, was partly a statement of intentions, and partly an attempt to appeal to Arab public opinion. The above-quoted article, when considered together with the signatories' pledge that 'in no case the adoption of a foreign policy which may be prejudicial to the policy of the League or an individual member state be allowed' is an early manifestation of the tension between state security and societal security in the Arab world. The point here is that the Alexandria Protocol had given priority to the principle of sovereignty but nevertheless mentioned Arab unity as a long-term objective. The LAS Pact was to put further emphasis on the former whilst omitting the latter (Hourani 1947: 132–3) – an act that indicated how jealously the principle of sovereignty was guarded by Arab policy-makers. Even the declaration of intent to coordinate foreign policies, which was stipulated in the Protocol, was removed from the LAS Pact.

The League of Arab States was set up a year later, with the Pact of the League being signed on 22 March 1945 by Egypt, Iraq, Jordan, Lebanon, Saudi Arabia and Syria. Yemen signed later in the year. It was noted in the preamble that the League was being formed in response to 'the wishes of Arab public opinion in all Arab lands'. The Pact stipulated that the League would

> support and stabilize [the ties which link the Arab states] upon a basis of respect for the independence and sovereignty of these states, and to direct their efforts towards the common good of all the Arab countries, the improvement of their status, the security of their future, the realization of their aspirations and hopes.[6]

Regarding the issue of inter-Arab relations, the main principle was that of non-intervention in the internal affairs of member states. Since it was the principles of sovereignty and non-intervention that were given priority, as noted above, debates on the issue of peaceful settlement of disputes proved controversial. After a lengthy debate between those in favour of establishing a strong machinery for the peaceful settlement of disputes and those who opposed the idea, it was agreed that the League's jurisdiction would not be compulsory over such disputes (see Hassouna 1975: 9; Gomaa 1977: 251–5; also see Shehadi 1997: 216–33). This relatively little evidence of attention paid to dispute resolution within the region betrayed an outward-directed conception of security (that assumed 'inside' to be secure and that threats came from 'outside'). As will be seen below, the Arab League Collective Security Pact, signed in 1950 in the attempt to relieve the deficiencies of the LAS Pact, also focused on the defence of Arabs (inside) from non-Arabs (outside).

However, notwithstanding this stress on statist concerns, in 1948 the Arab states joined forces to fight on behalf of the Palestinians – an action that showed how Arab policy-makers could not afford to be seen as leaving other Arab peoples to their fate. The argument here is not that the 1948 campaign undertaken by Arab states to help the Palestinians (or the 1967 and 1973 wars, for that matter) constituted an act of altruism that put the security of their respective states in danger – although the war did nothing to enhance their credibility regarding their ability to undertake effective military action. Rather the argument is that although Arab policy-makers prioritised the security of their respective states, they nevertheless found it difficult to act in total defiance of the concerns voiced by other Arab actors that were formulated in terms of Arab national security.

Indeed, although Arab policy-makers' practices were mostly statist, undertaken to enhance their own regime security under the mantle of state security, it is impossible to deny the fact that they were also concerned, if only at the discursive level, with the well-being of Arab peoples. The place accorded to the Palestine issue on top of Arab national security agendas (stated repeatedly at the end of LAS meetings since the 1940s), when viewed against the background of the decrease in the number of concrete actions taken to find a solution to the plight of the Palestinian peoples, could indeed be viewed as an indication of this delicate balancing act many Arab policy-makers engaged in in the second half of the twentieth century.

The Palestine issue was not only a flag raised by non-state actors in voicing their multiple security concerns, but also the source of a military threat, that is, the state of Israel. The unsuccessful military experience of 1948 and the formation of Israel in 1949 duly led LAS members to re-think the military dimension of their organisation. This culminated in the signing of the Arab League Collective Security Pact (ALCSP) in 1950. However, although the ALCSP was partly a response to the recognition of the need to create an effective collective security scheme to face an increasingly intransigent Israel, it was also a reaction to the advances Britain and the United States made to Arab policy-makers for the creation of MEDO. In this sense, the ALCSP was aimed to emphasise the intention of LAS members to remain non-aligned. Lastly, another consideration behind the conclusion of the ALCSP was to integrate the principles and vocabulary laid out by the United Nations so that the LAS would qualify as a 'Regional Arrangement' according to the UN Charter (Hassouna 1975: 13).

Thus, ALCSP sought to turn LAS into a collective security organisation to organise joint defence against external threats. Accordingly a Joint Defence Council (comprising the foreign ministers and ministers of defence of the signatory states), a Permanent Military Commission (composed of representatives of the general staffs of the signatory states) and a Consultative Military Council (composed of the Chiefs of Staff of the signatory states) were established. An annex to the ALSCP in 1950 provided for the appointment of a joint Arab commander-in-chief in the event of a war. The Pact did not envisage the creation of a permanent military command (Hassouna 1975: 15). Given the competition between the Middle Eastern and Arab national security approaches, the creation of the League of Arab States and especially the signing of the ALCSP signalled Arab actors' determination to prevail.

A struggle for prevalence

The chapter has so far showed how the two contending approaches to regional security solidified in the early years of the Cold War. The Middle East Defence Organisation, the Northern Tier, and the Baghdad Pact were designed to secure the Middle East, maintain access to bases in the region, and to make the region inviolable to Soviet influence or intervention. With the entry of the Soviet Union into the Middle East via the Egyptian–Czech arms deal struck in 1955, checking Soviet influence among Arab states became an ever higher priority for US policy-makers.

Nasser, following his rise to power, adopted a societal-focused conceptualisation of Arab national security, which 'came to coincide with the discourses of insecurity that informed the many pan-Arabist groups and activists who were challenging regional elites and Western colonial rule' (Niva 1999: 161). It could be argued that it was British and US policy of making economic and military aid conditional on Egypt's joining regional security schemes that led Nasser to put so much stress on a broader security agenda, defining anti-colonialism, political and economic sovereignty as well as the plight of Palestinian peoples as Arab national security issues (Niva 1999: 161; also see Khadduri 1957: 12–22). This is not to suggest that Nasser did not prioritise the security of Egypt (or that of his own regime); rather, he used the Israel/Palestine issue to flag other (perhaps more statist) security concerns.

It should be noted here that until the mid-1950s, US policy-makers had shied away from selling arms to Israel or its Arab counterparts in accordance with the Tripartite Declaration agreed among British, French and US policy-makers (1950). Assuming that the conflict could be managed if the parties to the Israel/Palestine conflict were prevented from entering into an arms race, the three allies had agreed to consider all applications for arms or war materials by these countries in view of their needs for the purposes of 'legitimate self-defence' (Ovendale 1998: 236). However, each of the three parties had different ideas as to what 'legitimate self-defence' might constitute, and France continued to ship arms (through non-official means) to Israel. This only added to Nasser's disillusionment with the United States, leading to the 1955 Czech arms deal (Dessouki 1989: 36).

Space does not allow going into the details of how the tension caused by the Soviet arms deal, US refusal to fund the Aswan dam project and Nasser's nationalisation of the Suez Canal culminated in the 1956 War (Dessouki 1989: 31–41). It should suffice to say that the war further increased Nasser's standing in the Arab world and gave credence to his resort to the Arab national security discourse. The support Soviet policy-makers provided to their Egyptian counterparts during the war, in turn, made it relatively easier for them to enhance their influence over some other Arab states.

However, the increase in Nasser's stature, perhaps paradoxically, enabled the United States to enhance its own influence over conservative Arab regimes. The policy-makers of conservative Arab states were sceptical of Nasser's articulation of a broader conception of Arab national security and felt threatened by the emphasis he put on its societal dimension. Indeed, following Suez, Nasser adopted increasingly more interventionist practices in an attempt to nudge conservative regimes into line with his policies. Nasser's interventions were not military but 'symbolic' (Barnett 1998); they were designed to use his influence over Arab public opinion to shape the practices of other governments. In his addresses to Arab peoples broadcast on Radio Cairo, Nasser urged Arab peoples to rebel against their leaders whenever the latter engaged in a policy that threatened Arab national security.[7]

By the end of the 1950s, the increase in Nasser's standing in the Arab world resulted in a division of Arab regimes into two camps: 'conservative' (Saudi Arabia, and other Gulf states, Iraq [until the 1958 coup]) and 'radical' (Egypt, Syria, Iraq [after the coup]).[8] Saudi Arabia took the lead in distancing itself from the Arab national security discourse and adopting that of the United States. The period of Saudi–US rapprochement also coincided with the Eisenhower Doctrine (1957) that was designed to reassure regional states that their sovereignty and independence would be protected by the United States 'against the predatory desires of "international communism", i.e. the Soviet Union' (Campbell 1958: 122; see also Little 2002: 127–37). The Doctrine signalled a shift in US policy-making from seeking to maintain regional security via constructing regional security schemes to that of supporting critical allies in the attempt to maintain status quo in the region. The United States pledged to provide military and economic aid to Middle Eastern states in return for their endorsement of the Doctrine. Eventually, Baghdad Pact members together with Lebanon and Libya endorsed the Doctrine and received aid. Jordan denounced 'international communism' but avoided endorsing the Doctrine. Israel, at this stage, was not supplied with arms by the United States so as not to destroy what was trying to be achieved with the new policy aimed at gaining the friendship of conservative Arab regimes. Although the Saudi policy-makers did not publicly endorse the Doctrine, they took up the opportunity provided by this shift in US policy-making. King Saud visited the United States in January 1957 and was 'persuaded to reassess his policy' (Dawisha 1984: 2).

The Saudi change of heart constituted another turning point in the struggle for prevalence between the two competing discourses. The division of Arab states into 'conservative' and 'radical' camps was followed by the members of the conservative camp moving to shape their practices more in line with the US approach to Middle Eastern security whilst purporting to uphold Arab national security at the discursive level. This, in turn, led to the emergence of what Bahgat Korany (1994: 174) called the gap between 'say' and 'do' in Arab politics, the discrepancy between the discourse of Arab national security and the practice of state security. The practices Saudi policy-makers adopted from the late 1950s onwards included conducting significant arms deals with the United States and Britain. They also launched a diplomatic campaign to alienate other Arab policy-makers from the 'radical' camp.[9]

Saudi policy-makers also sought to introduce another approach to regional security, namely the Islamist discourse. Instead of using LAS summits to discuss issues, King Faisal called for the convening of an Islamic summit. Despite Nasser's objection, he took the opportunity provided by the fire at Jerusalem's Al-Aqsa Mosque to convene an Islamic Conference in September 1969, seeking to create an anti-Israeli bloc under its own leadership (see Dawisha 1984: 3–4). Considering the centrality of the Israel/Palestine issue to the Arab national security discourse, the Saudi action constituted an attempt to appropriate it by interpreting the issue within its self-styled Islamist security discourse (Niva 1999: 165–70). Although the origins of what is referred to here as the Islamist security discourse go back as early as the mid-1960s, it will be dealt with in further detail in Part II, the point being that it was in the post-Cold War era that this perspective became more prominent. It should suffice to say here that Saudi security practices which were shaped by, and in turn shaped, the Islamist approach to security included providing aid to Islamist groups and movements abroad. In the 1970s, when Saudi Arabia was experiencing a boom in its oil-based income, the total value of grants and soft loans it promised to developing states was second only to that of the United States (Dawisha 1984: 19).

The 1960s also witnessed US policy-makers' re-conceptualisation of its approach to Middle Eastern security (already signalled by the Eisenhower Doctrine) by putting more emphasis on the regime security of the conservative states of the region. This re-conceptualisation resulted in a compartmentalisation of US regional security thinking and practices in that US policy-makers increasingly began to treat the regional status quo and the security of oil reserves (also referred to as Gulf security) in isolation from their other concerns, those of the Israel/Palestine issue and Israel's security. Indeed, although successive US administrations attempted to address the Israel/Palestine problem (for a brief overview, see Little 2002: 267–306), they did not put forward any region-wide security scheme.

The policy of de-coupling the issues of Israel/Palestine and Persian Gulf security crystallised during 1973–74 when US Secretary of State Henry Kissinger sought to de-link his efforts to bring an end to the 1973 Arab–Israeli war and the lifting of the OPEC oil embargo (which symbolised a rare moment of collaboration between the members of the 'radical' and 'conservative' camps) (Ramazani 1998: 49–50). This policy of de-coupling different dimensions of regional insecurity also had to do with increasing Israeli influence on US policy-making. Israel's influence on US policies had been on the rise since the 1967 war, when it proved itself to be a strong and dependable ally. Israeli policy-makers had for long sought to de-link the Israel/Palestine issue from other issues of concern to the United States and its Arab allies. The US policy-makers' compartmentalisation of their security thinking and practices to suit Israel's interests showed how detrimental Israel's military successes in 1967 and 1973 had been for the prestige of Arab states.

The beginning of the end for Arab national security discourse was marked by Egypt's defeat in the 1967 war (Sirriyeh 2000: 57). Although Nasser remained popular among Arab peoples, his society-focused conceptualisation of Arab national security began to give way to a more state-focused one. What was more decisive for Arab national security was Egypt's decision, following the 1973 war, to break ranks with other Arab states and sign a separate peace deal with Israel (for an insider's account of this period, see Heikal 1996: 180–289). Considering the fact that Egypt had flown the flag of Arab national security during Nasser's presidency, its move towards explicitly statist policies constituted a more significant blow than the 'loss' of Saudi Arabia.

The final decisive blow to Arab national security was struck by the members of the conservative bloc who decided to form the Gulf Cooperation Council (GCC) in 1981 (see Gulf Cooperation 1983). Although the formation of the GCC followed a heightening of the East–West tension regarding the region as a result of the Soviet invasion of Afghanistan (1978), the Iranian revolution (1978–79) and the Iran–Iraq war (1980–88), such a development would not have been considered possible had the Arab national security discourse not lost its grip over Arab actors. Although GCC members maintained that their action did not constitute a breach of the precepts of Arab national security, the security interests of the Gulf states clearly were more in tune with the US approach to Middle Eastern security that prioritised the maintenance of the secure flow of oil and military stability (which translated as 'regime security' as viewed through the lens of conservative Gulf leaders). One bone of contention between the United States and GCC members remained the status of Israel in the region.

During the 1980s, Gulf policy-makers sought to set a clear blue line between state security and Arab national security. Arguably, even the massive amounts of economic aid they provided to the Palestinian cause could be explained by their concerns about regime security. Given the centrality of the Palestinian issue to the Arab national security discourse, to be seen to be backing the PLO was one way of enhancing their legitimacy in the eyes of their citizens as well as other Arab actors. Such legitimacy was urgently needed given their stance towards the predicament of their poorer brethren during the 1980s. Indeed, during this period the practices of Arab policy-makers increasingly discredited the spirit of Arab national security; their discursive practices remained the only way to uphold the idea of Arab national security at the governmental level.

Conclusion

This chapter concludes Part I: 'Pasts', which sought to investigate the mutually constitutive relationship between (inventing) regions and (conceptions and practices of) security during the Cold War. Chapter 1 (representations) introduced two spatial representations, the Middle East and the Arab Regional System, which, it was argued, are rooted in contending approaches to regional security. Middle East is a geopolitical concept, the chapter argued, invented to help British and later US policy-makers to think about and organise action in that part of the world. Arab actors, in turn, pointed to the Western strategic origins of the Middle East and proposed an alternative, that of the Arab Regional System, which, in turn, was shaped by an alternative approach to security, that of Arab national security.

Chapter 3 (practices) looked at the practical manifestations of adopting particular representations of 'the region'. The aim here was to show how different security practices were shaped by and, in turn, shaped contending approaches to security and alternative spatial representations. It was argued that the three regional security schemes that the United States and its allies attempted to create were all military alliances designed to secure the Middle East against external actors, often to the neglect of regional actors' concerns. The British and US policy-makers' reasoning behind the creation of such regional security schemes, instead of backing the League of Arab States, it was argued, was to prevent the prevalence of the Arab national security discourse, which stressed issues such as decolonisation, state-building, economic and political sovereignty, and the plight of Palestinian peoples – none of which were high on the US regional security agenda.

The 1950s and 1960s were characterised by a struggle for predominance between these two contending approaches, which competed to shape the practices of multiple regional actors. Nasser's security practices during this period were designed to nudge conservative regimes into adopting his own broader and societal-focused conceptualisation of Arab national security – a path that they were hesitant to take. This policy backfired in the long run with conservative Gulf policy-makers breaking rank with their more radical Arab counterparts and choosing to shape their practices in line with the US approach to Middle Eastern (and Gulf) security (see Chapter 5).

Following Nasser's death, an explicitly statist conceptualisation of Arab national security prevailed. Nevertheless, many Arab policy-makers, including those in the Gulf, continued to justify their actions with reference to Arab national security in the attempt to enhance regime security. Such legitimacy was urgently needed given their stance towards the predicament of their poorer brethren during the 1980s. As Yezid Sayigh (1991: 501) noted, during this period 'famine was allowed to sweep Sudan and Somalia, locusts and drought to attack Yemen and Tunisia. Sudan and Egypt tottered constantly on the edge of bankruptcy'. In the attempt to prioritise state and regime security, Arab policy-makers failed to adopt long-term policies that could have addressed the inter-related issues of water and food security that were high up on the security agendas of regional peoples. The ways in which the Arab policy-makers tried to cope with these issues were manifestations of regional policy-makers' zero-sum and statist conceptions and practices of security. This point begs further clarification.

There are two dimensions to the problem of food security in the Middle East. On the one hand there are the oil-rich states of the Gulf such as Saudi Arabia and Kuwait, which are not self-sufficient but have the financial resources to pay for the feeding of their population. For example the Saudi policy-makers, as a part of the effort to achieve food security, sought to increase the country's wheat production to the point of self-sufficiency by paying their farmers six times the world market price. Needless to say, whilst doing this they caused further depletion of scarce non-renewable water resources in this arid region (Wenger and Stark 1990: 15).

On the other hand there are states such as Egypt and Sudan that had a less-developed agricultural sector and a weaker economy (Pfeifer 1993). These poorer Arab countries suffered from policy failures of the past such as lack of support for and heavy taxation of agriculture, as well as the increase in population, which has made it impossible for them to feed their population however much they increase food production (Duffield 1990: 4–5; Pfeifer 1993: 138). The issue of water scarcity only added to the predicament of these countries', already troubled, agricultural sectors.

Therefore, one dimension of food security in the Arab world was that faced by the poor peoples of the region, such as those in Sudan who sold their labour to purchase food necessary for survival (Duffield 1990: 4–5). The other dimension was the case of some Arab regimes, which were worried that the 'food weapon' might be used against them (as was the case with Iraq during the Gulf crisis) and therefore have adopted not-so-cost-effective techniques and have sought to grow water-intensive products to achieve agricultural 'self-sufficiency' and food security (Pfeifer 1993: 142). The significance of all this is that, notwithstanding the premises and promises of Arab national security, the practices through which regional states tried to address threats to water and food security were symptomatic of their unilateral (as opposed to cooperative), zero-sum (as opposed to common) and statist (as opposed to societal or individual-focused) conceptions and practices of security (see for example, Haidar 1996). This is also an illustration of the broader point (made in Chapter 1) that adopting broader conceptions of security is not enough in itself. After all, the Saudi regime (to name one example) was cognisant of the economic and political as well as environmental dimensions of security, but approached them from a statist perspective and adopted unilateral practices to address them. Taking re-thinking security seriously involves seeking to identify and overcome the shortcomings of Cold War approaches to security in theory *and* practice. Part II will further develop these points.

Part II

Presents

4 Representations of the Middle East in the post-Cold War era

Chapter 2 (representations) traced the trajectory of the Middle East from its invention in the late nineteenth century into the Cold War era and argued that the Middle East had its origins in British and US security thinking and practices. It also introduced an alternative that emerged during this period, that of 'Arab Regional System'. This chapter will continue to follow the trajectory of spatial representations 'Middle East' and 'Arab Regional System'. Two more representations will also be looked at, those of the 'Euro–Med Region' and 'Muslim Middle East'. The latter two representations have shaped and been shaped by the European Union's approach to security in the Mediterranean and the Islamist discourse on security, respectively. This is intended as a further illustration of the point (made in Chapter 2) that the origins of regions have had their roots in security thinking and practices of their inventors. It will further be argued that in the post-Cold War era, the competition between these four representations took place at multiple levels with non-state actors playing more active roles than they did during the Cold War.

Contending representations

In an article entitled 'Future Visions of the Arab Middle East', Saad Eddin Ibrahim (1996) identified four approaches competing to shape the future of regional security in the Middle East. These four approaches are 'four different visions of the future and four parallel geopolitical-economic projects: an Arab, an Islamic, a Middle Eastern, and a Mediterranean one' (Ibrahim 1996: 425). Ibrahim notes that of these four approaches, the first two are 'indigenous' to the region; 'both have roots reaching deep into the historical consciousness of Arab actors' (1996: 425). The third one, that of the Middle East, is the most established of them all and was, during the 1990s, identified with the Peace Process launched after the Gulf War. What Ibrahim identified as the Mediterranean approach is the most recent of the four and has lately received attention due to the Euro–Mediterranean partnership scheme initiated by the European Union.

Each of these approaches identified by Ibrahim gives primacy to different kinds of threats and uses a different spatial representation in discussing the 'region' they seek to secure. This is not to suggest that these
four representations exhaust the possibilities. One might add to the list of
alternatives the so-called 'Greater Middle East' – that was in vogue within
some US circles during the 1990s (see, for example, Blackwill and
Stürmer 1997; Khalilzad 1997; Pelletrau *et al.* 1998; Emerson and Tocci
2003). The 'Greater Middle East' was invented after the end of the Cold
War and the dissolution of the Soviet Union. It is used to represent those
states that are included in the Middle East as well as the former Soviet
republics of Central Asia. This, arguably, is indicative of the security conceptions and practices of its inventors that include securing the route to
Central Asian oil resources (in which there is now much interest) whilst
holding Islamism in check (which has become a persistent anxiety in the
United States since the 1978–79 revolution in Iran and especially the September 11 attacks) (see, for example, Chalk 2003). This new representation is yet to become established in the minds of people other than its
inventors. Still, increasing references to 'greater/wider Middle East' in discussions on US interests in the Middle East and Central Asia show how
central security interests are to the processes through which regions are
invented and reshaped.

Another alternative that emerged in the aftermath of the Cold War is
that of 'Middle East and North Africa' or MENA (see, for example, El-
Erian and Fischer 1996; Derviş and Shafik 1998; Zunes 1998). This label is
used to represent the same area covered in Cold War definitions of the
Middle East, i.e. members of the Arab League plus Israel, Iran and
Turkey. The fact that there is no change in the definition but its label
could be taken as an indication of a yearning on the part of north African
policy-makers to emphasise their difference from the rest of the Arab
world. It could also be taken as an indication of their increased bargaining
power – a power they derive from their close economic cooperation with
the European Union as a part of the Euro–Mediterranean partnership
scheme (see the section on the Euro–Med Region). This representation
will therefore not be treated separately.

Another spatial representation that emerged during the later years of
the Cold War and rose to prominence in the post-Cold War era is that of
'(Persian/Arabian) Gulf' (see Barnett and Gause 1998). Maintaining
security in the Gulf became more central to the security policies of the
United States and its allies in the aftermath of the Iranian revolution and
the Soviet invasion of Afghanistan. Viewed through the lens of US and
Gulf policy-makers, this spatial representation does not constitute an
alternative to that of the Middle East; it is rather viewed as a 'sub-region'.
Accordingly, the Gulf as a spatial representation will be analysed in the
section on the Middle East in the post-Cold War era.

In the following sections the development of the aforementioned four spatial representations, namely, the Middle East, the Arab Regional System, the Euro–Med Region, and the Muslim Middle East will be traced and the security conceptions on which they are based will be teased out. These representations have been shaped by four contending approaches to regional security – four approaches that have been competing to shape the future of regional security in the post-Cold War era.

The Arab Regional System

As Part I argued, the spatial representation Arab Regional System and the Arab national security discourse emerged in the aftermath of the Second World War in reaction to US practices designed to secure the Middle East. Arab Regional System was considered a better representation to be used when discussing the interactions among Arab states, with their neighbours and with the international system (Said Aly 1996: 26–7). As opposed to early representations such as the Arab homeland or the Arabian peninsula that downplayed the existence of sovereign Arab states, the Arab Regional System was a state-centric representation that rested on a statist conception of security; it appealed to Arab policy-makers who were concerned with consolidating their sovereign statehood and reducing their exposure to external influences. As Chapter 3 argued, since the late 1960s, Arab policy-makers, especially the more conservative Gulf leaders, have distanced themselves from the Arab national security discourse. Indeed during the 1990s, it was increasingly non-state actors whose practices shaped and were shaped by the Arab national security discourse.

Arab peoples have for long been collaborating across borders in order to escape intervention by their own governments that restrict their political activities at home. Given many Arab regimes' unwillingness to lift restrictions on political participation, Arab peoples have been making use of each other's human and technical resources when trying to bring about change at home. Indeed, part of the reason why Arab intellectuals chose to locate themselves in the Arab Regional System is because many have done 'much of their best work in exile' (Sadowski 2002: 148). Another part of the reason is rooted in their self-interest that is mediated through identity: Arab intellectuals remain 'quite wedded to their regional connections [because] they enjoy being read and recognised in neighbouring capitals' (Sadowski 2002: 148). Although there are some signs of cooperation with their Turkish and Iranian counterparts as well, if one is to judge by the titles of the organisations they set up, it is clear that they locate themselves in the Arab Regional System and not the Middle East. Such organisations include the Arab Association of Sociologists, the Arab Association of Political Scientists, Association of Arab Historians (1974), Association of Arab Universities (1964), the pan-Arab Organisation of Human Rights, the Beirut-based Center for Arab Unity Studies (1975), and the Jordan-based Arab Thought Forum (1985), among others. Arab women's organisations have also been active in strengthening civil society in the Arab world (see E. Boulding 1994: 43; Nasr 1997).

Although such non-state organisations existed during the Cold War as well, what has changed in the post-Cold War period is that they now tend to take less the form of stereotypical pan-Arabist movements that called for Arab unity during the 1950s, than the form of civil societal groupings that emphasise Arab identity, culture, homeland and nationhood whilst working towards democratisation and social justice at home. Ibrahim notes that the number of Arab NGOs and other civil associations has nearly doubled between 1990 and 1995 (see Ibrahim 1994, 1996: 427–8, for a sceptical view of the potentialities of civil societal actors in the Arab world). As will be discussed in Chapter 5, the activities of these non-state actors are more often than not designed to bring about change in the Arab Regional System by way of focusing on political and economic issues, calling for democratisation, increased political participation, an end to restrictions on human rights and better provision in fields such as health and education.

In the 1990s such sensitivity regarding the region's Arab identity has been more common among non-state actors than policy-makers. Indeed, the post-Cold War era witnessed the latter joining the Middle East Peace Process, the Middle East and North Africa (MENA) economic forum convened as a part of the Peace Process, and discussing potential membership to a Middle East Regional Development Bank, all of which involved the participation of Israel, Turkey and the United States.

Furthermore, there are some signs that the salience of the spatial representation Arab Regional System is beginning to fade even among some non-state actors, such as some Egyptian intellectuals who began to emphasise the Mediterranean dimension of Egypt's identity whilst others have emphasised the Islamic dimension. As the next section will argue, the debate over the Mediterranean, Arab and Islamic dimensions of Egyptian identity amongst the Egyptian elite dates back to the early twentieth century but had come to a halt following Nasser's rise to power in the early 1950s (Selim 1997; also see Karawan 2002).

As Chapter 3 argued, since the 1960s, the tendency among conservative Arab policy-makers has been that of distancing themselves from the Arab national security discourse. What has changed in the aftermath of the Cold War (and especially the Gulf War) is that regional policy-makers' references to Arab national security became even more sparse. During the 1990s smaller Gulf actors not only became less hesitant to identify with the US approach to Middle Eastern security but also prioritised maintaining security in the Gulf. This has meant further distancing themselves from Arab national security, which rests on the assumption that the security of Arab peoples is indivisible.

The September 11 attacks against New York and Washington, DC (2001) and the US-led war on Iraq (2003) seem to have contributed to the decline of Arab national security and the decrease in the number of references to the Arab Regional System. Reflecting upon Arab actors' reactions to the September 11 attacks, Michael Barnett (2002b: 81) noted that there was 'remarkably little attempt at sustained inter-Arab cooperation and only nominal calls for Arab unity'. Throughout the Iraqi crisis that culminated in the US-led war against Iraq in March 2003, references to Arab national security (amongst policy-makers and the public alike) were notable for their absence.[1] Although US policies were severely criticised both in terms of aims (regime change in Iraq) and methods (unilateralism), such criticisms were not followed up by calls for a 'no-alliance pledge' as happened when the Baghdad Pact was founded in 1955 (Barnett 2002b). Still, the parallels with the Baghdad Pact were not lost on some observers who characterised the emerging alliance between US, Pakistan, the Iraqi regime that is currently under construction, and Israel as 'the new Baghdad Pact' (Haşane 2003: 91; Al-Amrani 2003; Lewis 2003; Hamad 2003).

One significant impact of the war on Iraq has been that the rapprochement that characterised US relations with smaller Gulf states during the 1990s has been stalled. Although Arab policy-makers have failed to come together to constitute a united front in opposing US policies toward Iraq, many distanced themselves from US policies. Time will tell whether the 1990s would constitute a parenthesis or a break in Gulf policy-makers' relationship with the US approach to Middle Eastern security. What is more significant for the purposes of this chapter are the reasons why conservative Gulf states during the 1990s chose to locate themselves in the Middle East rather than the Arab Regional System.

The first reason is that the Iraqi invasion of Kuwait rendered it rather problematic to openly propound Arab national security. The fact that an Arab state (Iraq) invaded another (Kuwait) and threatened a third (Saudi Arabia) showed that threats to the Arab Regional System could be posed by Arab states from within the region as well as external actors (such as Iran, Israel, Turkey and the United States). This, in turn, challenged the outward-directed conception of security that has been at the root of Arab national security. During the US-led war on Iraq in 2003, references to Arab national security were very sparse indeed. This is not to declare the end of Arab national security. Rather, the point is that the Gulf War has clearly proven the bankruptcy of the inside/outside divide on which the Arab Regional System and Arab national security approach were built. Arab actors are yet to re-think the precepts of Arab national security and propose an alternative that comprises multiple dimensions of security as seen through the lenses of myriad actors (Arab and non-Arab).

The second and related reason for the decline of the Arab Regional System as a spatial representation is that the Iraqi invasion of Kuwait and the ensuing Gulf War served to discredit the arguments in favour of greater cooperation and collaboration among Arab actors. Since the Iraqi invasion of Kuwait, the term 'Arab nation' (*al-umma al-arabiyya*) has come to be identified with Iraqi pan-Arab expansionism (Tibi 1999: 51; see also Faksh 1993). The Iraqi aggression also strained the relationships among the members of the Arab League. For years, the Arab League has served as the backbone of the Arab national security discourse and the main institution that contained the Arab Regional System. The Gulf conflict, however, has left the Arab League divided (Awad 1994).

The US-led war on Iraq led to further marginalisation of the League of Arab States. Although LAS members declared their opposition to the war, they hesitated to put their words into action and did very little to prevent the war. One observer of Arab politics, comparing Turkey's refusal to allow the US and British troops to use its bases with the LAS declaration, characterised Arab states' position as 'ambiguous' (see Bedirhan 2003: 28). The deepening of the rifts between Arab states resulted in a relaxation of the Arab/non-Arab distinction that drew the boundaries of the Arab Regional System, to accommodate the increasing influence of non-Arab actors such as Iran, Israel and Turkey, as well as Britain, France and the United States. The aforementioned tendency among Arab policy-makers to locate themselves in the Middle East had already signalled such a relaxation of boundaries.

In sum, although the increasing involvement of non-Arab actors and especially the United States in the affairs of the Arab Regional System may not have too many opponents at the governmental level, the same cannot be said about actors at the sub-state level. As noted above, many non-state actors' practices continue to locate themselves in the Arab Regional System (see AbuKhalil 1992). The increasing prevalence of the Middle East or the 'New Middle East' has worried such actors who fear their Arab identity would be marginalised.

The Euro–Med Region

Mediterranean littoral peoples and societies were conceived as part of a total called the 'Mediterranean' in ancient Greece. Indeed, it is argued that the first uses of the concept the 'West' referred to peoples, societies and states surrounding the Mediterranean Sea, whereas the territories further to the east and south constituted the 'East'. Later, with the Muslim invasion of the territories to the south of the Mediterranean, as well as Asia Minor, Malta and Spain, and the entrenchment of the idea of Europe, the construct referred to as the 'West' shifted further to the west and those Mediterranean littoral peoples, societies and states to the south and east of the Mediterranean Sea came to be included in the (now vast) entity called the 'East' (and later the Middle East) therefore dissolving the unity of the 'Mediterranean' (Hentch 1996; also see Salem 1997).[2] This past unity of the Mediterranean was remembered rather recently to help facilitate the EU-backed project of constructing a Euro–Med Region.

Among Mediterranean littoral states of the Arab world, Egypt and

Lebanon are the ones that have been more in touch with the Mediterranean dimension of their identity than some others such as Syria. In Egypt, in the 1920s and 1930s, many Western educated and/or oriented intellectuals advocated the Mediterranean identity because it was viewed as 'neither completely European or Western nor completely divorced from the Arab-Islamic world' (Salem 1997: 38). However, Egypt's Mediterranean identity was de-emphasised in the post-Second World War era when it joined the League of Arab States and later took part in the 1948 war as a part of the Arab force fighting Israel. Gamal Abdel Nasser's advent to power (1954) was also decisive in this respect. During Nasser's presidency, the prevalent view was that any kind of affiliation with a Mediterranean institution would lead to dependence on the former colonial powers (Selim 1997).[3]

The debate between the proponents of Egypt's Mediterranean identity and those who emphasised the Arab and Islamic dimensions was revived following Egypt's defeat in the 1967 war. Nasser's death and Anwar al-Sadat's rise to power in the early 1970s further encouraged some intellectuals to dust off the arguments about the Mediterranean dimension of Egypt's identity and revive the early debate. Some well-known Egyptian intellectuals, disappointed with the losses against Israel and the lack of support provided by other Arab states for the Palestinian cause, had already begun to argue that 'the time had come for Egypt to stop fighting the battles of the Arabs' (Selim 1997; see also Salem 1997: 37–8).

Another factor that enabled Mediterraneanism to see the light of day once again was the peace treaty Sadat signed with Israel, which resulted in Egypt's isolation from Arab and Islamic institutions. As a result, Egyptian policy-makers sought alternative paths, one of which was 'Mediterraneanism'. Besides, since the independence of Tunisia, Algeria and Morocco, there had emerged more independent non-European Mediterranean-littoral states with which Egypt could collaborate within a Mediterranean framework. Lastly, its break with the Soviet Union in 1972 also enabled Egypt to re-establish close relations with the West in general and Mediterranean-littoral European states in particular (Selim 1997; see also Karawan 2002).

Egyptian intellectuals were not alone in locating themselves in the Mediterranean. During the 1950s some forthcoming thinkers of Lebanese nationalism also had voiced arguments favouring identification with the Mediterranean. Given Lebanon's multi-confessional and multi-ethnic make-up, locating their country in the Mediterranean could potentially have provided Lebanese policy-makers a solution to the dormant conflicts that threatened to break the society. Moreover, as did their Egyptian counterparts during the 1930s, they viewed Mediterraneanism as a tool to de-emphasise their links with the Arab-Islamic world and claim affinity with Europe and the West. Lastly, some North African intellectuals also favoured Mediterraneanism as a way of reinforcing the uniqueness of the

Maghreb's Arab–Berber ethnic mix and its historical links with Europe in general and France in particular (Salem 1997: 38).

Although the idea of the unity of the Mediterranean world dates back centuries, what is referred to here as the Euro–Med Region began to take shape from the 1970s onwards, largely in line with changing security conceptions and practices of the European Union (formerly the European Community). The EU's close interest in Middle Eastern affairs, in turn, was provoked by the OPEC oil embargo and the 1973 Arab–Israeli war. During this period, a change-of-heart on the part of some European policy-makers to adopt a more equivocal attitude towards the Arab–Israeli conflict resulted in the establishment of the Euro–Arab dialogue in 1973 (Jawad 1992).

The relationship between the EU and Arab states did not achieve much during the Cold War, partly because of the mistrust caused by some European states' colonial past and partly due to the atmosphere created by the superpower conflict. It should be noted that this period was also characterised by a change in the character of the EU itself, which had come a long way since the European Coal and Steel Community. An attempt was made to re-activate the Euro–Arab dialogue after the end of the Cold War. Although the Gulf Crisis (1990–91) interrupted the process, the dialogue resumed in 1992 (see Miller 1992: 7–13).[4] The links established as a part of the Euro–Arab dialogue formed the backbone of the Euro–Med Partnership Process in the following years.

It was not only the end of the Cold War but also a re-thinking on the part of some EU members that caused the re-activation of the Euro–Arab dialogue and the re-emergence of Mediterranean discourse of the EU. In the 1980s, changes in the societies of EU member states as a result of the growth of the Middle Eastern diaspora in Western Europe led EU policy-makers to re-think their priorities and come to consider stability in the Middle East (and especially the geographically closer North Africa) an integral part of their own security.

Over the years, Euro–Med cooperation schemes have taken various forms including the aforementioned Euro–Arab dialogue as well as the EU's 'Overall Mediterranean Policy', agreements with sub-regional organisations such as the Gulf Cooperation Council (GCC) and the Arab Maghreb Union (AMU), and more recently the still-born 'Conference on Security and Cooperation in the Mediterranean', and the ongoing 'Euro–Med Partnership' process (Jawad 1992; Joffé 1999). The Euro–Med Partnership scheme is hoped to encourage inter-state cooperation and increase regional interdependence as a way of maintaining security (understood as stability) in the Middle East towards enhancing security within the European Union. This theme will be further developed in Chapter 5. It should suffice to note here that the Gulf War only helped to reinforce the view that 'regional economic solidarity among all the peoples of the region' is 'a cornerstone for peace, stability, and development in the Middle East' which is, in turn, viewed as a necessary component of security in Europe (Miller 1992: 13).

The European Union's conceptualisation of the Euro–Med Region does not so far include non-Mediterranean Middle Eastern states (such as Saudi Arabia, Iraq, the Gulf states, Yemen and Iran). Moreover Mediterranean-rim states such as Turkey and Israel have participated only in some of the Euro–Med schemes.[5] This is partly because the EU's delineation of the Euro–Med Region reflects its aforementioned security concerns that have had less to do with the Gulf than the geographically closer North African states. Israel and other Eastern Mediterranean states have come into the picture due to EU interest in finding a peaceful solution to the Israel/Palestine issue.

The fact that non-Mediterranean Middle Eastern countries (such as Saudi Arabia or Iran) are not included in the Euro–Med Region does not seem to bother much the North African partners. This is arguably because the policy-makers of those Arab states that are a part of the Euro–Med process are interested in economic cooperation with the EU, not with their fellow Arab countries with whom they have attempted several projects of cooperation in the past. The only country that has so far expressed reservations about the exclusion of the Gulf countries is Egypt. Egyptian policy-makers have suggested that membership to the Euro–Med Partnership scheme should be left open so that non-Mediterranean Middle Eastern countries could become members in the future (Selim 1997). It is difficult to know whether the Egyptian policy-makers are genuinely interested in including all other Arab countries, or whether this was a tactical move designed to allay the worries of some non-state actors in the Arab World in general and Egypt in particular who fear that 'Mediterraneanism will dilute the Arab identity of the Arab Regional System and lead to its dismantling' (Selim 1997). It is significant to note here that such concerns again echo Heikal, Dessouki and Matar's criticisms regarding the spatial representation 'Middle East'.

Although the exclusion of some Arab and/or Muslim countries from the Euro–Med Region has its problems, their inclusion could also be considered problematic. It was such concerns that resulted in the shelving of another Mediterranean-focused scheme initiated by two EU member states, Italy and Spain. The proposal for the creation of a 'Conference on Security and Cooperation in the Mediterranean' (CSCM) was introduced in 1991,[6] but failed to take off largely because it was considered too ambitious in terms of both its objectives and scope (Miller 1992: 13; Niblock 1992: 245–51). The idea has been criticised on the grounds that it covered a very wide area (the proposal mentioned inviting any state with 'any substantial interest'). This would have meant bringing together all 12 members of the EU, the 17 non-EU-Mediterranean littoral states (Albania, Algeria, Bulgaria, Cyprus, Egypt, Israel, Jordan, Lebanon, Libya, Malta, Mauritania, Morocco, Romania, Syria, Tunisia, Turkey and [former]

Yugoslavia), nine Gulf states (including Iran and Iraq), three others (Canada, the Soviet Union and the United States), and one UN-recognised entity (Palestine) (Niblock 1992: 247). The CSCM proposal will be further discussed in Chapter 5. Suffice it to note here that the objectives of the scheme that included addressing issue areas such as 'security, economic cooperation and human rights' were found too difficult to achieve for such a large and diverse group of states (Aliboni 1997–98: 73–86).

Currently, Mediterraneanism does not have many proponents. Initially, both Syria and Israel had responded positively to invitations issued for the Euro–Med Partnership activities. However, as Israeli–Palestinian peace-making came to a halt in 2000 amidst increasing violence, existing partners such as Lebanon and Syria refused to partake in Euro–Med activities (Spencer 2001). However, notwithstanding the reservations of some, there are not many who are against Mediterraneanism. As Saad Eddin Ibrahim (1996: 431) noted,

> unlike the Middle Eastern paradigm, the partnership has not generated active hostility in the Arab world. This may be due to the absence of the USA and the fact that the Israeli question does not play dominant parts.

Indeed, some Egyptian policy-makers view the spatial representation Euro–Med Region as a convenient way of locating Arab states and Israel in the same geographical setting without moving too many stones. The inclusion of Southern European countries in the definition of Euro–Med Region also serves as a guarantee that Israel would not be able to dominate but would be balanced by European members (Kramer 1997: 102). The strength of the Euro–Med Region as an alternative spatial representation comes not from its supporters who are not too many or too enthusiastic, but from the fact that unlike the 'new' or 'Muslim' Middle Easts, it does not have too many enemies.

In the long term, the main problem with the Euro–Med Region is likely to be the conception of security in which it is rooted. After all, the Euro–Med Region is a geopolitical invention of the European Union designed to serve the EU's security interests. Although the EU's approach to security in the Euro–Med Region is rooted in a rather broad conception of security and prioritises non-military practices, its referent remains the EU itself. In other words, EU policy-makers have adopted a broad conception of security that encompasses its non-military dimensions not from the perspective of regional peoples but from that of their own in an attempt to stop Middle Eastern problems from becoming European problems. This, in turn, could turn out to be a major weakness in the long term.

The Muslim Middle East

The spatial representation referred to here as the Muslim Middle East is rooted in the Islamist discourse on security. The Islamist actors' own preferred term is the 'Muslim world'. However, defined as the sum of Muslim peoples around the world (the *ummah*), the 'Muslim world' is a trans-state community that encompasses a significant portion of the globe. As a result, the adoption of the term 'Muslim world' as an alternative to the other three representations looked at in this chapter is problematic for mainly two reasons. First, two of the states with the largest Muslim populations, Indonesia and Bangladesh are remote from the Middle East. Second, there are more Muslims in Central Asia, China, India, Southeast Asia and Africa than there are in the Middle East. As Nikki Keddie (1973: 269) maintained, if the 'Middle East is unsatisfactory as an entity, the Muslim world is scarcely more so'.

My preferred term Muslim Middle East is rooted in the observation that when Islamist actors in the Middle East refer to the Muslim world, they have a Middle East-centred definition in mind (Abū-Sulaymān 1993: xv). This is also discernible from their practices, which suggest that notwithstanding the global character of their discourses, they locate themselves in the Muslim Middle East when it comes to taking action.[7] What is meant by the globalist discourse is the rhetoric that has been employed by some Islamist actors (such as Ayatollah Khomeini, Osama bin Laden or the Hizbullah in Lebanon), which indicates that they imagine all Muslims to be their audience. Theoretically, then, all areas on which the world's Muslims live are included in their definition of the Muslim world. During the first decade following the Iranian revolution, Iran's practice seemed to live up to its discourse with its anti-Israeli and anti-US rhetoric being matched by the support it provided for the PLO, the Afghan Mujahedeen and other Islamist movements around the world. This has begun to change following the death of Ayatollah Khomeini and the end of the Iran–Iraq war. Since then, Iran has mellowed its globalist revolutionary discourse, and concentrated on mending fences at the international arena and emphasising domestic development whilst keeping the revolutionary spirit up at the home front (Esposito 1995: 151; Esposito 1990).

Likewise, despite their globalist discourse, most Islamist grassroots movements aim to bring about change at home – even though they may occasionally undertake action abroad to achieve this aim.[8] Indeed, practice indicates that the self-consciously Islamist regimes of Iran and Sudan, and non-state actors such as Hamas, Hizbullah, and Algerian FIS (Islamic Salvation Front) all address themselves first and foremost to the localities they live in (see Esposito 1995: 119–87 for a brief overview of Islamist organisations). In other words, the globalist outlook of the Islamist actors at the discursive level becomes locally oriented in practice. Hence my use of the label Muslim Middle East to refer to the spatial representation that seems to have shaped and has been shaped by the practices of Islamist actors.

The Islamist discourse on security was initially introduced by the Saudi leadership, as noted in Chapter 3, to balance off Nasser's Arab national security discourse. In other words, pro-status quo policies of the Saudi leadership are at the root of the Islamist discourse on security. The 1978–79 revolution in Iran has resulted in anti-status quo actors' appropriation of the Islamist discourse. They not only appropriated but also reconceptualised the Islamist discourse by focusing on 'the need to establish an authentic cultural basis from which to assert the sovereignty of Arab states and to achieve true decolonisation' (Niva 1999: 167). This reconceptualised Islamist discourse perceives threats as stemming from 'un-Islamic' influences that could stem from inside as well as outside the Muslim Middle East. However, when it comes to defining what constitutes 'Islamic' or 'un-Islamic', there is more agreement amongst Islamist actors as to what they are against than what they are for. Some would consider 'Western' influence over and intervention into the region as 'un-Islamic'. Some Islamists criticise the existing political and religious establishments (such as the Islamic Kingdom of Saudi Arabia that allowed US troops on the 'holy lands') as well as the forces of Arab nationalism as being 'un-Islamic' (Abu-Rabi 1996: 24). Lastly, there are those who define 'structural violence' as 'un-Islamic' and call for its erosion (see Satha-Anand 1990: 28; also see Abū-Sulaymān 1993: 160).

It is worth stressing that this conception of security is not a purely outward-directed one as suggested by prevalent conceptualisations of *dar-us-salaam* ('land of peace') and *dar-ul-harb* ('land of war'). It is indeed true that the Islamist discourse considers threats to security as 'un-Islamic' influences mainly stemming from the 'West', but it also emphasises how 'external threats have been internalised in the very practices of Middle Eastern states' (Niva 1999: 168). In this sense, the Islamist discourse that informs these actors' practices is more complicated than Samuel Huntington's conceptualisation of a world order based on civilisations would allow for. For, there is by no means unanimous agreement among the proponents of the Islamist discourse as to the ideal state of the relations between Muslims and non-Muslims. Moreover, *salaam* is a very rich concept that has multiple meanings within the Islamic context (as is the case for both concepts *security* and *peace* in the Western context). One important point made by some Muslim authors on this issue is that in order to make peace, the elimination of war (understood as inter-state violence) is not enough; it is only a beginning. Echoing peace researchers' broader conception of peace, Chaiwat Satha-Anand (1990: 25–8) has maintained that working towards peace includes the elimination of 'structural violence' as well as 'direct/personal' violence. Such a view, in turn, renders it rather problematic to present the Muslim world as the 'land of peace', or the rest of the world as the 'land of war'; for, structural violence does not recognise such conventional boundaries.

The proponents of the Islamist discourse have their reservations about the other three representations. Indeed, the very concepts region and regionalism invoke territoriality, which some Islamist actors consider to be offensive to the concept of the *ummah*. Some argue that the existing system which divides believers into separate (nation-) states is against 'Islam' and that the *ummah* should be revived as the primary political unit (for a discussion, see Piscatori 1986: 1–21). Building upon such assumptions one author labelled regionalism as the 'disease of the twentieth century'. He argued that 'establishing or promoting such ideas will never allow the *ummah* to revive and regain her status as the number one nation in the world' (Mustafa 1998). As is the case with some other projects propounded by the Islamist actors, the specifics of how this potential could be fulfilled are not clear. What is emphasised is that it cannot be achieved through the construction of a (New) Middle East, a Euro–Med Region, or the strengthening of the Arab Regional System. However, the proponents of such ideas often fail to note the fact that many Islamist actors have already accepted the reality of the state; they may look toward the *ummah* when emphasising their common Muslim identity, but direct themselves to their own milieu in practice (Esposito 1995: 433).

Pointing to the gap between the discourses and practices of Islamist actors, and their lack of consistent strategies, is not meant to suggest that their critiques are not worth considering. Rather the point here is that the violent practices of some Islamist actors such as the Hizbullah that aim to capture the state mechanism or the al-Qaida, whose aims are unclear, obscure their critiques of other approaches to regional security. For the greatest strength of the Islamist discourse stems from its critique of the other representations and the security discourses they shape and are shaped by. As Saad Eddin Ibrahim (1996: 433) noted, although the proponents of the Islamist discourse do not have the power to put their own visions into practice, they have the power to stall the others. Although the September 11 attacks and the series of terrorist bombings in the Middle East are not the only reason Arab–Israeli peace-making has stalled, they have nevertheless strengthened the hands of those who have argued that 'the Middle East is not Europe' (Zaharna 2003), meaning that the former may require the adoption of 'different' (more hard-line, military-focused) security policies.

The (New) Middle East

Before the Peace Process was derailed in the late 1990s, the Middle East seemed to be the strongest amongst the four contending representations of this part of the world. Its strength stemmed partly from its backers that include the United States, Israel and Turkey. But more significantly, its strength stemmed from the post-Gulf War environment that was characterised by the decline of Arab national security. As the section on the Arab Regional System argued, during the Gulf crisis three non-Arab states, Iran, Israel and Turkey played active roles in the US-led coalition formed against Iraq. Since the end of the Gulf War, non-Arab actors (the United States and the European Union) have played significant roles in inter-Arab relations in that the Arab/non-Arab divide (the distinction between Arab Regional System and Middle East, which Heikal, Dessouki and Matar, among others, were at pains to establish) became less and less central to Arab security policy-making.

During this period another spatial representation came to prominence: the 'Gulf'. Although the Gulf Cooperation Council (GCC) was created in 1981 (see Ramazani 1988), it was in the post-Gulf War environment that local actors became less hesitant to locate themselves in the Gulf. This is not to suggest that Gulf regionalism is gaining strength amongst smaller Arab states.[9] Rather, the point is that the decline of the Arab national security approach and the Arab Regional System has enabled local actors to locate themselves in a different geographical setting (the Gulf) that they share with like-minded actors who have similar (statist) security concerns. Although members of the Gulf Cooperation Council are also members of the League of Arab States, the policies of Gulf policy-makers in the post-Gulf War era have turned the 'Gulf' into a sub-region of the Middle East. For, following a brief moment of inter-Arab collaboration for maintaining security in the Gulf (Damascus Declaration; see Chapter 5), Gulf policy-makers turned to the United States for help thereby locating themselves in the US vision for security in the Gulf and the Middle East.

Although Iran could hardly be considered as accommodating the US approach to regional security in the Middle East, it nevertheless locates itself in the (Persian) Gulf, which it considers as a sub-region of the Middle East (see Kharrazi 2003). Whereas Iran or Iraq are not members of the Gulf Cooperation Council, both states play significant roles in Gulf (in)security. Indeed, the GCC was founded partly against the threat posed by (then) revolutionary Iran. Iraq too is a significant actor; recognising its aspirations for leadership in the sub-region, smaller Gulf states chose to establish the GCC during the Iran–Iraq war so that Iraq would not be able to join (see Barnett and Gause 1998: 166).

It was not only the role non-Arab actors and in particular the United States played during the Gulf War but also the Arab–Israeli Peace Process set in motion in the aftermath of the War that enabled the consolidation of Middle East as a spatial representation in the eyes of local actors. In the aftermath of the War, the United States was able to re-introduce itself to the region and be accepted largely due to the constructive role it played in the making of the Madrid Peace Process. The Madrid Peace Conference (1991) was convened after the Gulf War as a part of the pre-war deal the US policy-makers struck with international public opinion in general and regional policy-makers in particular. The pace generated by the Madrid talks opened the way for the Palestinian–Israeli Accords signed in Oslo (1993). The role US policy-makers played in the Peace Process, in turn, enhanced their credibility thereby lessening (albeit temporarily) the criticisms voiced against the US approach to regional security in the Middle East (Faour 1993: 93–6). As Chapter 5 will discuss in greater detail, US policy-makers took this opportunity to encourage Middle Eastern regionalism. Towards this end, a Regional Economic Development working group was set up as a part of the multilateral track of the Middle East Peace Process (see Kaye 2001: 110–57). Other US and World Bank sponsored activities included the convening of the Middle East and North Africa (MENA) economic forum, and proposing the formation of a Middle East Regional Development Bank (El-Erian and Fischer 1996).

During the Madrid talks, US efforts received a boost by Egyptian intellectuals as well. The ideas they put forward in support of regionalisation in the Middle East as a way of maintaining security is referred to as 'Middle Easternism'. Although there are very few Arab policy-makers who openly advocated Middle Easternism, the fact that most participated in the multilateral track of the Middle East Peace Process (Kaye 2001) is indicative of their changing policy preferences. One could tease out two main reasons for some Arab policy-makers' hesitance to locate their countries in the Middle East. The first reason stems from the opposition of the proponents of the Arab and Islamist perspectives at the sub-state level. Many non-state actors view Middle Easternism as a project that would de-emphasise the Arab and/or Islamic character of the region. Some even go so far as to warn that Middle Easternism might end up replacing Arabism. As Michael Barnett (1998: 231–2) noted, opponents of Middle Easternism in the Arab world tap into 'long-standing fears of the West and Israel'. This point takes us to the second reason behind Arab policy-makers' hesitance, that is Labour politician Shimon Peres' (1993) vocal advocacy of Middle Eastern regionalism.

In 1993 Peres published a book entitled *The New Middle East* in which he called for a 'regional-based' approach to security (1993: 33–4). The adoption of such an approach, he stressed, was crucial in the face of the threats posed by the weapons of mass destruction and long-range missile delivery systems against which there exist no foolproof means of national defence other than a wide-ranging regional arrangement (Peres 1993: 83). 'Outdated' approaches to security based on the concept of 'national defence, which depend mainly on military and weapons systems', argued Peres, should be replaced by a 'modern' concept 'which is of necessity based on political accords, and embraces international security and economic considerations' (1993: 33–4). Peres expected regionalisation in economic relations to have a spill-over effect into political relations thereby paving the way for the creation of a 'New Middle East', which he envisioned as a 'regional community of nations, with a common market and elected centralised bodies, modelled on the European Community' (1993: 62).

Although Peres's blueprint for the future was received favourably outside the region, to some in the Arab world the idea of becoming a part of the New Middle East is a precursor to an emerging Israeli hegemony. Indeed, as will be discussed in Chapter 5, the Jordanian leadership, that sought to locate Jordan in the 'New Middle East' in the mid-1990s was forced to revert back towards the end of the 1990s because of pressures from the public (Lynch 1998–99, 1999, 2002). As Marc Lynch (1998–99) has maintained, although there were economic reasons behind this policy reversal, it was mediated through identity.

Then, Israel's economic might, which Peres considers a magnet to pull other regional countries towards cooperation, seems to have produced a contrary effect on some regional actors who hear 'dependence' when Peres says 'interdependence' (Barnett 1996–97: 604; Barnett 1998: 231). Indeed, the opponents of Middle Easternism invoke Arab peoples' age-old suspicions when they argue that the idea of constructing a New Middle East is an attempt at 'imperialism by regionalism' (Barnett 1996–97: 604).

Then, one major reason why Arab policy-makers became less hesitant in locating themselves in the Middle East was the fact that there were significant financial and political resources available for strengthening Middle Eastern regionalism. However, although this constituted good enough a reason to convince many policy-makers regarding the virtues of cooperation within a Middle Eastern framework, it was not that easy to persuade many non-state actors. For, as noted above, unlike the Cold War years when it was Arab policy-makers and some intellectuals that refused to locate themselves in the Middle East, it was now mainly non-state actors and especially grassroots movements informed by intellectuals that opposed US attempts to strengthen Middle Eastern regionalism (for a discussion of the Jordanian debate, see Lynch 1998–99, 1999). In other words, however attractive creating links of interdependence in the Middle East as a way of building peace may have seemed to some, others opposed it for the same reason; they did not want to be a part of and/or dependent on any non-Arab or non-Islamic entity.

According to Bahgat Korany, if regional policy-makers were to embrace Middle Easternism against the wishes of their peoples, this would have a divisive effect on the Arab world. Korany (1997: 143) warns that

> a return to the concept of the Middle East as a mosaic region, a pure agglomeration of different races and cultures – where Arabs are to be treated interchangeably with other groups like Kurds, Berbers or Armenians – would revive old and powerful memories of 'divide and rule' tactics.

Such concerns echo those that were voiced by Heikal, Dessouki and Matar during the late 1970s. What has changed since then, according to Korany, is that it is no longer tenable to present this issue as a matter of making a choice between the two competing representations. The end of the Cold War and the marginalisation of many Arab actors, the alienation of many Arab regimes from one another, and the globalisation of economic relations, argues Korany (1997: 145), have created what he calls 'a regional Arab vacuum' which may result in the 'triumph' of the 'new Middle East ... not because of its own merit but rather by default'. Given non-state actors' misgivings about the (New) Middle East, such a development has already started to create divisions in the Arab world.

In sum, well until the September 11 attacks, the debates on the Middle East in the post-Cold War era focused on two major concerns: the future of the Arab and Islamic dimensions of regional peoples' identity, and the future of regional economies. The latter concern rates above that of the prior on many Arab policy-makers' agendas, but the vocal opposition of non-state actors against Middle Easternism has made it difficult for them to openly embrace it. The debate on Middle Easternism had already died down following the stall in the multilateral peace talks in the 1990s and Palestinian–Israeli peace-making in early 2000. Given the environment created by the US policies toward Iraq (see Ibrahim *et al.* 2003), it is difficult to imagine the revival of such a debate unless a breakthrough is achieved in Arab–Israeli peace-making.

In many ways, the 2003 'War on Iraq' marked the unquestioned prevalence of the US approach to regional security in the Middle East. Indeed, the war was fought for reasons that find their explanation in the security concerns that have, over the years, helped to shape the Middle East. What has changed in the aftermath of the September 11 attacks is that US policy-makers declared commitment to 'advancing freedom' in the Middle East as a way of 'confronting the threats to peace from terrorism and weapons of mass destruction' (Bush 2003a). The Iraqi war and the US effort to change the Iraqi regime were explained with reference to this new policy priority. At the same time, US policy-makers sought to give momentum to Israeli–Palestinian peace-making by presenting a new 'roadmap'. For, the peace process (that began in the aftermath of the 1991 Gulf War) had come to a halt towards the end of the 1990s for reasons largely to do with the incongruities between the US perspective of regional security and those of regional actors. Although declared commitment to democratisation of Iraq seems to signal a change in US security policy-making, the unilateralist ways in which this aim has been pursued and the stress put on military force to achieve military as well as non-military aims[10] has served to alienate Iraqi and regional peoples alike (see, for example, Attiyah 2003; Nuri 2003). Indeed, it has become difficult to imagine Middle Eastern regionalism gaining strength unless US policy-makers decide to adopt an alternative approach more cognisant of the concerns of Iraqi peoples that include 'security, the reconstruction of Iraqi institutions, respect for human rights and the rule of law' (Kaldor 2003a).

Conclusion

The aim of this chapter was to follow the trajectory of four alternative representations in the post-Cold War period, namely the (New) Middle East, the Arab Regional System, the Euro–Med Region and the Muslim Middle East. It was argued that in the post-Cold War era the competition between these four representations took place at multiple levels. For a while during the 1990s the Middle East was the prevalent representation at the governmental level thanks to US encouragement of Middle Eastern regionalism. The 2003 US-led war on Iraq has caused a backlash in this regard. Besides, certain segments of the Arab and/or Islamist elite as well as some grassroots organisations oppose regionalisation in the Middle East. The chapter argued that such little evidence of enthusiasm for regionalisation in the Middle East is not because of a lack of regionalism, but rather because of the presence of a multiplicity of regionalisms, initiated, supported and (at times) stalled by myriad actors at multiple levels. In other words, the proponents of the other three spatial representations oppose Middle Easternism not because they are against regionalisation in itself, but because they are against regionalisation within the Middle Eastern framework. As the chapter argued, many have voiced their concern that the economic might of Israel, coupled with the political, economic and military backing it receives from the United States, would enable it to dominate an integrated Middle East if the 'New Middle East' project were to be put into practice (Ibrahim 1996: 428–30; Korany 1997: 135–50).

Among the three alternatives, the Euro–Med Region is the more clearly defined one and has so far received positive response at the state as well as sub-state level. This is also because it is a relatively neutral representation. The other two representations, Arab Regional System and Muslim Middle East are popular among non-state actors, some of whom actively oppose Middle Easternism. The debates between the proponents of these representations have showed that the main divide of the post-Cold War period is not one of Arab versus non-Arab or Arab Regional System versus Middle East, but pro-status quo actors who seek to maintain security by encouraging economic regionalisation, and anti-status quo actors who seek radical change. The proponents of the Arab Regional System and Muslim Middle East do not offer clear-cut alternatives in the form of regionalisation projects, but unite in opposing Middle Easternism. They nevertheless pose a significant challenge in that although they do not have the necessary resources to put their own ideas into practice, they have the power to stall others as September 11 has made it clear to all.

5 Practices of security in the post-Cold War era

Chapter 5 concludes Part II. As with Chapter 3, this chapter looks at the practical manifestations of adopting particular representations of the region – namely, the 'Arab Regional System', 'Euro–Med Region', 'Muslim Middle East', and '(New) Middle East' – which are rooted in different conceptions of security. The aim here is not to cover the complete range of security practices, but rather focus on those practices that were adopted to address the problem of regional security. The overall purpose of the chapter is to show how spatial representations help to shape practice; how they enable some practices whilst marginalising others; how they address some insecurities while constituting others.

Security in the Arab Regional System

The Arab Regional System as a spatial representation is rooted in the Arab national security discourse, which has shaped and, in turn, been shaped by the security practices of Arab actors. Security practices of Arab actors during the post-Cold War era have taken different forms. On the one hand were Arab policy-makers whose references to Arab national security became more and more sparse. Although Gulf regimes had begun to make this shift from the Arab national security discourse to that of Middle Eastern security since the 1960s, as far as the rest of the Arab states were concerned, the watershed event became the Iraqi invasion of Kuwait. Since the Gulf War, conservative Gulf regimes have expressed their reservations regarding the concept of Arab national security. Taking such a stance publicly would have been unheard of until the 1990s. Jordan and the PLO took up the opportunity to break away from the rest of Arab states and sign individual peace treaties with Israel. Egypt consolidated its ties with the United States. Even Syrian policy-makers, long-time contenders for the leadership of the radical camp, considered (until the Peace Process broke down in the late 1990s) engaging in bilateral peace negotiations with Israel. Turkey and Israel grasped this opportunity to strengthen the strategic ties they established during the Cold War but kept under covers for fear of Arab reaction. As the Arab/non-Arab divide that once was the backbone of Arab national security discourse became less and less meaningful, Iran re-introduced itself to regional politics and sought to assume the leadership of Muslim states, particularly in 1997 when it took over the presidency of the Organisation of Islamic Conference (OIC) (see Korany 1999).

On the other hand were Arab non-state actors whose practices continued to shape and be shaped by their concerns regarding Arab national security. Whilst intellectuals and grassroots organisations cooperated across borders to demand increased political participation and respect for human rights from their governments, those economically worse off focused on issues such as unemployment, better health provision and education (Gubser 2002). This section of the chapter will seek to show how non-state actors continued, throughout the 1990s, to locate themselves in the Arab Regional System and sought to shape and constrain the practices of their policy-makers, who often stepped outside the boundaries set by Arab national security (Korany 1994: 161–78; Barnett 1996–97: 598–606).

The Gulf Crisis (1990–91) was a decisive event for inter-Arab relations. This had to do with the security practices of Arab governments, which were increasingly shaped by concerns regarding *amn qutri* (the territorial state) as opposed to *amn kawmi* (the Arab nation). As Bahgat Korany (1994: 164) wrote:

> At the root of the Arabs' different alignments during the Gulf War were differing perceptions of security requirements – and these, in turn, were determined by whether Arab actors thought of security primarily in terms of the individual territorial state (Amn Qutri) or in terms of the broader collectivity: Arabs versus non-Arabs.

During the Cold War there had already emerged a gap between 'say' and 'do', or 'the *doctrine* of (pan-)national security and the *practice* of territorial state security' in Arab politics (Korany 1994: 174). However, notwithstanding this discrepancy, many Arab policy-makers, until the early 1990s, continued to uphold the Arab national security discourse, whilst the rest of their security practices increasingly focused on maintaining state and regime security. Then, what has changed with the Gulf War is that since then not even the discourses employed by Arab policy-makers uphold Arab national security. Note the following statement by the Secretary-General of the League of Arab States (LAS) made in December 1992:

> Each state determines the needs and boundaries of its security on its own, because this concerns its people and its future. We should basically assume that there should be no interference in any country's security. We must acknowledge and proceed from this basic principle.
>
> (quoted in Barnett 1996–97: 602)

This is not necessarily what one would consider a controversial statement, rather a pronouncement of a statist approach to security. Nevertheless it would have been unthinkable to utter such a statement publicly during the 1950s and 1960s, when Nasser was in power and Arab nationalism was at its peak. The Gulf War, in this sense, helped to bridge the gap between 'say' and 'do' in Arab politics; representatives of Gulf states and others no longer seem to feel the need to resort to the language of Arab national security to justify their practices (see Sayigh 1991: 489; Barnett 1996–97: 605).

The Gulf War constituted a watershed in Arab politics also because this was the first time, in the history of the LAS, that an Arab state invaded another Arab state. Although there had been instances in the past such as Saudi Arabia providing financial backing to Islamist movements in other Arab states, or Syria's intervention into Lebanon during the civil war, respect for each other's sovereignty and especially territorial integrity had been a closely guarded rule (see Barnett 1996–97: 602). By invading Kuwait, Iraq not only broke this rule, but also sought to destabilise other Arab regimes by legitimising this action with reference to Arab national security in a way reminiscent of Nasser's 'symbolic practices' (Barnett 1998) of the 1950s and 1960s. In the immediate aftermath of the invasion, Iraqi president Saddam Hussein suggested that the Iraqi action was part of a large-scale process to attain Arab national security which – in his view – included the re-distribution of Arab oil wealth equitably between 'haves' and 'have nots' (Faour 1993: 61; Korany 1994: 165). This attempt to present the conflict between Kuwait and Iraq as one of Arab 'haves' against 'have nots', thereby playing up the resentment felt by the peoples of poor Arab states against their oil-rich neighbours did not prove to be very credible, not the least because Iraq itself was a 'have' state (with oil reserves second only to those of Saudi Arabia) (Faour 1993: 12) enjoying a GNP that was nine times that of Somalia, five times that of Sudan, and just less than four times that of Egypt (Korany 1994: 165–6).[1] Saddam Hussein's claim was made all the less credible by the fact that he had not come up with the idea of distributing oil wealth before the Gulf War (Faour 1993: 5; Korany 1994: 166).

Bahgat Korany (1994: 166) likened the Iraqi attempt to legitimise Kuwait's invasion with reference to Arab national security to a 'fatal bear hug', maintaining that Saddam Hussein's reference to the Arab national security discourse only helped 'downgrade' the ideal itself (also see Barnett and Gause 1998: 181). Gulf policy-makers were particularly vocal in expressing their disillusionment with Arab national security, especially its core assumption that threats to the security of Arabs come from non-Arabs. In a statement made after the Gulf War, the Secretary General of the Gulf Cooperation Council (GCC) Abdallah Bishara expressed his conviction that the basic threat to the security of the Gulf states emanated not from Israel, but from some Arab states:

> We in the Gulf and the people of Kuwait have paid the price of fixed
> emotional positions and of basing our policy on so-called solidarity . . .
> My view of the Arab future is based on a concept which destroys the
> myth of Arab fraternity, the myth of Arab security, and the myth of
> the one homeland. Future Arab links should be based on the Arab
> dimension of civilised interests, not on futile emotional theories.
>
> (quoted in Maddy-Weitzman 1993: 225)

As noted above, the very fact that an Arab policy-maker did make such a
statement, which would have been considered heretical if made a decade
earlier, signalled the diminishing hold the Arab security discourse had
over Arab policy-makers' practices.

Another example of Gulf policy-makers' increasingly bold disregard of
the premises of Arab national security was observed when they decided to
punish those states that they saw as taking Iraq's side by banishing their
migrant workers. Following the liberation of Kuwait, hundreds of thou-
sands of Palestinians, Iraqis, Yemenis and Jordanians were forced to leave
their homes in Gulf states. It should also be noted that Iraq and Jordan
also sent migrant workers back home because of their own economic
decline (Fergany 1997: 95–6; also see Faour 1993: 82–3; Karawan 1994:
444–6).

Gulf policy-makers' banishment of Arab migrant workers becomes all
the more striking when it is put in its historical context; for until the 1990s
labour migration had been perceived as 'a dimension of Arab economic
interdependence and an example of regional integration' (Karawan 1994:
445). The 'have not' governments, which exported work force, viewed this
as a way of claiming a share of the oil revenues of the 'have' states.
Workers' remittances not only helped to feed their families back home
but also helped to ameliorate the financial troubles of their governments.
Those 'have' states, which were on the receiving end of labour migration,
in turn, benefited from the services of their poor brethren (see Chaudhry
1997, for an elaborate analysis of the workings of this relationship within
the context of Saudi Arabia and Yemen; also see Fergany 1994: 93).
Although the 'have' states were always very cautious about the potential
destabilising effects of the migrant workers in their societies, not allowing
them to become a permanent part of the socio-economic fabric, they had
never before used migrant workers explicitly as a foreign policy tool – not
even during periods of strain (Karawan 1994: 445).

The Gulf War, then, could be considered to have resulted in the 'securitization' of labour migration in that since 1991 the issue has been treated
openly by Gulf regimes as 'a matter of national security, state sovereignty
and regime stability' (Karawan 1994: 446; see also Sullivan 2000). This, in
turn is a good illustration of how non-military issues, when put on the security agenda, could be approached from a statist perspective and met by traditional practices unless alternative practices are adopted in addressing them.

There is, as yet, little evidence of Arab actors adopting cooperative practices to address such problems. The 'oil sensitive' and 'remittance sensitive' countries of the Arab world have framed their sensitivities in 'security dilemma' terms rather than defining economic underdevelopment and lack of regional integration as threatening Arab national security. Over the years, regional economic cooperation in the Arab world has remained a 'political slogan without any real economic transactions'. What is more, 'most Arab countries are linking to non-Arab economic centres with little or no concern for their Arab neighbours' (Kubursi 2001: 151).

Another example of the 'atomisation' (Faour 1993: 77–97) of the Arab region and decline of Arab national security was observed when the Damascus Declaration (signed in the immediate aftermath of the Gulf War by Arab members of the US-led coalition) was allowed to wither. The Declaration was agreed on in March 1991 between Egypt, Syria and GCC member states in the attempt to take the issue of Gulf security in the hands of Arab states (Barnett 1996–97: 602). The Declaration was based on the principles embodied in the UN and LAS charters with special emphasis being put on state sovereignty and territorial integrity. In the economic sphere, the intention to establish an 'Arab economic grouping' was declared. Regarding defence, the Declaration envisaged the constitution of a 'nucleus Arab peace force' which was to be based on existing Egyptian and Syrian forces already stationed in Kuwait and Saudi Arabia, with the stated aim of safeguarding the Gulf as well as serving as 'an example that would guarantee the effectiveness of the comprehensive Arab defence order' (Maddy-Weitzman 1993: 226–7). In this way, Egypt and Syria were committing themselves to the security of Gulf states, whilst the latter were pledging $5bn in economic assistance to Egypt and Syria as part of a projected $10–15bn package (1993: 227).

The misgivings of Gulf policy-makers regarding the Declaration began to surface shortly, as they repeatedly postponed its ratification (Barnett and Gause 1998: 181–6). It soon became clear that in the eyes of the Gulf policy-makers the real value of the Damascus Declaration, as the Kuwaiti ex-Secretary-General of the GCC Abdallah Bishara put it, was 'its recognition of the legitimacy of the Arab states' borders, the right of each state to arrange its own security, and the exclusive claim to its resources' (Barnett 1996–97: 602). When Egypt and Syria withdrew their forces from the Gulf, tired of waiting, this served the purposes of Gulf states, which 'seemed intent on watering down the signed document without scrapping it outright' (Faour 1993: 88). Finally, on 16 July 1991 the foreign ministers of signatory states met and issued a revised version of the Declaration that no longer mentioned a 'nucleus Arab peace force' (Maddy-Weitzman 1993: 227–8).

A few months later Kuwait signed a ten-year security accord with the United States (September 1991). Bahrain (October 1991) and Qatar

(June 1992) followed suit. Kuwait sought also to broaden the net by signing 'defence cooperation accords' with the other four members of the UN Security Council (Barnett and Gause 1998: 182). In other words, the Gulf states were quick to turn away from an 'Arab collective security' scheme and towards a 'go it alone defence strategy' (Barnett and Gause 1998: 183; see also Barnett 1996–97: 608), with each seeking to buy security by concluding colossal defence contracts and negotiating individual security guarantees with the United States. They did not seek to coordinate their efforts even within the GCC framework let alone with other Arab states. Nor did they show any 'desire to come to understandings about burden-sharing, avoidance of duplication, or inter-operability' with other GCC member states (Barnett and Gause 1998: 182). The point here is that in stark contrast to the premises of Arab national security, Gulf policy-makers were not willing to allow any other Arab actor to interfere with their policies. Although attempts were made later in 1995, 1996 and 1998 to agree on the principles of a 'new Arab order' firmly based on the principle of sovereignty and non-intervention, its conduct was not regularised but remained 'issue-oriented'. In other words, Arab leaders came together as issues of concern to Arab states came up. These meetings often took the form of 'mini-summits' between a few Arab states for crisis management purposes (Sirriyeh 2000) whereas Gulf states turned to the United States for security cooperation. Hence the point made in Chapter 4 that 'the Gulf' as a spatial representation turned into a sub-region of 'the Middle East' and a component of the US approach to regional security in the Middle East during the 1990s.

However, although the fate of the Damascus Declaration did indeed highlight the decline (if not 'collapse', see Barnett 1998: 227) of Arab national security as far as Arab governments were concerned, this should not lead one to underestimate its centrality to the practices of many individuals, grassroots organisations and other civil societal actors.[2] For instance, when Saddam Hussein resorted to Arab national security discourse to justify Iraqi actions, his views were echoed by the demonstrators in the streets of the Arab world. He was received favourably by many when he appealed to Arab peoples and called for a unified Arab stance against the foreign (non-Arab) elements that have been usurping Arab oil and their regional allies who provided services such as keeping the oil prices down and helping maintain a stable international economy without eliciting a political quid pro quo (such as a less pro-Israeli stance in the Israel/Palestine conflict) (Khalidi 1991: 161–71; Said 1994b: 278–82). When he made his 12 August 1990 speech explaining the Iraqi presence in Kuwait by establishing linkages with the Israeli presence in Palestine, southern Lebanon and the Golan, and the Syrian presence in southern Lebanon, his arguments struck a chord with many people both within and outside the Arab world (Khalidi 1991: 17; see also AbuKhalil 1992). As Rouhollah Ramazani (1998: 50) put it, the fact that Saddam Hussein chose to justify his actions with reference to these linkages did not mean that they did not exist in the minds of other regional actors.

Non-governmental actors' protests against the US-led coalition took the form of street demonstrations, conferences, and the formation of delegations to try and solve the problem within an Arab framework. The demonstrators in Arab streets expressed support for Iraq not necessarily because they condoned the Iraqi invasion of Kuwait, but because they were, as Walid Khalidi (1991: 167) noted, '[disillusioned] with the Arab status quo – political, social and economic – as well as with the regional policies of the United States'. In their eyes, the Iraqi action 'constituted a deserved blow to the status quo (with all its domestic, political, socio-economic, and international dimensions) . . . which Kuwait was seen to symbolise' (1991: 204). Their protests were 'not so much pro-Saddam or anti-Kuwait as anti the socio-economic status quo, despite the merits of the Kuwaiti case' (1991: 168). To a certain extent, then, the pro-Iraq demonstrations of the Arab masses were a way of voicing their opinion against their governments that otherwise refused to listen to their concerns (Azzam 1991: 471).

Many Arab intellectuals, among them Edward Said, also refused to condone the Iraqi action, but at the same time opposed the US-led coalition and its resolve to bring an end to the crisis through the use of force (Said 1991a: 15–20). Arab intellectuals felt frustrated when the Arab world could not cope with an inter-Arab dispute by itself, that it displayed signs of dependence on the West (especially the United States), and that Iraq was allowed to be destroyed (Maddy-Weitzman 1993: 225). Said (1994b: 286) expressed the feelings of many when he wrote:

> No Arab country today can adequately defend itself or its borders, yet national security arguments are used to justify gigantically large outlays of money for imported weapons, standing armies, praetorian guards. Above all, the movement toward war today has overridden any rational consideration of what as Arabs we want out future to be. Where is the real discussion of 'Arab' wealth, poverty, society? All of us feel connected to an Arab nation, yet we allow massive amounts of polemic to cover hypothesized Arabs, while not enough detailed attention and care are given to individual, actual Arab lives and bodies.

Fatima Mernissi (1993: 9) voiced similar concerns, but from a feminist perspective, when she wrote:

> It is true that Mecca is still the centre of the world, even though it needs the American air force to protect it. But what can such a force protect against, against what deviation and confusion? What about the women in the city? . . . What will become of the women in a city where the defence of the *hudud* [boundary] is in the hands of foreigners?

Mernissi sought to emphasise how the Gulf War only added to the predicament of Arab women. The Arab national security discourse privileged militarised practices by way of invoking the need to secure Arabs (inside) from non-Arabs (outside). This, in turn, resulted in the marginalisation of women's concerns. In the aftermath of the Gulf War, women found themselves once again on the margins, unable to voice their concerns let alone put them on Arab national security agendas, because the boundary dividing Arabs from non-Arabs was once again under challenge.

Despite the prevalence of statist security practices that have been justified by regional governments' pro-Arab rhetoric, a more societal-focused conceptualisation of Arab national security has been upheld by Arab intellectuals and non-governmental actors. They have used Arab national security as a tool in shaping and constraining their governments' actions. For example, notwithstanding the Egyptian and Jordanian governments' policy of rapprochement with Israel, non-governmental actors in these two countries have effectively prevented normalisation. In the case of Jordan,

> A major force ... is the professional syndicates. They have their own policy forbidding their members from doing business with Israel. This policy is reinforced by the monopoly the syndicates have in licensing their members. Thus, a syndicate can disbar a lawyer or take away the license of a doctor if he/she does business with Israel – a powerful tool to say the least. Anti-normalisation has been the policy of the syndicates since the mid-1990s.
>
> (Gubser 2002: 145; see also Lynch 1998–99, 1999)

Then, Arab non-state actors continue to locate themselves in the Arab Regional System when they write and organise activities in collaboration with activists in other Arab countries to put pressure on their governments. Although not much cooperation is visible with their Iranian and Turkish counterparts,[3] Arab intellectuals regularly come together to address those problems overlooked (if not perpetuated) by their governments (see, for example, Nasr 1997: 16–18; Sharabi 1988; E. Boulding 1994: 43; Gubser 2002). Saad Eddin Ibrahim (1996: 428) observed that those of the socialist conviction put 'social justice' on top of their agenda; those with liberal convictions prioritise 'democracy' (see also Sharabi 1988: 6–7). Human rights is another significant issue upheld by Arab intellectuals and social activists (Osseiran 1994: 86–7). Needless to say, the agenda of non-governmental organisations are shaped, to a significant extent, by the donor's agenda. Whereas those funded by the European Union locate themselves in the Mediterranean and focus on human rights and democratisation issues, oil-rich Arab actors favour non-governmental actors that focus on welfare, health care and education.

It should also be noted that the late 1980s and especially 1990s saw the relative strengthening of civil society in the Arab world with an increase in the number of relevant organisations.[4] Arab civil society is considered to be more vibrant than ever, with grassroots organisations of all sorts emphasising their Arab character. Many Arab non-governmental organisations work on relief and survival issues, human rights, provision of health care and education (Norton 1993; Schwedler 1995; Gubser 2002). Lebanese and Palestinian NGOs have been doing crucial work in trying to alleviate the difficulties of life in civil war (Lebanon) or under occupation (Palestine) by 'nurturing a sense of community, solidarity and hope' (Bibi 1995: 26). These are also excellent examples of non-state actors acting to provide for their own and others' security where governments fail to do so.

What has changed with the 2003 US-led war on Iraq is that even Arab intellectuals' references to Arab national security became sparse. In the immediate aftermath of the war, one Arab author expressed his feelings as follows: 'It is even uncertain even if there is still such a thing as a collective Arab order. After all, the invasion and occupation of Iraq was only made possible because of some Arab countries' (Ezzat 2003; see also Huveydi 2003).[5] In the debates in the Arab media, references to Arab national security and Arab order were notable for their absence. On the decline of Arab national security, Barnett (2002b: 81–2; see also Seale 2003) made the following observation:

> At best, Arab states have refused to sanction or to join any American military campaign against Iraq (at least under current conditions). Nor have these events led to a significant tightening of inter-Arab strategic relations. Instead, Arab leaders have been quite interested in figuring how they can get Washington to alter its policies toward the region. Most of the major Arab actors have demonstrated a keen interest in seeing a greater coordination between them and Washington. Certainly because of the anti-Western sentiments there is a limit to how far they can go, but there has been no widespread demand for the prohibitions against relations with the West (that is, the United States) that characterised the early decades of the Arab state system, and there has been no tangible movement toward the coordination of Arab military relations.

Indeed, Egyptian President Husni Mubarak's immediate reaction to the beginning of the US operation on Iraq was to call for the United Nations Security Council to 'undertake its crucial role in managing the international mutual security system and safeguarding international peace and security' (Shukrallah 2003). One of the few Arab leaders who made reference to Arabism, Syrian President Bashir Asad (2003: 43) was also modest in formulating his plea to other Arab leaders: 'I am not calling for signing a Common Arab Defence Pact, closing off the foreign bases or expelling foreign forces', he said. 'This is a matter of national sovereignty . . . What is important is that these foreign bases and forces are not used in an attack against another [Arab] country'. In other words, asking his fellow Arab policy-makers to refrain from providing bases to US forces was the most Asad could do in the name of Arab solidarity. This, in turn, could be taken as an indication of the state of Arabism as a force shaping Arab politics in the beginning of the twenty-first century. Although it continues to shape the practices of Arab actors (some more than the others) it is no longer the major force it used to be. This, in turn, is likely to have implications for the future of regional security. One consequence of the decline of Arab national security might be that the Islamist discourse on security would take up the issue of the plight of the Palestinian peoples, thereby strengthening its hold over regional peoples provided that the Palestinian problem retains its significance for Arab peoples.

Security in the Euro–Med Region

As argued above, the Mediterranean as an alternative spatial representation began to take shape from the 1970s onwards largely in line with the development and changing security conceptions and practices of the European Union (previously the European Community). The EU's close interest in Middle Eastern affairs goes back to the early 1970s – a period marked by the OPEC oil embargo that intertwined with the 1973 Arab–Israeli War. Over the years, the EU's policies toward the Middle East have been shaped around three major concerns: energy security (understood as the sustained flow of oil and natural gas at reasonable prices); regional stability (understood as domestic stability especially in countries in geographically North Africa); and the cessation of the Israel/Palestine conflict (see Perthes 1997; Rhein 1997).

In the 1980s, changes in the societies of EU member states as a result of the growth of the Middle Eastern diaspora in Western Europe led EU policy-makers to re-think their priorities, and come to consider stability in the Middle East (especially North Africa) as an integral part of their own security (see Salamé 1994). Accordingly, EU policy-makers have sought to create cooperative schemes with the Mediterranean-rim countries of the Middle East to encourage and support economic development and growth (see Satloff 1997; also see Buzan and Roberson 1993: 131–47). Although non-EU actors such as the International Peace Research Association (IPRA), the IPRA Commission on Peace Building in the Middle East, and the European Peace Research Association (EUPRA) have also encouraged and supported the search for security within a Euro–Med framework (see E. Boulding 1994; The Commission Document 1994), the EU has almost single-handedly sought to construct a Euro–Med Region to meet its own domestic economic, societal, and, to a much lesser extent, military security interests.

This, however, is not to suggest that the members of the European Union have adopted a single common approach or that EU policy-makers speak with one voice regarding Middle Eastern issues. On the contrary, EU members do not all share the same sense of urgency or the need to adopt an independent and common European foreign policy towards the Middle East, or to assume a prominent role in Arab–Israeli peace-making. Whilst France and other southern European states press for more assertive policy-making and implementation, Germany, the Netherlands and the UK have cautioned against it (see Perthes 1997: 87).

The shift in the EU's priorities towards adopting a Mediterranean-centred approach, then, should be understood within a context created, over the years, by the convergence of domestic societal as well as economic concerns. The presence of a large and growing Middle Eastern diaspora in the EU has meant that the de-stabilisation of Middle Eastern societies, especially those in North Africa, could be detrimental to security and stability in the EU (Perthes 1997: 92; Marfleet 2000). The term 'time bomb' is used in EU texts to describe the character of the challenge the Mediterranean poses to security in the European Union; a bomb that might, if not defused, 'fuel the sort of repressive regime, anti-Western religious fundamentalism seen in Algeria' (Larsen 2000: 343). In short, the EU's turn towards a more Mediterranean-centred approach has its roots in the domestic societal concerns of EU policy-makers and a re-thinking of security in the European Union against the backdrop of migration from the Middle East; the increasing restlessness within the Middle Eastern diaspora in the EU that has at times taken the form of militant activism; and the civil war in Algeria, which accelerated the pace of the first two processes (see also, Parfitt 1997; Roberson 1998).

What is also new in the post-Cold War era is the gradual emergence of a division of labour between the United States and the European Union over regional security in the Middle East (Satloff 1997) – a division of labour based on the differences between EU and US priorities. Previously, there used to be a division of labour between Britain (that focused on the security of the route to India and other [former] colonies) and the United States (which prioritised making the region inviolable to the Soviet Union while securing the flow of oil at reasonable prices and Israel's well-being). The terms of the new division of labour are that US policy-makers concentrate on maintaining the security of the Gulf and the Arab–Israeli peace process, whereas the EU puts emphasis on security and stability in geographically closer North Africa.

However, these differences in priorities should not obscure the common interests that remain. Both the United States and the European Union still share an interest in the sustained flow of oil (and natural gas for the EU) at reasonable prices. EU members (with the exception of the UK) are considerably more dependent on Middle Eastern oil than the United States. The latter imports only 20 per cent of its total energy consumption from the Middle East whereas it is 50–90 per cent for some European states (Rhein 1997: 49). Indeed oil is the only Middle Eastern issue over which transatlantic relations have been relatively 'concentric and coherent' since the end of the Cold War (Perthes 1997: 88). The cooperative relationship established between the two during the Gulf War could be viewed as an example of this phenomenon (for a discussion, see Heisbourg 1997; Kugler 1997).

It should nevertheless be noted that although it is true that the EU, like the United States, seeks to maintain military stability in the Gulf, when security in North Africa is concerned it emphasises economic development and democratisation as well as stability. EU policy-makers are very sceptical about what military practices could achieve in influencing North African countries (that are included in the Euro–Med Region). Some (such as the United Kingdom, Italy and Spain) were less hesitant in following the US lead in the Gulf War (1991) and the war on Iraq (2003).

On the issue of security in the Euro–Med Region, EU members have maintained that 'economic, political, and diplomatic engagement can be of greater relevance' (Heisbourg 1997: 284). According to François Heisbourg (1997: 285),

> although the Europeans are just as prone – and possibly even more so, for reasons of proximity – as the Americans to emphasize the combined regional dangers of militant fundamentalism and terrorism (not least in Algeria, a prime French security concern), they do not usually see these as essentially military challenges.

In other words, the EU's practices towards achieving security in the Euro–Med Region are based on a broader conception of security that takes into account its non-military dimensions and seeks to adopt non-militarised practices.

The Euro–Mediterranean partnership that shaped the Euro–Med Region was institutionalised at the Barcelona Conference (November 1995) that brought together Algeria, Cyprus, Egypt, Jordan, Israel, Lebanon, Malta, Morocco, Syria, the Palestinian Authority, Tunisia and Turkey.[6] The Conference agreed on establishing a partnership between Mediterranean littoral states in three areas: political and security relations, economic and financial relations, and social, cultural and human relations. In order to give practical expression to this scheme, the Conference agreed on a work programme of activities in a multilateral framework that brought in the private sector to play a role in transferring additional resources, both technological and financial. The cornerstone of the Euro–Med partnership is the creation of a free-trade zone in industrial goods and services over a twelve-year period. The purpose behind this formation is stated as not only one of creating an expanded trading bloc, but also providing, incentives for sound economic and financial decision-making by Middle Eastern participants, to create a framework for labour-intensive European-funded development projects, and even reduce intra-Middle Eastern conflicts by providing a non-threatening forum for participation across divides.

(Satloff 1997: 23)

In this sense, the Euro–Med partnership scheme is based on liberal assumptions as can be deduced from British Foreign Secretary Malcolm Rifkind's address to the Barcelona Conference where he said that the Euro–Med had 'two main themes: political stability ... and economic growth. In reality these are actually only one subject' (Satloff 1997: 23). A similar logic was at the roots of the establishment of the multilateral negotiations of the Arab–Israeli peace process (see below).

The programme agreed at the Barcelona Conference, although less ambitious compared with a CSCE (Conference on Security and Cooperation in Europe) type organisation, nevertheless envisaged that the partners would discuss issues of human rights and fundamental freedoms. The partner states also called for exchanges at civil societal level as a key element of the implementation of the partnership programme.[7] So far, one key achievement of the partnership has been to bring together Syria and Lebanon with Israel as part of a multilateral scheme. Considering the fact that Syria boycotted the MENA (Middle East and North Africa) summits organised as a part of the Madrid Peace Process (Perthes 1997: 95) this is no small achievement.

The proposal to create a CSCE type organisation in the Middle East, a Conference on Security and Cooperation in the Mediterranean (CSCM), was an earlier attempt by two EU member states, Italy and Spain to create 'a stable system of regional cooperation' in the Mediterranean (1990) (Niblock 1992: 246). Later in the year a meeting on security and cooperation was held in Cairo, attended by representatives from Algeria, Egypt, France, Italy, Malta, Portugal, Spain and Yugoslavia. The long-term objectives and principles of the CSCM discussed at this meeting were modelled after the CSCE and aimed to achieve consensus, among the participant states, on a set of principles and rules dealing with issues of security, economic cooperation and human rights (Niblock 1992: 246–7). Although the CSCM proposal was well received by the International Peace Research Association, among others (E. Boulding 1994: 49), it was not followed up. Arguably, the formation of a CSCM was considered too ambitious a project. A CSCM would have set certain criteria to be met in terms of inter-state relations as well as state–society relations and would have created responsibilities which very few of the potential CSCM member states were willing to assume (for a critique of the CSCM proposal see Aliboni 1997–98). Furthermore, European policy-makers were more eager to adopt policies that would show immediate economic effects. This is because the European Union's conception of security in the Euro–Med Region takes the EU itself as the referent. EU policy-makers have broadened security not from regional peoples' but from the EU's perspective in the attempt to stop Middle Eastern problems from becoming European problems.

Although a Helsinki-type process was not initiated in the Euro–Med Region, non-state actors from Western Europe have been active in conducting people-to-people diplomacy. In February 1992 a meeting was organised in Paris entitled the 'Citizens of the Mediterranean' bringing together the peoples of the region and the Helsinki Citizens' Association (Osseiran 1994: 87). A similar bottom-up approach was the organisation of the three-day UNESCO-supported meeting of the Consultation on Educating for Peace in the Mediterranean that took place in Malta in November 1991. A network of peace educators has begun to be built by the Peace and International Education Programmes of the Foundation for International Studies at the University of Malta. Later in the year the 1991 Conference of the European Peace Research Association in Florence became the occasion for a workshop on this theme (Calleja 1994: 282).

Since it is relatively new, the Euro–Med partnership scheme does not have too many proponents at the sub-state level; nor does it have many enemies. Notwithstanding Israeli scepticism regarding the increased role for the European Union in security matters, the main strength of the Euro–Mediterranean partnership stems from the fact that it managed to bring together Syria and Israel as well as a wide spectrum of NGOs. Another one of its strengths is the assistance the EU has provided to NGOs. Between 1995 and 2002, the EU has set M€6803.4 to be granted to regional NGOs.[8] The point here is that although the Euro–Med partnership scheme does not have too many backers, if the EU policy to take civil societal actors on its side bears fruit in the long run, it may come to prevail over the other three approaches. Yet, although the EU side is resolute in its commitment to the centrality of civil societal actors for this project, the Mediterranean partners have their doubts (see Salamé 1994; Marfleet 2000; Jünemann 2002). Besides, given the mixed record of the EU in engendering civil society in the region (Youngs 2002), EU policy-makers might feel compelled to re-think their civil-society focused approach. Indeed, given the progress in European Security and Defence Policy and the EU's move to develop its own military force, the Mediterranean partners have already voiced their worries regarding the future of the Euro–Med partnership project.[9]

Security in the Muslim Middle East

The Islamist discourse on security is the most controversial among the four approaches looked at in Part II. This partly stems from the anti-status quo discourses and violent practices of some Islamist actors that include the Islamic Republic of Iran, Sudan, and organisations such as al-Qaida, the Hizbullah in Lebanon and Hamas in Israel/Palestine that constitute a challenge to the military stability in the region, which the United States and its regional allies have been keen to maintain. On the other hand, Saudi Arabia, a major US ally and a pro-status quo actor, does not only resort to the Islamist discourse to enhance legitimacy, but it has also been a major financial supporter of many Islamist organisations (Esposito 1993: 188; Eickelman 1997: 37–8) often regardless of their anti-status quo practices. This was done partly to weaken the grip of Arab national security discourse over Arab peoples' practices, and partly to prevent Iran from dominating the Muslim Middle East (Fraser 1997: 212–40). Such practices have, over the years, helped to maintain regime security for a Saudi leadership that has not been keen to allow political participation. However it is also such Islamist organisations that challenge the regional status quo. In other words, the very same practices designed to enhance Saudi security have at the same time challenged regional instability. This, in turn, is an example of how 'short-termist' (Booth 1999a) approaches to security sooner or later backfire; the support Saudi policy-makers provided to the Islamist actors have in the long run strained the Saudi–US relationship and led the latter to look for alternative bases and allies in the region.

The way Saudi practices seem to have rebounded could partly be explained with reference to the different, and at times clashing, conceptualisations of security adopted by Saudi policy-makers and the Islamist actors it has chosen to support. Indeed, there is more agreement amongst Islamists as to what they are against rather than what they are for. They often define 'un-Islamic influences' as the major threat to Muslims' security, but there is little agreement as to what constitutes 'un-Islamic' (or 'Islamic' for that matter). Some would consider Western influence over and intervention into the region as 'un-Islamic'. Some others would criticise existing political and religious establishments (such as the Islamic Kingdom of Saudi Arabia that allowed US troops to step on the 'holy lands') as well as the forces of Arab nationalism as being 'un-Islamic' (see Eickelman 1997: 27–46, for an overview of Islamist organisations). Lastly, there are those who define 'structural violence' as 'un-Islamic' (this point will be further developed towards the end of this section).

The practices of Islamist actors range from militant activism (such as the New York Trade Center bombing in 1993 or the September 11, 2001 attacks) to grassroots activities providing welfare services (such as the activities of FIS – the Islamic Salvation Front – in Algeria), and to advocating political violence aimed at establishing an 'Islamic' state (as with the Hizbullah in Lebanon) (see Esposito 1995; Eickelman and Piscatori 1996; Eickelman 1997). From the perspective of the governments of the United States, Egypt and Israel, most Islamist organisations constitute threats to regional security due to their anti-status quo discourses and (at times) violent practices. However, viewed through the lenses of some regional peoples, some of these actors serve as major security agents by providing welfare services that the state fails to provide its peoples. Indeed, their practices indicate that some Islamist organisations aim primarily at bringing about change at home although they do, at times, take action abroad to achieve their aims. Some Islamist organisations that target the United States, for instance, aim to bring pressure upon the US government so that it would cease supporting its regional allies, some of which (such as Egypt) suppress Islamist opposition at home (see Paz 2003). The point here is that the globalist outlook and discourses of some Islamist actors often become locally oriented in practice.

The difference between an Islamist actor with a domestic and reformist approach, and one with a more universal and revisionist orientation could be seen in the examples of AMAL (Lebanese Resistance Army) and Hizbullah (Party of God), both of which have used violence to achieve their aims that included fighting Israeli forces in south Lebanon. AMAL initially emerged as the military wing of the 'Movement for Dispossessed' that was founded in Lebanon in the 1960s to bring about political and economic parity for the Lebanese Shii community. The military wing (AMAL) eventually absorbed the socio-political movement, but it also adopted the political wing's goals and has concentrated on demanding reform at home. The Hizbullah, on the other hand, was founded in the 1980s following Israeli invasion of Lebanon (1982). It is an umbrella movement comprising like-minded groups and militias whose aims converge in the dismantling of the Lebanese state and the creation in its place of an Islamic state; the acceptance of Khomeini and Iran as the model to be emulated; a consensus that the enemies are the Lebanese government, other confessional groups, the United States, and France, as well as pro-Western Arab regimes such as Saudi Arabia and Kuwait; and the belief that it is a religious duty to destroy the 'enemies of God' through *jihad,* martyrdom and self-sacrifice (Esposito 1995: 148).

Al-Qaida is considered as a 'class of its own – more global and networked than probably any other violent or nationalist group' (Kaldor 2003b) and has a seemingly universal and revisionist agenda. In the aftermath of the September 11 attacks, Osama bin Laden declared:

> To America I say only a few words to it and its people, I swear by God, who has elevated the skies without pillars, neither America nor the people who live in it will dream of security before we live it in Palestine, and not before all the infidel armies leave the land of Muhammad.[10]

By its own deed, al-Qaida constitutes an example of what Mary Kaldor (2003b) calls 'regressive globalisation' meaning those 'new groups, which make use of and even promote globalisation, when it is in the interests of a particular religious or nationalist group'. In other words, although a primary aim of al-Qaida is rolling back globalisation, it flourishes in the environment created by the very process. Its primary goal, on the other hand, is rather traditional in that it wants to capture state power. Although it is difficult to imagine al-Qaida type actors capturing state power, what is important to note is that 'it is the struggle on which they thrive and the difficulty of achieving their stated goals will make the struggle even more plausible' (Kaldor 2003b).

Amongst those Islamist organisations that have acted as agents of security, the case of FIS is a telling example of how an Islamist organisation can muster domestic support notwithstanding the violent practices of its members (on FIS, see Esposito 1995: 163–83). FIS emerged as a political actor in Algeria during the social upheavals in the late 1980s, which were generated by the fall in oil prices and the economic crisis that ensued. In 1988 the Algerian government faced massive student protests and food riots. As the protests were brutally suppressed, FIS emerged as the 'self-proclaimed voice of the oppressed masses' (1995: 167) and went on to gain electoral victories in local elections in 1990 and the first round of the general elections in 1991. When it became clear that FIS had won the majority of seats in the parliament, the army intervened, the second round of the elections was cancelled, and President Chadli was forced to resign in January 1992 to be replaced by an army-backed government.

In achieving such popularity with the masses, FIS followed a two-pronged strategy. One part of this strategy was pointing to the failures of the state in fields such as education, housing and employment as well as governmental corruption – criticisms that found receptive ears in a society like Algeria with more than 60 per cent of the population under 25 years of age and high levels of unemployment (Esposito 1995: 168). Another popular FIS critique was that the government spent too much on arms. Slashing the defence budget to make more money available for social expenditures was one of its election promises (Sadowski 1992: 5). The second part of the FIS strategy was to proclaim 'Islam's message of social justice' and call for an 'Islamisation' of the society as a solution to the current ills. To get its message across, FIS undertook grassroots activism and set up a network of medical clinics and charitable associations to serve the poorest and most crowded neighbourhoods, provided housing, opened shops, created jobs, and cleaned up neighbourhoods (Esposito 1995: 174). Following the 1992 coup, the military wing of FIS engaged in violent activism in defiance of this non-violent past.

As seen in the case of FIS, some (but clearly not all) Islamist movements and organisations do not merely criticise the state for its failures in meeting the socio-economic needs of peoples, but also propose solutions, adopt creative practices and provide tangible economic, social and moral support to their members as well as others who have otherwise been neglected by their state for political or infrastructural reasons (see

Esposito 1995: 23, 100; Esposito 1993: 191–2). However, the fact that these organisations act as agents of security for some should not obscure the ways in which they constitute a major threat to women's security (among others). For, it is often women who get caught in the middle when Islamist actors – be it the Islamic Republic of Iran, the Islamic Kingdom of Saudi Arabia, the Hizbullah or Hamas – play up their 'Islamic' credentials (see Doumato 1999: 568–83). This, in turn, could be taken as an illustration of the point made by students of critical approaches that the very same actors that could be considered as engaging in emancipatory practices could, at the same time, create insecurity for others.

In sum, it would be a mistake to generalise about Islamist actors, for they have different and at times contradictory aims; they also adopt divergent practices. However, notwithstanding such differences, what seems to unite AMAL, Hizbullah, FIS, the Islamic Kingdom of Saudi Arabia and Saddam Hussein is that they all resort to an Islamist discourse to legitimise their practices, garner support for their own policies, or mobilise action to stall that of others. For them, 'Islam' provides a discourse of politics to reach Muslims, although they may seek to communicate radically different messages when using the same symbols. The ways in which the concept *jihad* was used during the Gulf War is a good example of the point I am trying to make here.[11]

The Iraqi president Saddam Hussein's practices during the Gulf Crisis were not limited to invoking the Arab national security discourse. He also employed symbols such as *jihad* or the 'holy lands' in the attempt to de-legitimise the US-led intervention and to put pressure on the Arab governments that cooperated with the United States (Heikal 1992: 295). In one instance he addressed the peoples of other Arab/Muslim states as follows:

> Oh, Arab, oh, Muslim and believers everywhere, this is your day to rise and defend Mecca, which is captured by the spears of the Americans and the Zionists. . . . Keep the foreigner away from your holy shrines.
> (quoted in Eickelman and Piscatori 1996: 15)

As the leader of the Arab Ba'th Socialist Party with its commitment to secularism and a record of suppression of Islamist groups in Iraq, Saddam Hussein was an unlikely leader to resort to Islamic symbolism. Yet he chose to refer to the 'infidels' of the West that arrayed against him and called for *jihad* to combat them (see Eickelman and Piscatori 1996: 13). Perhaps even more significant was the fact that notwithstanding his past record, peoples in the streets of the Muslim world heeded his call. It was not only Muslim peoples in the Arab world, but also those in Malaysia, Iran and Turkey, among others, that reacted to his calls.

Arguably it may not necessarily have been Saddam Hussein's invocation of Islamic symbolism that enabled him to receive a sympathetic hearing, but the alacrity of the manner in which the United States decided to come to Kuwait's aid and assembled a large number of troops in Saudi Arabia. In the eyes of some, the massive build-up of US troops transformed what was initially viewed as a defensive operation to free Kuwait into an offensive one set to 'destroy Iraq politically and militarily' (see Esposito 1993: 192–4). Some, with the experiences of Western colonialism at the back of their minds, viewed this as 'threatening' (see Azzam 1991: 479; Eickelman and Piscatori 1996: 15) others viewed it as an indication of a 'lack of respect for the sanctity of holy places' (Heikal 1992: 28).

Saddam Hussein's calls received support from some Arab policy-makers as well as peoples in Arab streets (Azzam 1991: 476; Esposito 1993: 192–3; Khadduri and Ghareeb 1997: 241). Some of the Iranian politico-clerical elite, the Jordanian *ulama* and Muslim Brotherhood also joined Saddam Hussein in calling for a *jihad* against 'foreign intervention' (Esposito 1993: 192–3; 1995: 226).[12] The London-based think-tank, the Islamic Council criticised the involvement of the United States in what was seen as an inter-Arab matter and the Saudi policy-makers' cooperation with the United States (see Azzam 1991: 480).

In the attempt to counter the anti-Saudi assault undertaken by some actors, Saudi policy-makers adopted a two-pronged strategy. On the one hand, they invited troops from other Arab and Muslim countries to provide what Mohammed Heikal referred to as an 'Islamic cover' to obscure their reliance on US troops (Heikal 1992: 282). Egypt and Morocco both sent troops to join the US forces amassed in Saudi Arabia. King Fahd invited Syria to send forces as well, to add a 'radical Arab' dimension to the 'Islamic cover' (Heikal 1992: 266–7; Khadduri and Ghareeb 1997: 131–3).

The second prong of Saudi strategy was to minimise the effect of Saddam Hussein's call for *jihad*. Saudi policy-makers sought to get a counter-*fatwa* to sanction their own practices. The contradiction between Saddam Hussein's call for *jihad* and the Saudi *fatwa* – the latter seeking to de-legitimise the former – triggered a theological debate over the religious dimension of the presence of non-Muslim troops in the Holy Lands. The Grand Mufti of Egypt sanctioned that the invitation extended by Saudi Arabia to foreign troops did not breach Muslim laws because it was 'in conjunction with an invitation to Muslim troops' and served 'the greater good' (Azzam 1991: 481). The Mufti of Saudi Arabia went even further and declared that 'even non-Muslims participating in the war were participating in *jihad*' (Azzam 1991: 481).

Thus, during the Gulf War 'Islamic' symbols were used by both sides in line with their discrepant aims, to legitimise their divergent practices and to de-legitimise each other's policies. Islamist actors resorted to 'symbolic exchanges' (Barnett 1998) rather than arms races or gunboat diplomacy in the attempt to prevail over each other. Such 'symbolic exchanges' were once again observed during the US-led war on Iraq (2003). Whereas an Islamic scholar issued a *fatwa* banning cooperation with the United States, the Islamic Research Agency based at Al Azhar University, Egypt declared it a must to *jihad* against the US invasion of Iraq (Bulut 2003: 72, 170–1).

What is clear from the above discussion is that there is little agreement among Islamist actors as to what security in the Muslim Middle East should look like. Saad Eddin Ibrahim had maintained in 1996 that the Islamist security discourse is 'more a promise than reality; it can "break" but does not "make"' (1996: 433). The September 11 attacks have proven him right.

Security in the (New) Middle East

The US approach to regional security in the Middle East has remained military-focused in the post-Cold War era. US policy towards Iraq before and after the Gulf War (1990–91) and particularly the 1998–99 bombing campaign directed at obtaining Iraqi cooperation with the UN team inspecting the Iraqi weapons of mass destruction programme could be viewed as examples of this military-focused approach. Furthermore, US policy towards regional security in the Middle East remains top-down. In following a policy of dual containment (Lake 1994: 45–55) US policy-makers presented Iran and Iraq as the main threats to security in the region, mainly due to their military capabilities and the revisionist character of their regimes that are not subservient to US interests. What has changed in the aftermath of the September 11 attacks is that US policy-makers declared their commitment to 'advancing freedom' in the Middle East as a way of 'confronting the threats to peace from terrorism and weapons of mass destruction' (Bush 2003a). The 2003 war on Iraq and the US effort to change the regime were explained with reference to this 'forward strategy of freedom in the Middle East' (Bush 2003b; also see Lemann 2003; Tanenhaus 2003). This top-down perspective that glosses over the concerns of regional actors, while revealing certain aspects of regional insecurity in the Middle East (such as terrorism) at the same time hinders others (as with economic underdevelopment, resource scarcity and environmental decay that constitute threats to human security). It was such incongruities between the regional security agenda of the United States and more human and societal focused agendas of regional (mostly non-state) actors that caused the Madrid Peace Process to come to a halt towards the end of the 1990s.

Notwithstanding the military-focused and top-down character of the US approach to regional security in the Middle East, the United States was able to reintroduce itself to Arab politics and impose its own security agenda. The 'atomisation' of the Arab regional order and the enhanced credibility of the US as a result of the triumph of US forces in the 1991 Gulf War both contributed to this development. The entrenchment of 'the Gulf' in the minds of local actors as a sub-region of the Middle East could be viewed as an instance of the prevalence of the US approach to regional security. For, during the 1990s, US policy-makers succeeded in their long-standing effort of separating the Gulf monarchies from the more radical Arab states through encouraging Gulf regionalism and strengthening bilateral ties with individual Gulf states. Indeed,

> the GCC now plays an unprecedented role in the Middle East security and diplomacy, backed by the United States. The GCC's power now surpasses the League of Arab states as the leading inter-Arab organisation, effectively placing any pretence of pan-Arabism, the long-sought dream of Arab unity – or at least a willingness to share oil wealth – to rest.
>
> (Zunes 2003: 65)

US policy-makers' success in creating a divide between Gulf monarchies and other states also constitutes a reaffirmation of the principle of compartmentalisation of regional security, which treats the issue of the security of oil reserves (Gulf security) and that of the Israel/Palestine issue and Israel's security as separate concerns (for a recent example see Pollack 2003).

During the Gulf crisis, in the attempt to garner support for the US war effort against Iraq, Secretary of State James Baker chose to break with this compartmentalised approach and acknowledged the linkages between Iraq's invasion of Kuwait and the Israel/Palestine issue – linkages Saddam Hussein pointed to (Sayigh 1991: 38–46; Ramazani 1998: 50). However, although Baker's acknowledgement of the linkages between the multiple dimensions of regional security seemed to signal a change of policy, the overall conduct of the US government during the war was more in line with its traditional approach. For, the United States sought to bring an end to the threat posed by Iraq to the security of Gulf oil by defeating Iraq with the help of an international coalition which it formed, forged and sustained, without inquiring into the roots of the Iraqi action. In other words, Baker's acknowledgement constituted a parenthesis rather than a break in the US approach to regional security in the Middle East, with the rest of the US policy establishment carrying on with business-as-usual. It is significant to note here that during the 1997–98 standoff between the United States and Iraq over the issue of Iraq's non-cooperation with the UN inspection team, Secretary of State Madeleine Albright kept with the tradition and refused to acknowledge the linkages between the stalled Arab–Israeli peace process and the difficulties the United States was facing in organising an Arab coalition supportive of the US stance (Ramazani 1998: 49). More recently, in tandem with their efforts to garner support for the US-led war on Iraq, US policy-makers put forward a 'roadmap' for peace in Israel/Palestine – a rare moment of acknowledgement of the linkages between different dimensions of security in the region. Yet, such acknowledgement remained in theory; in practice, US policy-makers allowed the roadmap to be sidelined while pushing forward with their agenda on Iraq.

The strategy of the US-led coalition during the Gulf War (1991) was to achieve air superiority, minimise coalition casualties, and expel Iraq from Kuwait (Freedman and Karsh 1991: 23). These aims were achieved by the end of the war. There was another less pronounced aim, that of debilitating the Iraqi military machine to minimise the threat it would pose to regional security in the future (Sadowski 1993: 5). In the aftermath of the war, as a part of the cease-fire agreement and in accordance with relevant UN resolutions, which Iraq had agreed to comply with, a UN investigation on the Iraqi weapons of mass destruction (WMD) programme was put into effect. With the experience of the Gulf War in mind (in the course of which Iraq fired Scud missiles to both Israel and Saudi Arabia) US policy-makers made it a priority to eradicate the Iraqi WMD programme and prevent other Middle Eastern states – except Israel – from developing nuclear weapons. They also sought to restrict existing chemical and biological weapons silos (Hollis 1994).

In the aftermath of the Gulf War, US policy-makers moved away from statements they had made during the crisis regarding the desirability of arms control and practising self-restraint on arms sales to the region. They banned arms sales to the two 'rogue states' (Iran and Iraq) whilst supporting the arms build-up of GCC states (Hollis 1994; Stork 1995: 14–19). The massive rearmament policies of the Gulf states enabled the Israeli and Iranian policy-makers to follow suit by providing a justification for further arms purchases (Sadowski 1992: 11). Turkey and Egypt were rewarded by the United States for their services during the Gulf War, in the form of military (and economic) aid. Israel and Turkey, in turn, chose to solidify their existing security cooperation (see Makowsky 1996; Altunışık 1999; on the background of Turkish–Israeli relations, see Nachmani 1987). What seems to bring Israel and Turkey together, apart from their cooperation in the military and intelligence fields, is the issue of scarce water resources. Indeed, the triangular relationship between Turkey, Syria and Israel (see Jouejati 1996; Makovsky 1996; Berikes-Atiyas 1997) is a textbook example of worst-case thinking, zero-sum conceptions of security and reliance on the military instrument to meet threats that are political (the Kurdish issue), or environmental (water resources) in character.

The 'atomisation' of Arab order also enabled the United States to impose its own vision for the (New) Middle East and the broadened security agenda during the 1990s. The term 'new Middle East' is associated with the notion of an integrated Middle East modelled after the European Union. As noted in Chapter 4, Israeli politician Shimon Peres (1993) put forward this proposal in the attempt to entice Arab actors to join the Peace Process. US policy-makers also supported Peres' vision thinking that this would be a way of getting 'moderate' Arab actors to cooperate with Israel. The assumption being that the need for direct US involvement in military and especially economic matters would be minimised. The multi-lateral track of the Peace Process was considered as the 'key channel' for building this cooperative relationship (Rubin 1995: 63).

It was partly the hope of constructing a 'new Middle East' and partly the acknowledgement of multiple dimensions of regional insecurity that enabled the United States together with Russia to convene the Madrid Peace Conference on 30 October to 1 November 1991, bringing together, for the first time, the representatives of all major parties to the Israel/Palestine conflict.[13] At the Madrid Conference bilateral negotiations were set up between Israel and Syria, Israel and Lebanon, and Israel and a Jordanian–Palestinian delegation. Subsequently, Israeli–Palestinian and Israeli–Jordanian negotiations were separated. The bilateral talks concentrated mostly on territorial control and sovereignty, border demarcations, the security arrangements, and the political rights of the Palestinians.

At the Madrid Conference it was also decided to set up multilateral Arab–Israeli negotiations alongside the bilateral track to bring the participants to the bilateral talks together with other regional states as well as those outside the region wishing to make a contribution (financial, technical, political) (Peters 1996; Kaye 2001).[14] The multilateral negotiations were also hoped to help build confidence among participants and facilitate progress at the bilateral level. Furthermore, they were intended to permit the discussion of issues that were perceived to be affecting the region as a whole. The assumption behind the establishment of the multilateral track alongside the bilateral one was the awareness that the need for cooperative arrangements to foster economic development, to preserve and enhance the supply of water, and to check environmental degradation is shared by all states in the region. It was felt that many of these issues did not demand, nor could they wait for, a comprehensive settlement to the Arab–Israeli conflict (Peters 1996: 5). It should be noted that this was a rather functionalist view of international cooperation in that progress in the multilateral track, where only the 'technical' issues were discussed, was hoped to have spill-over effects on the bilateral track, which was reserved for 'political' issues.

The first organisational meeting for the multilateral talks was held in January 1992 in Moscow. Five working groups were set up: 'Water Resources', 'Environment', 'Regional Economic Development' (REDWG), 'Refugees', and 'Arms Control and Regional Security' (ACRS). Each working group included actors from both within and outside the Middle East. Setting up a working group on human rights was also discussed but eventually rejected (Peters 1996: 15). Arguably, this showed how parties to the negotiations were not ready to acknowledge all dimensions of regional insecurity, especially those pertaining to the security of individuals and social groups. Indeed, the issues that were allowed on the agendas, as will be seen below, were those considered as 'security' issues by policy-makers;

non-military issues were almost always approached from a statist perspective. Let us briefly consider the progress made by the five working groups.

The working group on arms control and regional security (ACRS) was intended to complement the multilateral negotiations more than the other working groups by helping build confidence among the parties (Jentleson and Kaye 1998; Kaye 2001: 76–109). The main difficulties between the parties during the negotiations emerged over the issue of nuclear weapons, with Arab states under Egypt's leadership seeking to put the issue of Israel's nuclear capabilities on the agenda. Israel, on the other hand, emphasised the need to develop a set of confidence-building measures as the first steps in a long process at the end of which the issue of nuclear weapons could be discussed. The absence of Iran, Iraq, Lebanon, Libya and Syria from the negotiations also added to Israel's hesitance to discuss the issue (Peters 1996: 38; Feldman and Toukan 1997: 76–8). At the end, the setting up of the ACRS working group, which was the first region-wide attempt to address issues of arms control and confidence-building, remained its main outcome (Feldman and Toukan 1997: 73–96; Jones 1997; also see the statement prepared by the working group in Feldman and Toukan 1997: 103–7).

The working group on the environment focused on establishing codes of conduct, prepared 'The Bahrain Environmental Code of Conduct for the Middle East' (for the text see Peters 1996: 89–93), and formulated an Upper Gulf of Aqaba oil spill contingency plan. The working group on refugees was fraught with difficulties from the beginning, largely to do with the fact that the issue of refugees is a highly sensitive one. The issue was nevertheless included in the multilateral track for it concerns a number of countries and requires the support of actors outside the region. The discussions remained focused on the so-called 'technical' aspects of the issue such as databases, public health, child welfare, job creation and vocational training, human resource development, family reunification and economic and social infrastructure (Peters 1996: 29–35; Kaye 2001: 158–83).

The working group on regional economic development (REDWG) was the largest of the five groups and made substantial progress in formulating principles and defining region-wide projects. A major outcome of the REDWG was the convening of four Middle East and North Africa (MENA) economic summit meetings in Morocco (1994), Jordan (1995), Egypt (1996), and Qatar (1997). The first MENA summit in Casablanca, Morocco was attended by the representatives of 61 countries including Israel and the PLO (as well as 1114 business leaders).[15] The reasoning behind the setting up of the REDWG was rooted in the assumption that 'the rewards of economic cooperation will drive the search and strengthen the foundations for political agreements' (Peters 1996: 46; see also Kaye 2001: 110–57). The group also took on the responsibility of addressing the economic needs of the Palestinians in addition to establishing the Bank for Economic Cooperation and Development, the Middle East–Mediterranean Travel and Tourism Association, and the Middle East Business Council.

The water resources working group was fraught with troubles from the beginning because of the absence of Syria and Lebanon. This thwarted the hopes for an agreement to be reached on either the Tigris–Euphrates or the Jordan river basins. The discussions were also impeded by the disagreement between Israel on the one hand and Jordan and the Palestinians on the other as to whether 'water rights' should be included in the agenda. Arab states viewed the consideration of water rights as a precondition to cooperation and any regional water management agreement. The Israeli side, however, wanted to separate what they viewed as the 'technical' and 'political' aspects of the water issue and wanted to limit the working group to technical issues and joint water management. The Israeli policy-makers maintained that the issue of water rights was a 'political' issue and had to be addressed at the bilateral negotiations (Peters 1996: 17). Later the dispute was settled with Israel agreeing to set up a 'water rights' working group as a part of the bilateral negotiations (1996: 16–22).

Although substantial progress was achieved in the multilateral negotiations in terms of promoting dialogue, by the end of 1997 the stall in Israeli–Palestinian negotiations led to a halt on both tracks. Progress in the multilateral negotiations was stalled in the late 1990s for three main reasons. First, Arab policy-makers thought not enough progress had been achieved in the bilateral negotiations. Second, they were worried about Israel's domination in the economic and technological fields if they agreed to strengthen Middle Eastern regionalism. And third, they were frustrated with US policies, for they remained convinced that not enough pressure was being put on Israel, which continued to ignore UN resolutions on Palestine, whilst Iraq faced the threat of air attacks because of its lack of cooperation with the UN inspection team. US policy-makers' refusal to acknowledge the linkages between the two has been viewed as 'double standards' by many in the Arab world (Ramazani 1998: 51).

The case of Jordan is a telling example of the failure of the US approach to constructing a 'new Middle East'. Jordan was the first Arab state to take up the opportunity of concluding a peace agreement with Israel in the aftermath of the Gulf War. Although Jordan had cooperated secretly with Israel before, this was the first time relations became public. This change in policy was explained to the Jordanian public by locating Jordan in the 'new Middle East', which, in turn, was presented as a project of regional integration designed in response to the process of globalisation (Lynch 2002: 51–2). Notwithstanding the criticisms of those who considered Jordan's action as endangering Arab security, Jordanian policy-makers were able to defend this change in policy so long as the Peace Process was on track and Israel seemed intent on transforming regional economic relations. However, as Israeli–Palestinian peace-making came to a stall in the late 1990s, it became more difficult to sustain Jordan remaining located in the 'new Middle East'. When, for instance, Jordanian policy-makers decided (after much deliberation) to attend the last Middle East and North Africa summit in Doha, this caused an outrage; the government, no longer able to make use of the power of ideas, had to rely on coercive power to prevent effective opposition to its decisions (Lynch 2002: 55).

Then, the multilateral negotiations failed to produce the spill-over effect as suggested by the logic of functionalism due to lack of progress on bilateral negotiations. The argument here is that the problem with the set up with the two-track diplomacy was not that the linkages between several aspects of the problem of regional insecurity in the Middle East were not addressed, but rather that this was not done in a way that was acceptable to both sides. The multilateral negotiations were reserved for discussions on 'technical' issues, whilst the 'political' issues were discussed at the bilaterals to which not all Arab states participated. As the negotiations in the working group on water resources showed, the 'political'/'technical' divide did not prove to be sustainable. Moreover, some issues, such as that of nuclear weapons, were left out of the negotiations, and only certain 'technical' aspects of the other issues, such as water or refugees, were discussed. The problem was not only that the cooperative process was not successful enough in redefining 'otherwise politically charged issues as technical' (Kaye 2001: 3) but that neither the US nor Israel were ready to acknowledge as many linkages as the Arab side would have liked to establish. The multilateral negotiations also showed that no regional policy-maker was ready or willing to establish interrelationships between all aspects of regional insecurity as non-state actors would have wanted. The multilateral track of the Middle East Peace Process came to a stall as progress on the bilateral track slowed down.[16]

The US approach to regional security in the Middle East was seemingly altered by the George W. Bush administration in the context created by the September 11, 2001 attacks. Although US understanding of regional security in the Middle East remains unchanged, there has been a change in methods in that 'democratisation' in Iraq was attempted by the George W. Bush Administration. Although the professed aim of the operation was that of ridding Iraq of weapons of mass destruction, another major aim was 'democratisation'. Indeed, since September 11, US policy-makers no longer seem to prefer stability to democratisation; rather, they have declared their intention of seeking stability through democratisation. It is not yet clear how far the US is willing to take this policy of democratisation. It seems likely that US policy-makers would seek to set an example with Iraq and hope that the others would be inspired (see Lemann 2003).

The critics of the US approach to regional security in the Middle East have pointed to the parallels with the 1950s policies when the US encouraged the formation of the Baghdad Pact. Currently, the critics argue, US policy-makers are trying to establish links between Iraq and Israel, while backing Bahrain and Qatar (among other GCC member states). Such efforts are considered by the critics as steps taken towards setting up a 'new Baghdad Pact' (Al-Amrani 2003; Hamad 2003; Haşane 2003; Lewis 2003).[17] As Chapter 3 argued, the problem with the Baghdad Pact was that it prioritised the security concerns of the United States and some of its allies (as with Turkey, Iran and Iraq that sought security through closer cooperation with the United States) and not that of other regional actors. Similar criticisms could be raised regarding the current efforts that build upon a conception of regional security that prioritises US security interests. Although the security interests of some regional actors are also considered (as with regime security in Bahrain and Qatar and Israel's security), this is done from a state-centric perspective and through militarised means.

Conclusion

This chapter sought to investigate the relationship between (inventing) regions and (conceptions and practices of) security by looking at how post-Cold War security practices have been shaped by and, in turn, shaped contending security discourses and spatial representations. The first section of the chapter looked at those practices that were shaped by the representation 'Arab Regional System'. It was argued that in the post-Cold War era it was mainly non-state actors that continued to uphold the Arab national security discourse. Although the Gulf War served to further alienate Arab governments from one another, the chapter argued that the practices of Arab peoples and civil societal actors have continued to shape and be shaped by the Arab national security discourse. Focusing on issues such as political participation, respect for human rights, unemployment, better health provision and education, they have sought to shape and constrain the practices of their policy-makers, who have adopted increasingly more statist practices.[18]

The chapter also looked at the security practices of the EU, the locomotive of the Euro–Med partnership process. It was argued that it was the EU's adoption of a broader conception of security that led to its involvement in this process. In the attempt to prevent Middle Eastern problems from becoming European problems, EU policy-makers sought to maintain stability in the geographically closer North African countries. The instrument chosen to do this was non-military in character; they sought to maintain stability by encouraging Euro–Med regionalism. It was hoped that encouraging economic liberalisation and accelerating economic growth would eventually lead to increasing political participation and democratisation. However, it was the security of the EU rather than that of North Africa that was the referent for this approach.

The third section of the chapter turned to look at the security practices of Islamist actors. It is difficult to generalise about the practices of the Islamist actors, which range from Saudi Arabia's pro-status quo practices to the Hizbullah's search for state power in Lebanon; from FIS grassroots activities in Algeria to provide basic services to peoples, to the September 11 attacks against New York and Washington, DC. It was further argued that what is common to all these Islamist actors is their employment of Islamic symbolism, although they may seek to achieve radically different aims through invoking the same symbols. The example of *jihad* as a symbol was used to illustrate this point. The section concluded that in the post-Cold War era, the Islamist discourse has been appropriated by anti-status quo actors who have sought to bring about radical change at home.

The last section of the chapter looked at those practices shaped by the Middle Eastern security discourse. It was argued that many Arab policy-makers joined the anti-Iraq coalition and later the Madrid Peace Process; this indicated the prevalence of the US approach to regional security at the expense of Arab national security. It was argued that despite a momentary acknowledgement by Secretary of State Baker of the linkages between the problem of regional stability and the Israel/Palestine issue, the US approach to regional security remained top-down and compartmentalised.

The difficulty of sustaining this compartmentalised approach was illustrated in late 1997 when the MENA economic summit convened in Doha to discuss regionalisation coincided with a stall in the peace process because of the Netanyahu government's intransigence and the US bombing of Iraq in the attempt to attain Iraqi compliance with UN resolutions. Many Arab policy-makers refused to attend the summit; others sent low-level delegations. The overall message was that there was a limit to which Arab policy-makers could overlook the suffering of other Arab peoples (such as those of Iraq who continued to suffer under UN sanctions)[19] and carry on cooperating with Israel (that remained defiant of UN resolutions) and the United States (which punished Iraq for not abiding by other UN resolutions). This, in turn, showed that even at a time when Arab inter-governmental relations were at a low, Arab policy-makers could not completely disregard the concerns raised by non-state actors at home and abroad. It is also significant to note that the multilateral ('technical') track, which was hoped to have a spill-over effect on the bilateral ('political') track through strengthening regionalism, not only failed to generate the expected spill-over effect but also came to a stop itself because of lack of progress in bilateral negotiations.

As noted in Chapter 4, the main post-Cold War divide in the region emerged not between the Arab national security discourse and that of the Middle East, but between stability-focused approaches of the United States and its allies and the anti-status quo discourses of myriad non-state actors. The launch of the Euro–Med partnership process and the two-track negotiations of the Madrid Peace Process, the chapter argued, marked attempts by the EU and the US to use economic tools to increase economic regionalisation and maintain stability in the region. Both processes prioritised stability over other concerns such as democratisation and human rights as emphasised by non-state actors. Concerning stability in the Gulf, both the US and the EU prioritised military stability and privileged militarised practices, as was the case with the Gulf War and subsequent bombing of Iraq. It was noted that such stability-oriented practices that privilege the stable flow of oil and market economies over human rights and political participation evoke memories of a colonial era in Arab peoples' minds. This, in turn, makes it difficult for their governments to participate in region-wide schemes, as the stall of the multilateral negotiations showed.

When these multiple approaches to regional security and the discrepancies between the security needs and concerns of actors that adopt them are considered, it would be highly unlikely for their proponents to come to an agreement on one of them. The question then becomes, if they cannot agree on the representation of the region, how could they ever agree on common security practices? This is where the argument comes back full circle; for, conceiving the relationship between (inventing) regions and (conceptions and practices of) security as mutually constitutive enables me to make the next step. This is to argue that critical approaches to security could inform alternative practices and thereby help to alleviate regional insecurities. This argument will be fully developed in Part III: 'Futures'.

Part III

Futures

6   Alternative futures for security in the Middle East

Whether s/he is aware of it or not, one always has some ideas about the future that inform his/her practices. For instance, those who think that the future will be no different from the past shape their practices based on this premise, which constitutes some kind of knowledge based on one's understanding of what the past was like. Students of Cold War approaches to security, who conceived world politics as an endless process of balancing and bandwagoning in the struggle for power expected the future to be more of the same. The point being that we all operate based on our (often unthinking and unquestioned) knowledge about the future. This is because, as Kenneth Boulding (1995: 1) wrote, 'unless we at least think we know something about the future decisions are impossible, for all decisions involve choices among images of alternative futures' (see also Bernstein *et al.* 2000).

Thinking about the future becomes all the more relevant given the conception of theory adopted by students of critical approaches to security as constitutive of the 'reality' it responds to. Our knowledge about the future – our conjectures and prognoses – may become self-constitutive. This, however, is not to suggest that it is totally in our hands to shape the future. 'Men make their own history', wrote Marx (1997: 300), 'but they do not make it just as they please; they do not make it under circumstances chosen by themselves, but under circumstances directly encountered, given and transmitted from the past'. Furthermore, thinking about the future is only one form of shaping the future, and, admittedly, is not enough in itself. It should be compounded by other forms of practice. As Fatima Mernissi (1996: 8) wrote, 'it is by and through action that the future is shaped'. Having said that, Mernissi (1996: 1–7) herself would endorse the argument that thinking (and writing) about the future is a crucial task if the aim is to shape the future.

Towards this end, that is, shaping the future, students of critical approaches to security have so far looked at 'desired' futures: security as emancipation (Booth 1991b; Wyn Jones 1999). This is partly because 'being able to picture a desired future is empowering in the present' – as Elise Boulding (1995: 97) argued. In order to be able to make a change, one has to have some knowledge as to what s/he wants to achieve, to shape his/her practices in the attempt to shape that desired future. This, however, is not to suggest that emancipation is an endpoint. As Ken Booth (1999b: 41) has maintained, 'emancipation is best likened to a political horizon: something to aim for, something that establishes perspective, but something by definition can never be reached'. Nor does the security community approach necessarily constitute a blueprint. The creation of security communities could constitute only a beginning. The security community approach, in this sense, should be viewed as the start of a path that could take peoples from an insecure past to a more secure future.

Thinking about the future from a critical security perspective need not be limited to 'desired' futures only. Students of security could also try and shape the future by pointing to what some futures may bring if no preventive action is taken in the present – as Ulrich Beck has done in *Risk Society* (1992). According to Beck, if threats to security are 'threats to the future', as is the case with many environmental threats (such as depletion of natural resources), then, it is imperative that they be addressed in the present. For,

> through our past decisions about atomic energy and our present decisions about the use of genetic technology, human genetics, nanotechnology and computer science, we unleash unforeseeable, uncontrollable, indeed even, *incommunicable* consequences that threaten life on earth.
>
> (Beck 2003: 257)

'As conjectures, as threats to the future, as prognoses, [such threats] have and develop a practical relevance to preventive actions', notes Beck (1992: 34). However, one problem with trying to mobilise action to meet such threats is that they only exist in the future as conjectures. It is only through thinking and writing about such threats that one could raise peoples' awareness regarding what the future may bring, and what needs to be done in the present to prevent them from happening. When issues such as threats to the environment are concerned, thinking (and writing) about the future becomes crucial; otherwise they have the potential to cause destruction on 'such a scale that action afterwards would be practically impossible' (Beck 1992: 34).

Although Beck's thesis is about the environment, the points he makes in explaining the way human agency has been complicit, via the production of knowledge, in exacerbating (if not creating) 'threats to the future' could be adopted and adapted to further develop the critique students of critical security present of prevailing security discourses in general and US discourse on regional security in the Middle East in particular. Beck (1992: 183) writes:

In contrast to all earlier epochs ... the risk society is characterized by a *lack*: the impossibility of an *external* attribution of hazards. In other words, risks depend on decisions ... Risks are the reflection of human actions and omissions, the expression of highly developed productive forces. That means that the sources of danger are no longer ignorance but *knowledge*; not a deficient but a perfected mastery over nature.

Beck's point is made within the context of environmental politics, where the grip of 'scientific' knowledge over practice is even stronger than in the less 'scientific' Security Studies. Nevertheless, as noted above, knowledge about the future, presented in terms of obstacles and opportunities, both constrains and informs actors' practices thereby helping constitute the future. Then, given the ways in which the Middle Eastern security discourse has, in the past, been complicit in shaping regional insecurity in the Middle East, it could be argued that uncritical adoption of existing knowledge produced by prevailing discourses that do not offer anything other than more of the same does itself constitute a 'threat to the future'. Accordingly, students of security who fail to reflect upon the self-constitutive potential of their thinking would be complicit in perpetuating regional insecurity in the Middle East.

Chapter 6 looks at alternative future scenarios and their possible implications within the Middle East context. The point being that given the conception of theory adopted by students of critical approaches as constitutive of a future 'reality', it is vital that they do not limit their thinking to 'desired' futures but criticise existing knowledge about the future that informs myriad actors' practices in an often unthinking manner. Indeed, the thinking of the students of critical approaches to security does not evolve in a vacuum. All approaches to security in the Middle East incorporate some image of the future, which constitutes the knowledge that informs practices at present. Thus, if students of critical security hope to help invent alternative futures, their task is both to produce knowledge about desired futures, and present critiques of existing knowledge in terms of its emancipatory potential.

Each one of the scenarios looked at here raises an alternative set of possibilities on thinking about the future of regional security. Despite certain overlaps, they present quite distinct images and would prescribe different policies as to how to achieve and maintain security in future worlds. The critical security approach introduced in Chapter 1 will be utilised here to criticise future scenarios. By looking at the strengths and weaknesses of other ideas about the future the chapter will seek to identify the difficulties facing the future. It will also seek to point to unfulfilled potential immanent in regional politics.

The Middle East in a globalising world

In the 1990s, it became commonplace to present the future of world politics as one of increasing globalisation, with the term itself becoming a 'buzzword' – often invoked but rarely defined (Scholte 1996: 44–5). Here, globalisation is understood as a process of increase in the extensiveness and intensity of relations between peoples, social groups, organisations and institutions that has been leading towards a global interpenetration of the political as well as economic and military sectors (Robinson 1998; Held and McGrew 1999). Although it is often the economic factors, in particular the global integration of production and finance, that are viewed as the driving forces behind globalisation, the impact that has been made by the revolution in communications and information technologies (especially the expansion of the World Wide Web) in increasing peoples' awareness of each other whilst diminishing the significance of the physical distance separating them (time–pace compression) is also recognised as a crucial factor in accelerating this process. More recently, the world woke up to the impact of globalisation on security in that the September 11 attacks were understood within the framework of globalisation (see, for example, Held 2001; Friedman 2002a; Halliday 2002; Rasmussen 2002). Indeed, the attacks were 'constructed as a scenario for security threats in the twenty-first century' (Rasmussen 2002: 327) and were interpreted as signalling the need for 'reinforcing the security dimension of globalisation' (Halliday 2002). Halliday (2002) wrote:

> Globalisation cannot be seen only in terms of trade, investment, travel and communications: it requires a security dimension, the responsibility above all of states, and one that is both effective and under legal and democratic, control.

Yet, notwithstanding the criticisms of those who point to the economic and security implications of the global integration of production and finance in peripheries of the world (see, for example, Hurrell and Woods 1995; UNRISD 1995; Thomas 1997: 1–17, 2000), those who firmly believe in its virtues maintain that increasing globalisation fosters economic efficiency and helps provide a remedy to the very problems it perpetuates (Friedman 2002b, c). In this new world united in its search for new markets and higher profits, the argument goes, markets would demand and help produce common ways of thinking or even a new global culture, and peoples' identities as producers and consumers will overshadow most, if not all, other interests and identities (Friedman 1999a, b). In such a world, myriad actors are expected to solve their conflicts via non-military means, not only because they would achieve common ways of thinking but also because a breakdown in business relations would simply be regarded as too costly (see Ohmae 1994: esp. pp. 13–14). Hence the expectation of global security as a side effect of further globalisation.

One problem with such interpretations of globalisation is that they bear striking resemblance to the neo-functionalist writings of earlier decades with regard to the emphasis placed on cooperation over certain (technical) issues eventually leading to the emergence of a 'superstructure of political behaviour' (Clark 1997: 18).[1] Moreover, they often ignore how increasing globalisation also leads to a perpetuation of inequalities worldwide (Hurrell and Woods 1995; UNRISD 1995). Indeed, the proponents of increasing globalisation do not account for the processes of 'structural violence' perpetuated by the globalising forces so far as the latter do not disrupt the course of the former. In this sense, what they mean by the attainment of global security is the creation of some form of 'macropeace' (Barber 1992: 62) based on the maintenance of the status quo by way of exercising social control through the global communication and information networks and the entertainment industry (see Der Derian 1992: esp. pp. 19–39).[2] The kind of security that could be achieved as such would at best amount to an absence of war – 'negative peace' in Johan Galtung's (1969) terms.

The identification of al-Qaida as the actor behind the September 11 attacks has led to a questioning of such expectations in that recent studies which presented the future of world politics in terms of globalisation are far less optimistic regarding the emergence of 'negative peace' let alone 'positive peace' as a side effect of globalisation (see, for example, Rasmussen 2002; Beck 2003; Kaldor 2003b). Mary Kaldor has proposed the term 'regressive globalisers' to describe those who make use of the opportunities provided by the process of globalisation and even promote it when it serves their interests. Kaldor writes:

> 'Regressive globalisers' on the one hand feed on the insecurities generated by globalisation and are organised as global networks in ways similar to other global organisations in civil society or the business world. On the other, their goals are rather traditional – they want to capture state power or construct new regional or new secessionist states, and they envisage states in traditional terms as 'bordered power containers'. In other words, they want to roll back globalisation, while making use of the instruments of globalisation.
>
> (Kaldor 2003b: 5)

The best strategy for dealing with regressive globalisers, argues Kaldor, is reducing their 'recruiting power and to minimise the damage they are able to inflict' (Kaldor 2003b). Given the 'negative trends' and the 'mass anger' further exacerbated by the US-led war on Iraq (Khouri 2002) it would require a comprehensive approach cognisant of the factors that regressive globalisers feed on, in order to begin addressing issues of regional security in the Middle East.

For, the Middle East has so far had an uneven balance sheet in keeping up with an increasingly globalising world. On the one hand, it is closely linked to world markets via oil sales, financial flows and arms purchases. The Gulf being the hub of world oil production means it is fully integrated into the world economy. On the other hand, the level of integration of the Middle East in general is still below the expectations of the proponents of increasing globalisation (El-Erian and Fischer 1996). This being the case despite the increase in the density of financial and trade connections between the Middle East and world markets, especially since the 1970s boom in oil prices, suggests that the region has had very little to offer with the exception of oil. The point here is that in a globalised future where oil may not be as significant a commodity as it currently is, the future of the Middle East in general and the Gulf in particular may be rather bleak (Derviş and Shafik 1998).[3] Alternatively, in a future where the significance of oil as a commodity does not decrease, the Middle East might still lose its attraction as a source of oil and natural gas since regional reserves are expected to diminish in about 45 to 70 years time (Schaffer 1998).

The relatively low level of integration between world markets and Middle Eastern economies has had partly to do with the fact that the latter were geared towards import-substitution in the post-colonial era. Although some (such as Tunisia and Turkey) have switched to export-promotion in the last decades, many others have either hesitated or failed to make this shift.[4] As Chapter 3 noted, Syrian and Saudi policy-makers have chosen to seek self-sufficiency in basic foodstuff production for reasons of food security – that is, fear of having to rely on external supplies at times of crises. For others, such as Egypt, the transition from import-substitution to export-promotion was hampered by the lack of infrastructure and financial resources. Furthermore, some regional actors' negative disposition towards the forces of globalisation has also played a role in delaying this shift. Indeed, many regional actors, with the memories of the colonial era still fresh in their minds, feel threatened by the very enmeshing and interpenetration that is part and parcel of the process of globalisation. The growth of so-called 'Islamic banking' is exemplary of some regional actors' misgivings regarding the process of globalisation, which some view as a 'colonisation of the future' (see Sardar 1985: 10). On the other hand, the satellite networks and other information technologies that underpin the communications revolution have been dubbed by one author as 'cybernetic colonialism' (Miskin 1995: 28).

Although the proponents of increasing globalisation are not wholly unaware of regional actors' misgivings, their response would be to say that Middle Eastern regimes would sooner or later have to give in. This is necessarily because, they would argue, 'the only thing worse than being a part of the evolving economic hierarchy is being excluded from it' (Henwood 1993: 8; see also Beinin 1999: 22). If this statement is taken to its logical conclusion, it could be argued that if Middle Eastern actors

were to go against the wishes and expectations of the forces of globalisation, they would find themselves marginalised in an increasingly globalising world. For example, in a hypothetical future world where oil prices fell
drastically, the Middle East (with the possible exception of Israel, Tunisia
and Turkey) would find itself on the margins of the world economy with
the marginalisation of Gulf economies resulting in a loss of crucial financial support for the rest of the Arab countries.[5]

If oil prices were to remain stable, the Gulf (including Iraq) would
remain a part of the globalised world economy. Southern Mediterranean
states should also be expected to integrate with the global markets largely
due to the European Union's interest in and continued resource input
into their economies.[6] In this hypothetical world, only Syria and Iran
should be expected to become marginalised – unless, that is, they agree to
adopt the recommended stabilisation and structural adjustment packages
and open up their markets. In such a future world, one should not expect
much improvement in regional security. Given the intimate links between
Arab societies, it would be very difficult to conceive of security being established in some Arab states whilst the rest are still on the margins. Yet, such
a scenario is in line with the main precepts of the George W. Bush administration's approach to the Middle East, which has sought to de-couple its
policies towards the Israel/Palestine conflict and the Gulf. The problem
with this compartmentalised approach is that it risks alienating regional
peoples as well as some regimes. The Saudi regime, for instance, is likely
to be alienated if and when US policy-makers turn to Iraq as the source of
stable oil-flow. As Rosemary Hollis (2003: 32–3) pointed out, 'the result
could easily be a unification of the forces of nationalism, anti-Americanism and pan-Islam'.

In the 1990s it was this threat of marginalisation in an increasingly globalising world that helped to persuade regional governments such as those
of Egypt, Jordan and Morocco to remove the obstacles in front of free
trade (Pfeifer 1999). So far this has involved the implementation of stabilisation and structural adjustment programmes by regional governments in
line with the 'Washington consensus'.[7] Some Gulf economies have also
taken steps towards privatisation and reducing governmental subsidies
(see Richards 1999: 65). Yet, as Yezid Sayigh (1999: 229) has maintained,
so far 'liberalisation has remained a tactic to relieve pressure rather than a
goal, and has not been allowed to threaten the established order'. Besides,
the fact that many Middle Eastern actors seem to have given in to the
forces of globalisation should not be taken to suggest that the outcome is
likely to lead to security (understood as stability) as the proponents of
increasing globalisation hope. On the contrary, the recent trend towards
economic liberalisation in the Middle East could also be viewed as a sign
of helplessness and fear of being marginalised, and not necessarily
commitment to achieving security by way of doing business. There has
indeed emerged some local resistance against the presentation of

increased globalisation as the only option to escape marginalisation. Hasan Hanafi (2000: 5) has expressed his frustration as follows:

> There are only two alternatives: to compete or to retreat, to produce or to consume, to create or to imitate, to invent or to assimilate, to give or to take, to export or to import, to be in the center or to be in the periphery.

The point here is that the problem with presenting increased globalisation as the only option is that it constitutes a 'primary form of alienation' (Cox 1999: 27) and could lead to further fragmentation and instability – the very developments the proponents of increasing globalisation would want to avoid. In the past decade the emergence of some Middle East actors as regressive globalisers pointed to the ways in which the excesses caused by the uncontrolled character of globalisation feeds into the tendency towards fragmentation.

The Middle East as a breeding ground for fragmentation?

Notwithstanding Thomas Friedman's (1999b: 124) claim that 'the wretched of the earth want to go to Disneyworld, not to the barricades', Robert D. Kaplan (1994b, 1996, 2002a) has maintained that the very uniformity that is imposed by the global communication and information networks and the entertainment industry has, at the same time, given rise to a proliferation of particularisms that manifest themselves as cultural and racial clash, increasing erosion of states and inter-state borders, and refugee flows. Although Kaplan is not alone in his conception of globalisation and fragmentation as two mutually reinforcing processes (see, for example, Rosenau 1995: 49; Clark 1997: 4),[8] his approach is singular in its celebration of globalisation in the developed world and warning about the 'coming anarchy' in the developing world.[9]

   Kaplan's thesis is that environmental dynamics could, in the future, further reinforce the process of fragmentation.[10] As a result, argues Kaplan (1994b: 46), the lines dividing the realm of globalisation (represented by the travellers of his metaphorical stretch limo) and the realm of fragmentation (made up of the majority of the world's peoples who travel on foot and are therefore more amenable to the effects of environmental degradation) would further deepen, leading towards a future which would be characterised by spreading diseases, population upsurges, unprovoked crime, scarcity of resources, increasing erosion of states and inter-state borders, and the augmentation of private armies, security firms and transnational criminal organisations (such as drug cartels).

   While certain elements of Kaplan's argument remain valid – such as the need to pay more attention to developments in those parts of the world that are suffering from environmental and societal stress – he suggests very little as to how to alter these dynamics to prevent the 'coming anarchy'. In fact, given the tone of environmental determinism hidden between his lines, it is not clear whether he deems these dynamics to be alterable at all. For, by way of presenting the causes of the 'coming anarchy' as mere 'environmental' (i.e. 'natural') dynamics, as opposed to human decisions, actions and omissions (as seen in Beck's analysis), Kaplan glosses over the role human agency has played in exacerbating them. To put it in other words, Kaplan is oblivious to the ways in which the developed world (the passengers in the stretch limo), through economic interactions, usurped raw materials, depleted natural resources and polluted rivers affects the developing world (on this point also see, Dalby 1996: 489).

By way of failing to account for the role human agency has played in perpetuating these problems, Kaplan also fails to see how human agency may intervene to reverse these trends. Even NGOs (that are treated as agents of security from a critical security perspective) are allocated with the task of 'wound-binding' in Kaplan's scenario (1996: esp. pp. 432–3). This has partly to do with Kaplan's fatalism – a trait he shares with Huntington, as will be discussed below – and partly from his problem-solving approach to international phenomena as opposed to the critical approaches that point to unfulfilled human potential and call for change.[11]

At the first glance, the Middle East does not seem a likely candidate for fragmentation in the way depicted in Kaplan's scenario. After all, many Middle Eastern countries have got rich oil and natural gas resources, are better off economically than some relatively deprived parts of the world, and could therefore be expected to remain largely immune to the effects of such fragmentary forces that affect other parts of the Third World. On the other hand, it could be argued that environmental factors could push the Middle East into the realm of fragmentation with, for example, the scarcity of water in quantitative terms coupled with a deterioration in its quality (due to excessive use) fuelling already existing divisions between parties that share the same river basins.[12] Although the impact changes in the global climate would make cannot be predicted, it is estimated that the Middle East would emerge as one of the problem areas in the not-so-distant future.

Furthermore, fragmentation could also be caused by a crisis in the economies of the oil-rich countries of the region that currently desalinate and/or import water at very high costs. A fall in the oil prices could push Saudi Arabia, for instance, into the club of water-scarce countries.[13] In other words, not even the capital-rich countries of the Middle East would be immune to the kinds of dynamics emphasised in Kaplan's scenario if the existing scarcity were to be compounded by environmental factors (such as the 'greenhouse effect') and demographic trends (unchecked population growth coupled with rapid urbanisation). The future may indeed bring 'water wars' if no preventive action is taken (Starr 1991; Bulloch and Darwish 1993; Gleick 1994). Or, alternatively, the world may witness a Middle East where some are living in cities and suburbs leading comfortable lives, whereas the shanty-town dwellers or rural populations that sustain themselves by agriculture are 'doomed by a lack of water to drink, soil to till, and space to survive in' – a future in line with Kaplan's stretch limo analogy (Kaplan 1994b: 54). And, as Kaplan (2002b) reminds us, such environments would be likely to become a breeding ground for particularisms.

However, although the emerging particularisms and the challenge they pose to the state system may seem like the 'coming anarchy' to some, the same processes are considered as novel forms of resistance that could constitute a solution to the very problems perpetuated by the economic straitjacket forced onto regional economies in line with the 'Washington consensus'. According to Robert Cox (1981: 56), globalisation's perpetuation of inequalities worldwide could set social forces (such as social coalitions, labour movements, democratisation struggles) that might in the future lay down the groundwork for an alternative ('postglobalisation') world order. Although Cox is not unaware of the potential for fragmentation and violent conflict dormant in the struggles led by the social forces, he maintains that the disintegration of some units could result in the formation of new alliances thereby bringing about a new order.

Part of the problem with relying on the agency of social forces within the Middle Eastern context is that, when faced with economic hardship, they may show little resistance against the globalising forces' efforts to buy them off in an attempt to strengthen their grip over the populace (as was the case with the EU plan to channel resources into Southern Mediterranean NGOs to harvest support for increasing regionalism among Mediterranean-rim countries of the Middle East and the EU). In sum, given the fact that they have to operate under the double burden of restraint exercised by both their own governments as well as the pressure put by external actors (such as the United States or the EU) for increasing global integration (see Pitner 2000), social forces in the Middle East face a difficult task if they were to fulfil Cox's expectations from them.

However, although it is always possible to be sceptical about the relevance of Cox's scenario within the Middle Eastern context given the restraints imposed upon the activities of non-state actors by regional governments, there are also instances of non-state actors undertaking crucial roles in working towards alternative futures (Bilgin 2002). In the case of the Israel–Palestine issue, for instance, women's movements helped make the *Intifada* on the part of some Palestinian women, while some of their Israeli counterparts helped enhance its impact by way of questioning the moral boundaries of the Israeli state (Sharoni 1993, 1995, 1996; Mikhail-Ashrawi 1995). This, however, is not to suggest that all social forces would be fit to be considered as agents for change. On the contrary, some have emerged as 'regressive globalisers' in recent years. Nor is this to suggest that an uncritical adoption of their agendas would not be problematic. Rather the argument is that Cox's scenario introduces an element of human agency to reverse the trends set by the forces of globalisation – a factor that is missing from Kaplan's scenario of a 'coming anarchy'. Still, not all are as positive as is Cox concerning the transformative role social forces could potentially assume. Samuel Huntington is one who shares Kaplan's fatalism regarding the future of world politics.[14]

Clash of civilisations?

As the universalism of the West fostered by the globalising forces brings it into conflict with non-Western states, as argued by Samuel P. Huntington (1993, 1998), the latter would increasingly choose to form coalitions to stand against the West thereby challenging the Western civilisation – hence his scenario of the future of world politics as a 'clash of civilisations'. Huntington has maintained that this clash would not remain at the macro (inter-state) level only; at the micro-level groups belonging to different civilisations vying for power would also clash with each other. Accordingly, submits Huntington, the future of world politics would be characterised by cooperation within and conflict between civilisations.

It is significant to note here that, as opposed to Kaplan, Huntington does suggest a way to reverse this trend. The two-pronged strategy Huntington recommends requires the West to hold on to its own in the short-term by promoting close cooperation and further integration within its own civilisation, whilst exploiting the differences within and between other civilisations thereby preventing the formation of anti-Western coalitions (Huntington 1993: 48–9; Huntington 1998: 19–39, 301–21). For the long-term Huntington prefers a more accommodationist policy and calls for developing a more profound understanding of other civilisations to identify the elements of commonality in between. The adoption of a long-term strategy is a must, maintains Huntington, or else the futures of both peace and civilisation (understood as the opposite of Kaplan's 'coming anarchy') would come under threat (Huntington 1998: 321). What is surprising is that it does not seem to strike Huntington that the two prongs of his strategy may be contradictory; the pursuance of the short-term policies he advocates may make it harder to follow the long-term policies. Put crudely, if the West holds on to its own and seeks to sow the seeds of division within and between non-Western civilisations, it may end up alienating them, thereby making it more difficult – if not impossible – to follow the long-term policy of accommodation.

Leaving aside the contradictions within Huntington's argument (that have been pointed to by others; see, for example, Binyan 1993; Kirkpatrick 1993; Mahbubani 1993; Rubenstein and Crocker 1994; Ó Tuathail

1998; Said 2001: 139–43), it is his conception of theory that should also be criticised. Huntington's is a 'problem-solving' approach to international phenomena (as was the case with Kaplan's approach). He conceives the role of theory as one of explanation. When presenting the future of world politics as a 'clash of civilisations' he assumes that he is representing what he sees, albeit in an admittedly 'simplified' fashion (see Huntington 1998: 37). However, his is too 'simplified' a representation that, for the sake of explanation, glosses over many important aspects of international phenomena and leaves 'a great deal of dignity . . . on the cutting room floor', to use Cynthia Enloe's (1996: 188) words. Lastly, by way of failing to reflect upon the potential of his thinking to become a self-fulfilling prophecy, Huntington fails to see how his scenario could contribute to a deepening of the differences between civilisations that have historically had porous borders (for similar points, see Rubenstein and Crocker 1994: 128; Cox 1999: 144; Said 2001: 139–43). The reaction his thesis has received within the Middle Eastern context attests well to this.

Although Huntington's thesis has come under criticism, its implication for the Middle East stems not necessarily from its consistency (or lack of it) but from the fact that it is by building upon the declarations of Islamist actors, examples of terrorism and inter-denominational conflicts from within the Middle East, that Huntington substantiates his argument on the need for a new world order based on civilisations. It is worth noting that Huntington borrowed the phrase 'clash of civilisations' from Bernard Lewis (1990), a noted student of Middle Eastern history. The problem is that Huntington's scenario could 'unwittingly play into the hands of the fundamentalists' (Tibi 1998b: xii) and/or be utilised to license interventions and violent practices by extra-regional actors (from other civilisations). The argument here needs further clarification. I will make two points.

First, the propagation of Huntington-type arguments has so far played into the hands of such Islamist actors (such as Osama bin Laden) who have been trying to convince their supporters that the 'Western' and 'Islamic' civilisations cannot peacefully coexist and that they should seek to strengthen their side to prepare for the coming clash by rallying around their own civilisation (see Said Aly 1996: 38) – a call Huntington would recognise as one of his own. The failure of the mass media in the West in general and in the United States in particular to distinguish between Islam as a religion and Islamism as an ideology and political movement only adds to the sense of siege prevalent among some Muslims and substantiates the claims of some Islamist actors that Muslims have been chosen as the enemy to replace the communist threat and that they will be victimised no matter what they do.[15]

Second, Huntington's scenario not only plays into the hands of Islamist actors in propagating their own perspective on regional security, but it also licenses certain kinds of security practices whilst marginalising others.

If people do indeed 'rally to those with similar ancestry, religion, language and values, and institutions and distance themselves from those with different ones', as Huntington (1998: 126) thinks they would, then the best US policy-makers, for instance, could do would be to seek to maximise friction among the Muslims on the one hand, and the Muslims and peoples of non-Muslim civilisations on the other, whilst holding the West together. In the region, one view is that this is what the United States has begun to do by way of occupying Iraq, keeping Muslim/Arab states divided whilst making sure the regional balance of power tilts toward Israel. Otherwise, a closely coupled community of Muslim/Arab Middle East, if it were to emerge, could challenge US dominance in the region (this may or may not constitute a challenge to Israel's security depending on the conceptions and practices of security adopted by actors on both sides). Although it may be argued that the US policies do not require a licence by Huntington, it nevertheless is true that Huntington's scenario could be used to explain, for instance, the futility of the search for a region-wide peace agreement, or to help legitimise reliance on the use of militarised practices in the Middle East whilst other (non-military) practices are becoming the norm in some other parts of the world.

Establishment of democratic peace in the Middle East?

The so-called democratic peace theory has been prominent in International Relations since the 1970s (see, for example, Doyle 1986; Russett 1995). Since the end of the Cold War it has become more and more commonplace among US policy-makers to refer to the democratic peace phenomenon – that very few democracies in the last hundred years or so have gone to war with one another – to justify the US policy of supporting the spread of democracy (see Barber 1995: 14, 313 n. 22–3; Farber and Gowa 1995: 123). For instance, Anthony Lake (1993), former Assistant to the President on National Security Affairs, maintained that what should replace the policy of containment is a 'strategy of enlargement – enlargement of the world's ... community of market democracies'. President Clinton (1993) concurred: 'democracies rarely wage war on one another'. More recently, the George W. Bush administration embraced 'a focused strategy of freedom in the Middle East', the initial steps of which were building 'democracy' in Iraq. The democratic peace assumption behind this policy is clear: 'As in Europe, as in Asia, as in every region of the world', declared President Bush, 'the advance of freedom leads to peace' (Bush 2003b).

There are two main assumptions behind US policy-makers' statements. First, that free markets and democracy are twins, and that the spread of one strengthens the other – hence the popularisation of the term 'market democracies' (for a critique, see Cox 1996a: 303–5). Second, that democracies do not fight each other – the core argument put forward by democratic peace theorists. Although the democratic peace theory has come under criticism in the literature, especially regarding the definitions of its two core concepts – 'democracy' and 'war' (Layne 1994; Spiro 1994) – this second assumption has nevertheless acquired the 'status of a received truth' (Cohen 1994) in that it has been used to encourage transition to free markets and democracy worldwide.

Thomas Risse-Kappen (1995a) provided a constructivist explanation of the democratic peace phenomenon. Shared norms, maintained Risse-Kappen, renders the security dilemma far less significant among democracies in that the element of ambiguity and uncertainty that is characteristic of the security dilemma could be played down when states perceive each other to be bound by similar rules and norms. However, as Tarak Barkawi and Mark Laffey (1999) pointed out, what is missing from Risse-Kappen's argument (along with some other proponents of democratic peace theory) is an account of how peaceful relations between democracies have historically been made possible by the threat and use of force against non-democracies. Barkawi and Laffey (1999: 423) maintain that by way of failing to historicise and contextualise the emergence of the 'zone of peace' or account for the absence of democracies elsewhere, the democratic peace literature 'betrays a deeply unreflexive attitude to analysis'.

The future scenario drawn from the democratic peace theory is that the encouragement of more consensual modes of social control under the rubric of democratic peace would help maintain domestic stability thereby smoothening the process of opening up heretofore protected markets. Worldwide transition to free market economies, in turn, is expected to contribute to global security. Viewed as such, the future scenario presented by the proponents of the democratic peace theory may not be very different from that of increased globalisation in that peace is defined as the absence of war (i.e. 'negative peace') and issues such as 'structural violence' are sidelined. Moreover, the very definition of democracy adopted by those who propound this scenario is a 'limited' or 'exclusionary' one. In order for free markets to operate freely in the developing world, what is required is not necessarily fully-fledged democratic systems that could render the freedom of market forces vulnerable by imposing restrictions in line with the demands of political groups, but rather 'low-intensity democracies'[16] that would enable the restriction of decision-making power to 'elements acceptable to the financial market' (Cox 1996a: 304). US Cold War policy towards the Middle East was one of encouraging modernisation and increasing political participation, whilst supporting 'limited' or 'exclusionary' democracies (such as Egypt and Jordan) along with Gulf sheikhdoms (who allow for no or very limited political participation), that has helped to maintain the status quo and make the region secure for the transition to a free-market economy.

This has seemingly changed in the aftermath of the events of September 11, 2001 in that US policy-makers proclaimed a new willingness to democratise the Middle East in the attempt to rid the region of the roots of terrorism. US policy-makers seem to hope that regime change in Iraq will set off a domino effect on the rest of the region, thereby democratising the Middle East, albeit gradually. Leaving aside the issue of the feasibility of this project, let us discuss its potential implications.

The desirability of this option for US policy-makers rests on the assumption that democracy could have a pacifying effect in the Middle East. One could identify two problems with this assumption. The first and widely acknowledged problem is that it would be rather difficult to envision the establishment of democratic peace in the Middle East, as the region has so far proven to be rather 'resistant to democratisation' (Ray 1995: 3). However, although it is true that the region (with the exception of Israel and Turkey) has so far remained relatively immune to democratisation, to assert that the Middle East could be an exception to the democratic peace phenomenon is to let one's thinking be trapped in the present state of affairs, not realising the potential for change that exists. Indeed, in the aftermath of the Cold War, there has been some movement towards democratisation in the Middle East with some Arab policy-makers responding to their populations' demands for the adoption of liberalisation and democratisation measures. In the last decade or so, multi-party competition for elected legislative assemblies has been either introduced or expanded in Algeria, Egypt, Jordan, Kuwait, Lebanon, Morocco, the Palestine Authority and Tunisia (El Sayyid 1994).

However, although it is possible to argue that a beginning has been made, there are significant problems with these developments. For one thing, executive posts in some of these countries remain uncontested or at times unelected. Moreover, Bahrain, Kuwait, Oman and Saudi Arabia do not have universal suffrage.[17] Libya does have universal suffrage but elections are not held. In Kuwait suffrage is limited to males aged 21 or above who resided in Kuwait before 1920, their sons, and sons of naturalised citizens. Finally, the few elections that have been allowed to take place with limited suffrage are often engineered in line with the wishes of the ruling elite (Pripstein-Posusney 1998). Indeed, it has been suggested that the elected assemblies are there not to enable genuine political participation but to enhance domestic and international legitimacy. Still, even engineered elections are elections and they constitute a deviation from past practices by handing a certain degree of control to the public over the executive's actions and lending them an opportunity to get their voices heard. It is also worth noting that even those regimes that engage in electoral-engineered democracy are viewed as threats to regime security by Saudi policy-makers who have so far shied away from such reforms (Pripstein-Posusney 1998: 13).

The second problem with the democratic peace theory within the

Middle Eastern context is that it is difficult to know whether giving Arab peoples, for instance, more say in policy-making would have led to more or less clashes with Israel. It could be argued that, if Arab non-state actors had more say in their countries' policy-making, they could have pushed for more support for the Palestinian cause, not less. Likewise, they could have demanded (and indeed achieved) some degree of integration between Arab countries and/or more uniform responses to Israel's actions. Accordingly, if the future was to bring increasing political liberalisation and democratisation in the Middle East, this could lead to strained relations with both Israel and the United States. Indeed, it was this very unpredictability of democratic systems that had, throughout the Cold War, led the United States to shy away from supporting democratisation whilst backing 'friendly tyrants' (Pipes and Garfinkle 1991) and 'low-intensity democracies' (Robinson 1996) that have helped to maintain the status quo and make the region secure for the transition to free-market economies (see Kaplan 2002c). This, in turn, provides empirical backing to the point made by Barkawi and Laffey (see above) that the establishment of a 'zone of peace' in one part of the world should be understood within the context of 'low-intensity democracies' or authoritarian regimes elsewhere.

A Middle Eastern security community?

From a critical perspective, the process of imagining, creating and nurturing security communities could constitute emancipatory practices. Indeed, given global changes and the effects of the twin processes of globalisation and fragmentation, the argument for regionalism is fairly strong. The end of the Cold War and the marginalisation of many Arab actors, the 'atomisation' of the Arab regional system, and the globalisation of economic relations have indeed led some to conclude that it may no longer be possible to avoid regionalisation in the Middle East (see, for example, Maddy-Weitzman 1993; Guazzone 1997; Korany 1997; Hudson 1999). Although the stall in Arab–Israeli peace-making and the US-led war on Iraq have served to dishearten some (see, for example, Sayigh 1999), others have insisted that 'regional problems require regional solutions' (Hollis 2003: 34).

What shape such a regional solution should take, on the other hand, is an issue of controversy. Since the issue of choosing between contending approaches to regional security (or competing regionalisms) is a contentious one, one way of avoiding the problem of choosing between them is to come up with an alternative. An alternative conception of security could give rise to a new approach to regional security that could be acceptable to all. This new approach could be based on the perception of a common threat, that is, regional insecurity, and the need for the creation of a security community.

It is one thing, of course, to state this in abstract terms, but quite another to try and envision how this might happen. This section of Chapter 6 will try and present a preliminary assessment of the potential for the creation of a security community in the Middle East. In what follows, I will present a brief overview of the security communities approach as developed by Karl Deutsch. Next, I will explain the constructivist twist Emanuel Adler and Michael Barnett gave to the security communities approach. Finally, I will try to evaluate the potential for the creation of a security community within the Middle Eastern context. For this purpose, I will adopt the three-tier framework developed by Adler and Barnett and use it as a checklist to assess the potential for the creation of a security community in the Middle East.[18]

Karl Deutsch and the security communities approach

What Karl Deutsch and his colleagues (1957) were interested in when formulating the idea of a security community in the 1950s was the cessation of inter-state violence and the creation of dependable expectations of peaceful change by way of strengthening relationships among a group of states. In *The Political Community in the North Atlantic Area*, Deutsch and his colleagues set out to map the road to the creation of security communities. Their conviction was that once the conditions and processes that give rise to security communities were identified, it would be possible to replicate them in other parts of the world so that (the preparations for and the idea of) war would not enter into the calculations of those states (Deutsch *et al.* 1957: vii, 3, 20–1).

In this pioneering work, Deutsch and his associates (1957: 5) defined a security community, as 'one in which there is real assurance that the members of that community will not fight each other physically, but will settle their disputes in some other way'. They distinguished between two types of security communities, 'pluralistic' and 'amalgamated'. While both developed based on expectations of peaceful change, the latter emerged when states decided to merge (as in the case of the United States of America), whereas in the case of the former members retained their independence. Some kind of integration (defined as the creation of a sense of community and the construction of institutions and practices to sustain that 'we feeling') took place in both cases, but it is in the case of the prior that states decided to forego their independence and merge under a unitary or federal government (1957: 6–9).

Although Deutsch *et al.* were positive regarding the potential for security communities to travel to different parts of the world, their ideas remained largely on paper for four decades until they were revived by Adler, Barnett and the other contributors to their edited volume, which came out in 1998. In the meantime, the security communities approach was 'often cited but rarely emulated' (Adler and Barnett 1998b: 9).[19]

The constructivist turn in the study of security communities

The recently revamped literature on security communities also busied itself with the creation of pluralistic security communities. This is largely because Adler and Barnett (1998b: 5) deem pluralistic security communities as 'theoretically and empirically closest to the developments that are currently unfolding in international politics and international relations theory'. However, Adler and Barnett, while adopting and re-working Deutsch's conception of a pluralistic security community, dropped his behaviouralist outlook, giving the study of security communities a constructivist twist.

Adler and Barnett argued that one of the reasons why Deutsch's study was not replicated was because Deutsch, despite his initial collaboration with historians in the project, remained behaviouralist in outlook and prioritised quantitative methods in his research into international transactions in the attempt to understand the processes and conditions that foster the creation of security communities. Deutsch maintained that transactions generate responsiveness, reciprocity and mutual predictability of behaviour and lead to the discovery of new areas of interest and identifications thereby resulting in the creation of security communities. However, as Adler and Barnett (1998c: 48–9) argue, although focusing on quantitative research into transactions may help establish the relationship between increased transboundary movements and greater interdependence, it would not help 'detect a greater sense of cohesion and community based on mutual responsiveness, value orientation, and identity'. In other words, Deutsch's emphasis on quantitative methods when analysing the relationship between transactions and the shaping of interests and identities, although constituting a major contribution, nevertheless did not enable him to develop a better understanding of the 'social relations that are bound up with and generated by those transactions', or the complex and dynamic way in which identities and interests are shaped and reshaped to enable, further or forestall future transactions (Adler and Barnett 1998b: 7–8).

Thus, Adler and Barnett (1998b: 15) justified the need for the adoption of a constructivist approach with reference to the need to have a better understanding of the 'relationship between structure, social interactions, and the possible transformation of that structure that leaves its mark on security practices'. In other words, they maintained that in the absence of an account as to how actors' willingness to enter into transactions with each other could be moulded by transnational forces, interactions and structures that emerge and evolve due to the actions of the very same (state and non-state) actors, the potential for the creation of security communities worldwide could not be fulfilled (for further elaboration on this point, see McSweeney 1999).

Evaluating the potential for the creation of a security community in the Middle East

In an attempt to understand the emergence and development of security communities, Adler and Barnett (1998c: 37–48) developed a three-tier framework: precipitating conditions (tier one), facilitating conditions (tier two), and necessary conditions (tier three).

Tier one: precipitating conditions

Tier one comprises what Adler and Barnett term the 'precipitating conditions'. These may include a change in the external environment, technology, demography and economics. Such changes, argue Adler and Barnett (1998c: 38), 'can propel states to look in each other's direction and attempt to coordinate their policies to their mutual advantage'. The two authors are aware that not much may come out of these initial interactions; but, alternatively, states may succeed in developing social bonds, which could lead them to further improve their relations and proceed to tier two.

Some of the following developments in the post-Cold War Middle East could be viewed as constituting precipitating conditions for the formation of a security community in the region.

For instance, changes in the *external environment* caused by the end of the Cold War and the ensuing dissolution of the Soviet Union could be viewed as having contributed to a re-thinking of security relations in the Middle East. Indeed, the demise of the external threat posed by the Soviet Union brought about a relaxation in regional security relations not only because of a relative decline in external interventions (direct or indirect, by the United States or the Soviet Union) but also due to the end of Soviet support for anti-status quo forces (such as Iraq and Syria). Changes in the regional environment caused by the Iraqi invasion of Kuwait, the Gulf War and the US-led war on Iraq could also be considered to have precipitated a re-thinking of regional security relations. In the 1990s, Gulf policy-makers became increasingly convinced that they should pay more attention to military threats posed to their security stemming from inside the Arab world (as was the case with the Iraqi aggression). The now defunct Arab–Israeli Peace Process was also helpful so far as it helped to break taboos by bringing about Arab states' recognition of Israel and the gradual Israeli acceptance of the PLO. The multilateral negotiations organised as a part of the Peace Process brought many regional states together to discuss 'arms control and regional security', 'water', 'environment', 'refugees' and 'regional economic development'. Although not much has come out of this process, the initial progress of multilateral negotiations helped to strengthen the voices of those who call for common security practices (see Feldman and Toukan 1997).

Changes in the *natural environment* is another factor that could bring regional actors together if they choose to interpret, for instance, global warming and the increasing scarcity of water resources as a threat to their security. After all, these are what Ulrich Beck (1992: 34) terms 'threats to the future', to cope with which action would need to be taken in the present. However, although a working group addressing this issue was formed as a part of the multilateral track of the Madrid Peace Process, there emerged very little evidence of regional actors' willingness to adopt cooperative practices. On the contrary, changes in the global environment so far seem to have stiffened some actors' positions (as is the case with the conflict surrounding the use of the Tigris–Euphrates river basin shared by Iraq, Syria and Turkey). In sum, there is some potential for cooperation on this issue should regional actors choose to think differently about the long-term future and adopt cooperative practices that could enhance their gains. Environmental politics need not be a zero-sum game where one side's gain is the other side's loss. All parties stand to gain if they agree to cooperate, for instance, on the optimisation of water transportation and irrigation techniques, and minimisation of evaporation.

Technological changes could have contradictory effects in the Middle Eastern context. The increase in the range of surface-to-surface missiles, for instance, could be viewed as bringing regional states together by making it difficult to defend against them. However, they could also be viewed as increasing suspicion and threatening stability thereby pushing for more balance of power politics and arms build-up instead of cooperation. Another technological factor is the revolution in communications technology, which has enabled non-state actors to join efforts and cross (physical and psychological) boundaries, and organise coalitions pushing for more political participation, democracy and respect for human rights (see Green 1999). If such non-state actors, with their creative practices, could be channelled towards constituting a security community, they could indeed help build and sustain it. Still, it is conceivable that the very same factors could accelerate the process of fragmentation (as suggested by Robert Kaplan among others).

Transformations in *economic patterns* such as the increasing pace of the globalisation of production and finance have also made an impact on regional politics. Faced with the danger of marginalisation in a globalising world economy, some regional policy-makers have chosen to adopt structural adjustment and liberalisation programmes to integrate themselves into world markets. The threat of marginalisation in an increasingly globalising world economy could indeed be viewed as a precipitating condition for the creation of a security community should actors choose to view it as such. There is some potential for increased economic integration (in trade as well as agricultural and industrial sectors) should regional actors choose to tap them (see Shafik 1999).

Finally, *demography* is another factor that could be viewed as a precipitating condition. On the one hand, it could be argued that the population explosion in many Arab states, coupled with the effects of (internal and cross-border) migration, would strengthen the forces of fragmentation in the Middle East. Moreover, issues such as birth control could create a divisive effect by polarising activists of Arab nationalist and Islamist convictions who view the increase in Arab/Muslim population in this part of the world as a point of strength vis-à-vis Israel. On the other hand, the issue of birth control could be viewed as a potential common ground for women's movements throughout the Middle East to form coalitions (see Mernissi 1996: 46–62).

What has become clear in the preceding discussion is that most of the factors enumerated above could indeed precipitate the creation of a security community; they could also lead to fragmentation and even chaos. In other words, the same set of factors could both encourage increasing cooperation and collaboration, or lead regional states to resort to militarised practices such as balance of power politics, deterrence and arms build-up. The point here is that in order for new interpretations of such dynamics to emerge in a way that would 'propel states to look in each other's direction and attempt to coordinate their policies to their mutual advantage' as Adler and Barnett (1998c: 38) expect, there is a need for human agency to intervene and provide actors with an alternative reading of their situation – a reading that would need to be informed by an alternative conception of security. This is because the threat of further marginalisation of Arab countries, or increasing scarcity of water as a result of global warming, exist as 'threats to the future', to use Beck's phrase. Since they only exist in the future, the only way to prevent such threats from becoming 'reality' is to take action at present. Indeed in the absence of human agents that could provide such alternative readings, actors may choose to remain oblivious to changes enumerated above, thereby failing to take cooperative measures that could potentially be to their mutual advantage.

Tier two: facilitating conditions

In Adler and Barnett's framework, tier two comprises factors that facilitate the creation of a security community. Adler and Barnett categorise these factors under structure (power and knowledge) and process (transactions, organisations and social learning).

Following Deutsch *et al.*, Adler and Barnett stress power and knowledge as structures central to the development of security communities. Their conception of power includes the conventional understanding of power (i.e. the size and strength of states in terms of material resources) as well as the power of shared meanings (such as a 'we feeling'). Knowledge, in turn, refers to shared meanings and understandings that license and legitimate practices. Adler and Barnett (1998c: 39–41) maintain that the interplay between power and knowledge has an impact on the construction of security communities in that some understanding into the workings of the relationship between the two is essential.

Regarding the category of process, Adler and Barnett look at transactions, organisations, institutions and social learning as contributing towards the development of trust between members as well as the creation of collective transnational identities and shared understandings. Adler and Barnett expect tier two to help create trust and collective transnational identities that make transition to tier three possible.

In Adler and Barnett's framework, the significance of *power* stems from the fact that those politically, administratively, economically or educationally more advanced states could form the core around which a security community might develop. These states could create a 'magnet' effect by attracting other members, getting the existing members to agree on certain issues and creating an overall we-feeling in the community. Shimon Peres (1993) considered Israel as a candidate for this job. Another candidate would be the Israeli–Turkish alliance. The human as well as material resources and experiences in cooperation that these two states have could indeed be considered to have the potential to constitute the core for a security community.

One major problem with relying on these two states constituting the core is that their relationship is based on military strategic cooperation (alongside its non-military dimensions) and its anti-Arab image has already generated suspicion at best and hostility at worst. Indeed, Jordan has been hesitant to strengthen its relationship with these two states notwithstanding the willingness of Kings Hussein and Abdullah (see Lynch 2002). In other words, Israel and Turkey lack the non-material dimensions of power such as the ability to generate a we-feeling. Arguably, this could be compensated for if they were to be joined by an Arab state such as Egypt that has the necessary pan-Arab credentials.

Here, the role third parties (non-members) could play in creating the magnet effect should also be emphasised, for, the involvement of and commitment by third parties such as the United States and the European Union would considerably enhance the project's chances for success. This is not only because US and/or EU involvement (in one form or another) would encourage many regional actors to join in (due to the attraction of their material resources) but also because the two have the power to use carrot and stick policies to nudge regional actors in the desired direction when negotiations are stalled. Furthermore, they could also help maintain stability in the region by taking up the role of a 'pacifier' (Joffe 1984) to enable reconciliation to continue without interruption – as did the United States in Western Europe in the aftermath of the Second World War.

This, however, should not be taken to suggest that a collective identity should be forced upon the regional states in accordance with the wishes of external powers.[20] Rather, the argument here, following Deiniol Jones

(1999), is that external actors could fulfil the role of a 'cosmopolitan mediator' bolstering 'communicative action' in regional politics. Such an approach would involve overcoming obstacles to dialogue through strengthening civil society, the assumption being that 'dialogue arises out of necessity and that where power operates to shape a political context dialogue is rendered redundant' (Jones 1999: 94).

Arguably, it would be better if both the United States and the European Union were involved, because they appeal to different actors at multiple levels. Whilst the support of the United States is crucial for the participation of Israel and the Gulf states, the EU ranks higher in the eyes of the policy-makers of North African states, Syria and the Lebanon, who have remained outside the multilateral track of the peace process but participated in the Euro–Med partnership scheme. Moreover, the EU has so far proven itself willing and better endowed to conduct people-to-people diplomacy, which has served to strengthen its position vis-à-vis a significant portion of NGOs in the Arab world (especially in North Africa) (see Jünemann 2002). The problem here is that the United States and the European Union have had their differences regarding regional security issues; their relationship has, throughout the 1990s, been characterised more by rivalry than cooperation.

Lastly, the power of non-state actors should not be underestimated, for they could contribute to community building. Their power largely stems from their ability to work at the grassroots level and their familiarity with the needs and concerns of people on the ground. Intellectuals could also play important roles by presenting regional actors with alternative readings of their situation and imagining alternative futures.[21] This is especially relevant in parts of the world such as the Middle East where there is little support for the formation of a security community at the governmental level. However, the issue of the agency of non-state actors is an issue Adler and Barnett's framework is relatively weak on. The role non-state actors could play is potentially larger in the Middle Eastern setting than some other parts of the world where there is evidence of enthusiasm for regionalisation at the governmental level. Still, at the end of the day, action on the part of both state and non-state actors would be required if a security community is to be created.

Non-state actors could also assume important roles in the production and dissemination of the kind of *knowledge* that would be required for the formation and the nurturing of a security community. In Adler and Barnett's framework, liberalism and democracy are expected to constitute the shared meanings and understandings that would form the basis of communication and trust in a security community. The authors also note that there may evolve alternative paths to security communities and that in the absence of shared knowledge based on liberalism and democracy, regional actors could build their community based on alternative notions such as 'developmentalism' in the South-East Asian case.

In the absence of shared meanings and understandings that would help shape actors' practices and legitimate their activities, the most promising option for community-minded actors in the Middle East seems to be to build their security community based on their one commonality, i.e. their desire to address the problem of regional insecurity. However, as noted above, in order for them to come to view the problem of 'regional insecurity' as a commonality, regional actors would need to be presented with an alternative reading of their situation; they would need to be made aware of their shared interests and shown how coordinating their policies could be to their 'mutual advantage'. The production and dissemination of knowledge on futures of regional security, what futures may bring, and alternative strategies that could be adopted to meet 'threats to the future' could propel states to each other's direction. This raises the issue of agency – the need for community-minded actors to intervene and provide people with alternative readings of their situation.[22]

It should also be noted that although their shared project could constitute the minimal common ground required to initiate the project in the short-run, in the medium to long-run shared meanings and understandings as well as knowledge and practice of conflict resolution and non-violent action techniques would have to be generated and disseminated in order to create dependable expectations of peaceful change. One challenge that would be facing regional actors would be that of generating this knowledge whilst remaining sensitive to different conflict cultures that exist in the region. There is some knowledge and experience of conflict-resolution and non-violent techniques generated outside the region which regional actors could tap into. But they would also need to turn to their own heritage to anchor this knowledge if they wish these practices to be widely adopted by different actors at multiple levels. This is not meant to suggest that grounding knowledge of conflict-resolution, and non-violent resistance techniques in regional actors' own (cultural and historical) heritage would automatically help to solve the problem of regional insecurity. Rather, the hope is that pointing to unfulfilled potential in terms of knowledge that already exists in the region could help popularise the cause for a security community and facilitate its creation.[23]

This, of course, is not meant to downplay the existing structures that make it difficult for people to re-think their cultural and religious heritage and choose reconciliation and coexistence instead of conflict and war. Here, human agency would need to step in and present peoples with alternatives that exist, possibilities imminent in world politics. By way of doing this, students of critical security aim to challenge the claim to knowledge monopolised by the prevalent discourses. This, in turn, requires paying more attention to the workings of the power/knowledge relationship than Adler and Barnett seem to have done.

The use of processes (transactions, international organisations and institutions, and social learning) to entrench security communities was the point emphasised by Deutsch *et al.* when initially writing about the subject. Deutsch's particular focus was on the significance of *transactions* and the spill-over effects the establishment of trust in one sector could have in other sectors, thereby strengthening mutual identification and contributing towards the gradual emergence of dependable expectations of peaceful change. A major problem here is that relying on transactions to transform social relations could prove to be futile in the Middle East, for the region ranks very low in terms of intra-regional transactions. In fact, it is the very links of interdependence that are created through international transactions that some regional policy-makers want to avoid. The solution to this problem could be found in the creation of an organisational framework for such transactions to take place. With the involvement of third parties such as the United States or the European Union, the issue of potential Israeli hegemony – a major concern for most Arab actors – could be checked until regional actors build relationships of mutual trust.

Indeed it is conceivable that if successful cooperation over one core issue area could be developed, cooperation over other issues would follow. This argument does not necessarily entail buying into the logic of spill-over that implies the deterministic power of cooperation in one sector leading states to upgrade their interests to enable cooperation in another sector. Following Bill McSweeney (1999), the argument is that successful cooperation over one issue area may not only persuade other states to upgrade their interests but also lead domestic actors to redefine their identities within the framework of a common identity by 'seducing' them into further cooperation and collaboration. McSweeney maintains that the concept of seduction does away with the mechanical, material and deterministic connotations of spill-over by way of integrating an element of human agency (conceptualised with reference to the state as well as sub-state level) and stressing the 'processual character of the project in question ... rather than the discrete moment suggested by spill over' (McSweeney 1999: 169). Accordingly, if cooperation over one issue area such as arms control were to successfully take place, this could not only persuade governments to upgrade their interests, but also seduce non-state actors (such as individuals, social groups and grassroots organisations) to redefine their identities within the framework provided by the common identity of the security community, thereby making further cooperation and enmeshment possible (see McSweeney 1999: 166–72, for further elaboration on this point). This, in turn, would require paying more attention to the agency of non-state actors – more than Adler and Barnett's framework would allow.

Without wishing to de-emphasise the significance of transactions, Adler and Barnett underline the role institutions/organisations and social learning play in helping build trust and collective identity. Building upon the CSCE/OSCE experience in Europe, Adler and Barnett stress the role *organisations* could play to disseminate knowledge, contribute to the development of trust and mutual identification, and ' "engineer" the very conditions that assist in their development' by fostering a regional culture that, in turn, helps fortify their links (see Adler 1998b; Adler and Barnett 1998c: 42).

Proposals have already been made for the creation of a Conference on Security and Cooperation in the Mediterranean (CSCM) to deal with issues of 'security, economic cooperation and human rights' (Niblock 1992: 245–8; see also Galtung and Fischer 2003). Coupled with a Helsinki Citizens' Assembly-type organisation to ensure peoples' involvement, the CSCM could provide the much-needed setting for regional actors to come together, exchange views, build mutual trust and develop bonds. In other words, the creation of a CSCM could be a good starting point for the creation of a security community. The institutional power of the CSCM could not only work as a magnet to pull other members but it could also help reinforce the belief of the already existing members in the value and viability of the project. Lastly, institutions such as the CSCM also help disseminate knowledge necessary for the creation of a non-violent conflict culture.

Social learning is another process that is crucial in the development of dependable expectations of peaceful change. It involves not only the dissemination of knowledge of conflict resolution and non-violent techniques but also the moulding of existing identities within the framework provided by the common identity of the security community. Adler and Barnett (1998c: 45) expect social learning processes to promote 'shared definitions of security, proper domestic and international action and regional boundaries' as well. However, the emergence of common conceptions of security is something that cannot be left to emerge and be disseminated at such a late stage. It is through the adoption of a new conception of security that new interpretations of the social reality could emerge thereby helping precipitate the making of a security community.

In the non-so-distant past, some exploratory steps were taken to promote peace and reconciliation through education (see Calleja 1994: 282). Such meetings, at the moment, should not be expected to generate any substantive product other than helping parties get used to communicating with each other and exchange views in a non-confrontational setting. Indeed, the first few meetings of the Arms Control and Regional Security (ACRS) working group of the Middle East multilateral negotiations was spent on introducing parties to each other and making general statements. Given the achievements of the first three years that surpassed parties' expectations, the issue of arms control could be viewed as a potential core area to start with.[24] Although it is possible to be pessimistic about the potential for such a development, it is worth remembering that the setting up of a working group on arms control and regional security is a development few would have expected a few years ago.

Tier three: necessary conditions

In Adler and Barnett's framework, tier three builds upon the dynamics generated by the previous two tiers. It is expected that mutual trust and a common identity, which Adler and Barnett view as the 'necessary conditions' of dependable expectations of peaceful change, would flourish at this stage. The assumption here is that if actors start trusting each other, they would also start identifying with each other, which would, in turn, feed into the development of a common identity. The defining feature of this tier is that the relationships that are created through tier two are expected to be strengthened and actors are expected to begin to identify with each other so that they would 'no longer rely on concrete international organisations to maintain trust but do so through knowledge and belief about each other' (Adler and Barnett 1998c: 46). This, however, would take time as well as effort. As noted above, collective identity formation in a security community is a process that requires the agency of community-minded actors. Moreover, the process involves the creation of a common identity as well as the moulding of existing (individual, group, national, ethnic) identities by inscribing the common identity of the security community into other identities.

Although it is difficult to imagine such progress taking place given the current state of inter-community relations in the Middle East, there still are no grounds to assume that Middle Eastern peoples cannot show the flexibility required to remould their identities and commit to the creation of a new and more inclusive common identity (as did their Western European counterparts after the Second World War). After all, peoples of Saudi Arabia, for instance, moved from being Muslim subjects of the Ottoman Empire to being (albeit half-hearted) Arab nationalists in the 1920s, and then *khalijin* ('of the Gulf' in Arabic) in the 1980s and 1990s. On the other hand, in Egypt, the forerunner of Arab nationalism under Nasser's presidency, the Arab identity has never been beyond contention. Some Egyptian intellectuals have stressed the Mediterranean and African dimensions of Egyptian identity, downplaying the Arab and Muslim dimensions. In other words, there could always be found some element within peoples' existing identities to enable identification with a more inclusive community should peoples choose to do so (and provided that the necessary material resources, some of which have been outlined above, are put into effect).[25] Finally, becoming a member of and identifying with a security community need not mean the 'betrayal' of Arabism, or the downplaying of the Muslim character of some regional peoples. For example, the common identity of a security community could be a part of the identity of a Coptic woman living in Egypt whose other identities may include being an Arab, woman, Christian and Egyptian.

Indeed, as noted above, one strength of the security communities approach stems from the fact that it enables one to avoid the problem of the incommensurability of existing security discourses by way of coming up with an alternative perspective, the adoption of which need not mean the rejection of the others. There is no reason why the League of Arab States, the Organization of Islamic Conference, Middle East and North Africa (MENA) Common Market, Conference on Security and Cooperation in the Mediterranean (CSCM), and a Helsinki Citizens' Assembly-type organisation should not coexist (as is the case in Western Europe). After all, each would address different aspects of regional insecurity in the Middle East. However, in order for these alternative perspectives to peacefully coexist, a broader framework of non-violent conflict culture would need to be created within which myriad actors could put their perspectives into practice without depriving the others of their own security.

The membership of the community is a matter to be decided with reference to the core issue(s) the actors choose to focus on. One major problem involved in imagining the formation of a security community in the Middle East is that there is yet to be found a core issue over which initial negotiations and cooperation could begin. In other words, Middle Eastern actors have yet to come up with their own version of the European Coal and Steel Community, which marked the beginning of cooperation in Western Europe. Indeed, the very absence of such a core issue in the Middle East could prove to be the biggest obstacle on the road to the formation of a security community.

During the 1990s, the issue of arms control proved to be the most fertile among the five issue areas addressed by the multilateral negotiations of the Madrid Peace Process. Indeed, the progress made in its initial years 'was greater than many expected, or even deemed possible' as Bruce Jentleson and Dalia Dassa Kaye (1998: 205) have argued. It is also noted that 'compared to other regional security processes such as the European Conference on Security and Cooperation (CSCE) in its early stages, ACRS progress was noteworthy' (Jentleson and Kaye 1998: 205).

The issue of arms control is a promising core area where cooperation could be initiated. It is relatively promising not necessarily because regional policy-makers are committed to achieving regional security via arms control, but rather because they (Arab policy-makers in particular) view arms control as a way to deny their adversaries those weapons they cannot afford themselves (see Sadowksi 1993: 40). In other words, the reasoning for focusing on arms control could be found in the economic dimension of security within the Middle Eastern context. However, it should be pointed out that the logic behind such approaches to arms control is not based on common security thinking where security is sought *with* the adversary in an attempt to achieve stable security.

It is widely known that the Middle East has the highest military expenditure as a percentage of GNP in the world.[26] The Middle East also includes some of the most indebted countries of the world (such as Egypt, Morocco, Sudan, Algeria, Syria and Yemen). Even oil-rich states have been facing difficulties since the 1980s; they have begun to post regular budget deficits in recent years. Yet they continue to pour money into arms purchases often with encouragement from major arms sellers that include the United States and some EU member states. The point here is that given the willingness of arms sellers to sell and the willingness of buyers to buy notwithstanding their economic conditions, it would be very difficult to break out of this cycle of increasing debt and armament in the Middle East. This, in turn, raises the question of relationships between security communities – a topic that remains to be addressed in the literature.

A promising development took place in the 1990s when Jordan decided to break out of this arms and debt cycle and opted for unilateral arms reductions. Seeking to make the most of unilateral arms reductions (and in an attempt to avoid further weakening of their military vis-à-vis their neighbours) Jordanian policy-makers proposed an 'arms-for-debt swap' in line with which states that agree to become a part of a region-wide arms control process would qualify for a reduction of their debts (Sadowski 1993: 46).

Emphasising the state of Middle Eastern economies, Yahya Sadowski argued that the 'arms-for-debt swap' could prove to be the long-sought incentive necessary to get regional policy-makers to commit to arms control. He wrote:

> What has been missing in the Middle East is not some vision of what arms control arrangements are possible but the appropriate milieu for putting them into effect. Regional security plans and economic incentive programs supply the missing ingredient. They could foster an environment in which states approach arms control talks with less fear and more favour.
>
> (Sadowksi 1993: 55)

Sadowski's argument resonates with the call by students of critical security for adopting a broader conception of security, cognisant of the security concerns of myriad actors at multiple levels. For this vision to be put into practice, external actors (such as the United States and the EU) and non-state actors across the region would need to be brought in. The involvement of external actors is crucial, for they would be instrumental in cancelling the debts of Middle Eastern countries that agree to get involved. It is also them that stand to lose valuable business if and when the Middle Eastern arms market contracts as a result of a comprehensive arms control agreement. In this sense, the United States and other arms-producing states would also need to adopt broader conceptions of security cognisant of the interrelationships between the security concerns of actors at multiple levels if they are to agree to support such a process. Lastly, the involvement of the United States would be crucial in securing Israel's involvement in the process. Israel's nuclear status is likely to cause disagreements and US involvement and guarantees to both Israel and its Arab counterparts would be crucial to facilitate cooperation.

The involvement of non-state actors across the region would also prove crucial because, as noted above, in order for cooperation over arms control to generate interest in and cooperation about other issue areas, peoples' interest in and identification with a broader community would have to be generated. Non-state actors, especially women's movements and networks, could assume crucial roles in this process. For, it is women who suffer disproportionately as a result of militarisation and the channelling of valuable funds into defence budgets instead of education or health (see Mernissi 1993).

Still, it is important to note that not all regional policy-makers would benefit from a decisive end to the Arab–Israeli conflict. Especially those front-line states (such as Syria) or hard-line actors in most states that have, over the years, derived legitimacy from this conflict could be expected to stall the progress of the peace process. Furthermore, actors (such as Egypt) that have assumed the role of the only open channel of communication between the Arab states and Israel also stand to lose some stature if a region-wide peace settlement was to be reached (for a discussion, see Guazzone 1997: 239; Jentleson and Kaye 1998).

Conclusion

Chapter 6 presented a critical overview of existing ideas about the future and their potential implications within the Middle Eastern context. By looking at the practical implications of these scenarios, the chapter sought to identify the threats facing a critical security future. This also enabled me to point to unfulfilled potential in regional politics – a potential the 'problem-solving' approach of some (but not all) of the above-discussed scenarios has tended to overlook. Adopting the three-tier framework developed by Adler and Barnett as a checklist to assess the potential in regional politics, this final section of the chapter sought to point to those dynamics that could be viewed as conducive for the creation of a security community in the Middle East. It was argued that the same dynamics that could be viewed as propelling regional actors to look towards each other (such as the end of the Cold War, integration of world markets and global warming) could also be viewed as pushing them further apart from each other. In order for these dynamics to propel regional actors to look towards each other, as Adler and Barnett expect them to do, actors would need to be presented with an alternative reading of their situation – a reading informed by an alternative conception of security that shows them as 'victims of regional insecurity' rather than each other. This, in turn, would require the security community approach developed by Adler and Barnett to be reworked from a critical perspective.

I will make three inter-related points here. First, the concept of 'security' remains undertheorised in the literature on security communities. In fact, the conception of security in which the security community is rooted could be considered as rather narrow. What Deutsch and his colleagues sought to do when first exploring the concept was to find ways to min- imise inter-state violence. Although Deutsch put stress on the elimination of preparations for and the idea of war and stressed the use of non-mili- tary instruments, his main concern remained the maintenance of security understood as the absence of inter-state war. Adler and Barnett's revamped version of the security community approach is also rooted in a rather narrow conception of security. The co-authors mention in passing the increasing prominence of non-military dimensions of security such as 'economic, environmental and social welfare concerns' (Adler and Barnett 1998b: 4), but other than that, they remain surprisingly silent on the issue of conceptualising security. The point here is that defining secur- ity merely as the absence of inter-state violence and the creation of dependable expectations of peaceful change may not enable one to con- sider the structural roots of insecurity (that is, 'structural violence'). Being sensitive towards the structural causes of insecurity is even more crucial in parts of the world such as the Middle East that are at the peripheries of the world economic system.

Furthermore, in order for the 'precipitating conditions' to precipitate the creation of a security community in the Middle East, the dynamics identified above would have to be interpreted within an alternative frame- work rooted in an alternative conception of security cognisant of the mul- tiple and contending security discourses that exist in the region. Indeed, 'security' is a concept that would need to be defined and re-defined by dif- ferent peoples in different social and historical contexts. A common con- ception of security should not be expected to emerge at a later stage and as a side effect of increasing cooperation and collaboration on other fronts. On the contrary, in order for actors to view themselves as victims of regional insecurity rather than each other, they would need to be pre- sented with an alternative reading of their situation that stresses 'threats to the future'.

From a critical security perspective, writing about 'threats to the future' – to use Ulrich Beck's (1992) terminology – and pointing to sites and agents of change is crucial when one considers the ways in which human agency has been complicit – via the production of knowledge – in exacer- bating if not creating these threats. Beck's point is made within the context of environmental politics where the grip of 'scientific' knowledge is stronger. Nevertheless, knowledge about the future presented in the form of obstacles and opportunities by way of constraining and shaping myriad actors' practices thereby helps constitute the future.

The second point is about the relative lack of attention paid in the liter- ature to the global context in which security communities emerge and flourish. Indeed, the emphasis Adler and Barnett put on liberalism and democracy as the knowledge base of security communities betrays a 'state-centric' (if not statist) perspective that fails to take into account the extent to which the Western European security community owes its existence to the absence of security communities elsewhere around the world. To adopt and adapt a point made by Tarak Barkawi and Mark Laffey (1999: 404) in their critique of the democratic peace thesis, such an approach obscures the 'mutually constitutive relationship between so called zones of war and peace'. Indeed, the centrality of arms exports to many Western European economies could be viewed as an example of the core–periphery relations that are at work in the making of security communities. Accordingly, if the European Union, for instance, is going to play a role in helping build a security community in the Middle East, our understanding of the structural relations of power between the core and the periphery and the role these relations have played in the making and maintenance of the Western European security community should be better conceptualised.

This leads me to the third point, which is about Adler and Barnett's conceptualisation of power and the power/knowledge nexus. It could be argued that their conceptualisation is inadequate not because they stress the material dimension of power, but because they fail to adequately conceptualise 'representational power'. Indeed, as Janice Bially Mattern has argued (2000: 306–7),

> it is plainly not true that 'sticks and stones can break my bones but names can never hurt me'. In fact, one might argue that threats posed by representational force are a greater normative challenge because their insidious nature makes them harder to resist or neutralize.

Bially Mattern's point strikes a chord within the Middle Eastern context where representational power has been utilised to keep potential issues outside security agendas thereby exacerbating 'structural violence', or for representing the Middle East as a 'hotbed of conflict and war' thereby marginalising the calls for regional disarmament whilst privileging practices such as massive rearmament. The need to pay attention to the representational dimension of power becomes more apparent when we consider the ways in which language and knowledge were used to re-inforce existing power imbalance between the two parties at the Oslo negotiations (see Jones 1999). Hence the need to seek the roots of regional insecurity not only in 'world politics' but also in 'word politics' (Bilgin 2000–01).

Conclusion

This book set out to present a framework for thinking differently about regional security in the Middle East. This was attempted by adopting a critical security approach that seeks to reconceptualise security in theory and practice by broadening and deepening; looking below and beyond the state for other referents and agents; and suggesting emancipatory practices toward shaping alternative futures. Contesting those accounts that present the Middle East as only amenable to realist readings, it was argued that critical approaches present a fuller account of regional security in the Middle East. This is not to suggest that the items of the traditional agenda have lost their pertinence. As the US-led war on Iraq has shown, military concerns retain their place on regional security agendas, and military instruments remain useful in meeting certain kinds of threats. Rather, the point is that such traditional concerns should be addressed within a comprehensive framework cognisant of the dynamic relationships between multiple dimensions of security (including basic needs such as subsistence, health and education, and issues such as religious and cultural identity, democratisation and human rights). Although US policy-makers' view – that military instability in the Middle East threatens global security – retains its validity, focusing on military issues to the neglect of others risks further exacerbating those structurally-based (economic, political, societal) security concerns. Dealing with the military-security agenda is a must; yet, a military-focused and determined approach to security (in theory and practice) results in a diversion of already scarce resources into military build-up. The militarisation of the region during the Cold War not only made it more difficult to meet the traditional agenda, but also undermined regional states' capacity to provide welfare to their citizens thereby exacerbating non-military threats and rendering intractable regional conflicts.

Critical approaches to security have not received sustained attention in the Middle East Studies literature. Whereas a number of studies tackled the issue of regional security in Southern Africa (Booth 1994a; Booth and Vale 1997) and security in Africa (Thomas and Wilkin 1999), students of the Middle East remained somewhat silent until very recently (see Barnett

1998; Jones 1999; Lynch 1999; Kaye 2001; Jacoby and Sasley 2002; Bilgin 2004a). Building on these contributions as well as the more theoretical literature on critical security studies, this study sought to develop a critical perspective to study regional security in the Middle East. It was argued that when re-thinking regional security from a critical perspective, opening up 'security' is not enough; both 'region' and 'security' should be opened up to reveal the mutually constitutive relationship between the two. The structure of Parts I and II reflected this idea; Chapters 2 through 5 explored the mutually constitutive relationship between (inventing) regions and (conceptions and practices of) security. The idea being that, if inventing regions amounts to epistemological conquest of territory, the task for students of critical approaches becomes one of '[reconquesting] ... that territory, [doing] it initially epistemologically' (Said 2001: 252).

The book tried to achieve three more specific aims. The first aim was to present a critique of prevailing security discourses in theory and practice with reference to regional security in the Middle East and point to unfulfilled potential immanent in regional politics. The second aim was to explore the mutually constitutive relationship between inventing regions, and thinking about and practising security. The third aim was to show how a critical security approach might allow one to think differently about futures of regional security in the Middle East.

Chapter 1 laid out the basics of a critical security approach after briefly tracing the development of security thinking in the Cold War and post-Cold War eras. It was argued that Cold War Security Studies focused on the security of states, emphasised the military dimension and privileged the maintenance of the status quo. Although some alternative ways of thinking about security emerged during the Cold War years, they were marginalised by the prevalent approaches. The latter, 'armed' with an objectivist conception of theory, claimed command over knowledge, labelling the views of its critics as 'political' at best and 'propaganda' at worst.

Next, Chapter 1 turned to look at security thinking in the post-Cold War period by focusing on two key debates, namely 'broadening security' and 'appropriate referent(s) for security'. Building upon Peace Researchers' broadening of the concepts 'violence' and 'peace' that took human beings as referent, students of critical approaches broadened security to become aware of threats faced by referents in all walks of life. First, Walt's argument for keeping a military-focused agenda was criticised for his prioritisation of the coherence of Security Studies as an academic discipline at the expense of gaining insight into the security needs and concerns of individuals and social groups. Regarding Wæver and Deudney's critique (who have argued against adopting broader security agendas to prevent non-military issues from being addressed through traditional practices) it was noted that their worries are caused by the adoption of a particular Cold War mindset characterised by statist, zero-sum and militarised thinking and practices by all those who seek to broaden the security agenda. It was argued that re-conceptualising practice would allay their worries. For, this would enable students of security to suggest ways in which the use of traditional (statist, zero-sum, militarised) thinking and practices to meet non-military threats could be avoided. The need for re-conceptualising practice becomes all the more acute when one considers the fact that Third World policy-makers in general and Arab policy-makers in particular have for long adopted broad conceptions of security but have approached non-military issues such as food and water security from a statist perspective, and have sought to address them through traditional practices. The fact that some governments have already broadened their security agendas, the chapter argued, not only challenges Walt's call for a narrow military-focus, but also underlines how essential re-conceptualising practice becomes when non-military issues are put on the security agenda.

It was further argued that although it is possible to question whether 'desecuritization', or taking issues out of the realm of security, may be a better strategy, this would amount to leaving a useful tool (in terms of its mobilisation capacity) to the monopoly of state elites, who have not always been concerned with the security of individuals and social groups. It was further argued that desecuritization would amount to remaining uncritical of the ways in which the military dimension of security has been addressed. Here, Feldman and Toukan's approach was used to point to how the unilateral and zero-sum approaches of the Cold War years have only served to deepen mistrust and have led to the further militarisation of societies in the Middle East. Mernissi's critique was utilised to point to the effects military-focused thinking and practices have had on women's lives by sidelining their concerns.

Turning to the debate on appropriate referent(s) for security, Chapter 1 suggested that it is because of the state's unchallenged status as the main agent for security that it is still treated as the primary referent. Following an overview of Buzan's approach to the study of security, the chapter suggested that Buzan's thesis (since it is states that act for security, their security should be central to our analyses) could not be sustained. This is not only because states often fail to fulfil what they promise, but also because there already are non-state agents striving to provide for their own and others' security. The chapter also noted that producing state-centric analyses does not only reflect a world 'out there' but ends up reinforcing statism in Security Studies by making it difficult to move away from the state as the main agent for and referent of security. This, in turn, underlines the need to pay more attention to the relationship between theory and practice.

Chapter 1 also considered Ayoob's call for more not less statism in Security Studies. It was argued that the argument Ayoob makes to justify privileging the security of states in the developing world is symptomatic of the tendency among students of Third World security to emphasise the different security needs and interests of developing states. The chapter suggested that by emphasising the different 'nature' of developing or 'weak' states and the need for them to 'grow up' and become 'strong' states, Ayoob has failed to explore the interconnections between state building and security maintenance in different parts of the world. Following Thomas, it was argued that in order to be able to understand the problem of insecurity in the developing world, some of its roots should be sought in the developing world and especially in the structural relationships between the two.

The final section of Chapter 1 introduced critical security thinking. This section sought to clarify the key analytical moves of critical approaches to security, namely 'broadening security' and 'deepening security'. It was noted that broadening security should not be taken to mean putting more issues on governmental agendas and meeting them through 'traditional' (militarised) means based on zero-sum assumptions. Rather, it should be understood as opening up security to provide a richer picture that includes all issues that engender insecurity. Deepening security, in turn, involves investigating the links between security discourses and the worldviews from which they derive; the point being that conceiving security in a narrow manner merely with reference to military concerns and the state betrays a statist approach that could only (re)produce regional insecurities. Deepening security, however, leaves open the possibility of the transformation of political community at the regional level.

The chapter also sought to develop critical security thinking by focusing on three main themes I identified as the silences of post-Cold War debates on security, namely, 'constitutive theory', 'practice' and 'agency'. It was argued that students of critical approaches to security could make use of the constitutive role played by theories by presenting a fundamentally different approach to security in theory and in practice in the attempt to open up space for political action to take place. Here, the role students of security could play through 'thinking about doing' as well as critical self-reflection becomes crucial. The chapter also sought to show that a broader security agenda necessitates looking at agents other than the state in order to avoid falling back upon the agency of the state in meeting non-military threats. Pointing to this need becomes all the more crucial in the Third World context where security agendas have always been kept broad and threats were often met through militarised means by prioritising the security needs and interests of states over those of individuals and social groups. Lastly, the chapter looked at the issue of practice, and pointed to the need for re-conceptualising practice to meet a broader security agenda. Here, emphasis was put on the security community approach and the need to re-think this approach from a critical perspective.

Parts I and II of the book utilised the critical security perspective introduced in Chapter 1 to criticise conceptions and practices of regional security in the Middle East. Part III looked at what the future of regional security in the Middle East may look like when viewed through critical security lenses.

Part I: 'Pasts' looked at the Cold War pasts of regional security in the Middle East, and investigated the relationship between representations of the region (Chapter 2), and practices of security (Chapter 3). Chapter 2 traced the trajectory of the Middle East as a geopolitical invention from its origins in the British India Office into the Cold War, when the term entered the public discourse within the region itself. It was argued that the Middle East was invented to help British and later US strategists to think about and organise action in maintaining security in this part of the world. Chapter 2 also presented an alternative representation, that of the 'Arab Regional System', which challenged not only the colonial origins of the Middle East, but also the Cold War security discourse by which it was shaped. By way of looking at this alternative representation, the chapter laid bare the way regions are shaped by the security thinking and practices of their inventors. It was argued that the spatial representation Arab Regional System was shaped by an alternative security discourse, that of Arab national security, which criticised the top-down, outward-directed and pro-status quo approach of Cold War Security Studies. Instead it emphasised the need to look at the domestic political and developmental dimensions of security. Students of Arab national security maintained that the relationships between Arab states could not be understood simply as one of 'black box' states balancing each other through military build-up. Their shared Arab identity, they argued, rendered relations between Arab states different from any other group of states which did not share such similar characteristics.

Whilst welcoming their critique of the Cold War security discourse, the chapter argued that students of Arab national security adopted this altern-ative conception of security when studying the security needs and interests of Arab states only, but remained content with an outward-directed, mili-tary-focused and zero-sum conception when thinking about security rela-tions between Arab states and their non-Arab neighbours. It was further argued that non-military dimensions of security were almost always approached from a statist perspective, which resulted in the privileging of military and non-military threats to the security of Arab states whilst mar-ginalising the concerns of individuals and social groups.

Chapter 3 concluded 'Cold War pasts' by bringing together earlier arguments in the attempt to further illustrate the relationship between representations and practices. It looked at different security practices within the framework of the spatial representations that they shaped and were shaped by. It was argued that the practices of Britain and the United States shaped and were, in turn, shaped by the Middle Eastern security discourse. These practices, the chapter argued, were designed to secure the Middle East against threats from outside. The Middle East Defence

Organisation (MEDO), the Northern Tier, and the Baghdad Pact were all regional security schemes designed to maintain access to bases in the region and to make it inviolable to Soviet influence or intervention. The chapter further argued that the reasoning of British and US policy-makers behind the creation of such regional security schemes, instead of backing the League of Arab States, which was an indigenously-generated regional security organisation, was to prevent the prevalence of the Arab national security discourse. The latter stressed issues such as de-colonisation, state building, economic and political sovereignty and the plight of the Palestinian people. Needless to say, none of these issues were high on the agenda shaped by the Middle Eastern security discourse.

Chapter 3 continued by examining practices that shaped and were shaped by the Arab national security discourse. It was argued that during the 1950s Egyptian president Nasser adopted a broader and societal-focused approach to Arab national security, and sought to use his influence over Arab public opinion to shape the security practices of other Arab governments so that the last remnants of colonialism could be eradicated from the Arab Regional System. The issue of the plight of the Palestinian people became a 'symbolic' tool that helped Nasser (along with other proponents of Arab national security) to voice numerous concerns such as de-colonisation, sovereignty and economic development. Nasser's evident popularity among Arab peoples, perhaps paradoxically, led to the decline of Arab national security; Saudi Arabia and other Gulf states distanced themselves from Nasser's 'radical' approach and moved closer towards the pro-status quo approach of the United States.

Following the failure of MEDO, the Northern Tier and the Baghdad Pact, US policy-makers sought to re-shape their approach to regional security in the Middle East. Rather than trying to create regional security schemes, they focused on key states such as Iran, Israel, Saudi Arabia and Turkey. They also adopted a compartmentalised approach, avoiding acknowledging the linkages between different dimensions of regional security such as the Israel/Palestine conflict, oil and military stability. Considering how central these linkages were to the Arab national security discourse, the adoption of this compartmentalised approach by US policy-makers coupled with Gulf policy-makers' increasingly statist approaches, and Egypt's decision to break ranks with the rest of the Arab states to sign an individual peace treaty with Israel, marked the decline of Arab national security at the governmental level. Indeed the 1980s were characterised by more statist practices, with the Israel/Palestine issue being pushed further to the background.

Overall, Part I sought to advance the aims of the book by presenting a critique of the Cold War security approaches in theory and practice, based on an overview of Cold War critiques of Security Studies as well as critical approaches to security. The issue of the mutually constitutive relationship between theory and practice has been central to the latter. It was argued that the relationship between theory and practice is never neutral, and that security discourses help shape 'reality' by privileging certain practices whilst marginalising others. In these ways, Part I sought to present an alternative reading of the pasts of regional security in the Middle East. It was argued that the region took its current shape not because there were no alternatives, but because choices were made in history, which resulted in the Cold War security discourse prevailing over other discourses and consequently shaping security practices in the region.

Part II: 'Presents', which examined regional security in the Middle East in the post-Cold War era, adopted a parallel structure to Part I. Chapter 4 traced the development of the Middle East and the Arab Regional System in the post-Cold War period. It introduced two more spatial representations that came to prominence during this period, the 'Euro–Med Region' and 'Muslim Middle East'. These, it was argued, have been shaped, respectively, by the European Union's discourse on security in the Euro–Med Region and an Islamist discourse on security. It was argued that the competition between these four representations took place at multiple levels in the post-Cold War era. The Middle East as a spatial representation seemed to be on the rise for a while until the stall in Arab–Israeli peace-making in the late 1990s and the war on Iraq (2003) caused a backlash. During this period conservative actors of oil-rich states increasingly began to locate themselves in the Gulf, which emerged as a sub-region of the Middle East, reflecting the convergence of the economic and energy security concerns of the US and regime security concerns of Gulf policymakers. The ensuing relaxation of the Arab/non-Arab distinction that had been central to the making of the Arab Regional System meant that more and more Arab actors could locate themselves in the (New) Middle East. Although the break-up of violence in Israel/Palestine and the stall in Arab–Israeli regional economic cooperation brought the decline of Middle Easternism, the emerging void has not yet been filled by any of the alternatives. During this period the Euro–Med Region gained some backing from Arab actors, partly due to it being a relatively neutral representation and partly due to the resources the EU poured into its construction. It was noted that the other two representations, Arab Regional System and Muslim Middle East, have been shaped mainly by the practices of non-state actors, many of who actively resist their leaders' attempts to locate their countries in the (New) Middle East.

The overall conclusion of Chapter 4 was that the competition between the contending representations of the region took a different turn in the post-Cold War period. The main divide is no longer between the proponents of the Arab Regional System versus Middle East (as was the case during the Cold War), but one between pro-status quo actors who seek to establish security by increasing regionalisation (such as the United States and the EU via their respective projects) and anti-status quo actors that seek radical change. It was further argued that this competition no longer takes place mostly at the governmental level. The pro/anti-status quo divide cuts through boundaries forming coalitions between state and non-state actors in a struggle for prevalence.

Chapter 5 sought to investigate the relationship between representations and practices. Like the previous 'practices' chapter (Chapter 3) it was organised along spatial lines; security practices were looked at within the framework of the (spatial) representation they shaped and were, in turn, shaped by. It was argued that the US approach to regional security in the Middle East remains top-down and military-focused. The Gulf War, the subsequent bombings of Iraq, the Madrid Peace Process and the US-led war on Iraq were used as illustrations to make the point that the compartmentalised approach to regional security in the Middle East adopted by US policy-makers could not be sustained if the aim is to achieve stability in the long run. The chapter maintained that although Arab policy-makers did participate in the Madrid Peace Process, little progress was made in the attempt to create regional institutions (such as a Middle East Common Market) or in arms control negotiations, because of US (and Israeli) policy-makers' refusal to acknowledge the linkages between the multiple dimensions of regional security. In this regard, it is important to remember that, notwithstanding the decline in the Arab national security discourse, the interplay between state and societal security makes it very difficult for Arab policy-makers to totally overlook the concerns of other Arab peoples (such as those in Iraq and Israel/Palestine), and to carry on cooperating with an Israel (that remains defiant of numerous UN resolutions) and the United States (which punished Iraq for not abiding by other UN resolutions).

The US-led war and the US efforts to democratise Iraq were also looked at to make the point that current practices continue to prioritise the security interests of the US and its allies at the expense of those of some regional actors. Hence the label used by the critics of the US approach to regional security in the Middle East – 'the New Baghdad Pact' – to stress the top-down character of the US approach. The chapter also reinforced the argument made in Chapter 4 that the post-Cold War era has been characterised by a pro/anti-status quo divide. The US policy of encouraging economic regionalism in the Middle East and the European Union's approach to security in the Euro–Med Region were pointed to as being top-down and stability oriented. It was argued that both the US and EU have designed their respective regional security agendas by keeping their own concerns in mind, leaving those of regional peoples to be addressed in time as a side-effect of economic liberalisation and regionalisation. It was noted that such approaches (that sideline regional actors' concerns) evoke memories of a colonial past; as a result they strengthen the anti-status quo rhetoric of the proponents of the Islamist discourse. The latter put issues such as social and economic justice, human rights, identity and democratisation as well as more basic needs such as subsistence, illiteracy and unemployment on their security agendas. It was argued that these are all security concerns for some people, and would need to be addressed by putting them on security agendas, by adopting alternative practices, and by making use of the agency of non-state actors to address them.

Overall, Part II sought to advance the aims of the book by presenting a critique of post-Cold War security thinking and practices. This was attempted by drawing the contours of post-Cold War debates on Security Studies and offering a critique from a critical perspective. Taking 're-thinking security' seriously requires not only broadening security, but also considering the practical implications of adopting a broader security agenda. One problem with simply broadening the security agenda from a statist perspective without re-conceptualising agency and practice is that these new issues are approached not from the perspective of individuals or social groups but from that of states, and are addressed through tradi-tional practices. The Gulf states' approach to the issue of labour migration was identified as an example of adopting a broader security agenda from a statist perspective. The European Union's approach to security in the Euro–Med Region was criticised for broadening security but not from the perspective of regional actors.

Part II also pointed to non-state actors' practices and argued that they not only voice but also seek to address their own and others' concerns. It was argued that there exists unfulfilled potential in terms of human as well as material resources that could be tapped towards constituting alternative futures. Grassroots organisations (such as the FIS in Algeria and Hamas in Palestine) were pointed to as potential agents to meet a broadened security agenda. However, reliance on their practices could be problematic, it was noted, not the least because some seek to achieve security by creating insecurity for women. This, in turn, highlighted the need for studies to inform the practices of non-state actors and empower them to constitute themselves as agents for emancipatory change. This point was developed in Part III: 'Futures'.

Chapter 6 began by presenting a critical security perspective on think-ing about the future. Here I utilised Beck's argument regarding 'threats to the future' to make two interrelated points. First, it was argued that it is only by thinking and writing about the future that one could raise actors' awareness as to 'threats to the future', what future outcomes may result, and what needs to be done in order to prevent them. Second, the chapter suggested that, as knowledge about the future both shapes and constrains practices, thereby helping constitute the future, an uncritical adoption of existing knowledge produced by prevailing discourses – those that have been complicit in perpetuating regional insecurity in the Middle East – could in itself be construed as a 'threat to the future'.

Indeed, given the conception of theory adopted by students of critical approaches to security (that theory is constitutive of the 'reality' it seeks to explain) it is vital that its proponents do not limit their thinking to 'desired' futures, but also criticise existing knowledge about the future that informs actors' practices in an often unthinking manner. The latter task was taken up in the following section of the chapter, which looked at other plausible futures and their potential practical implications within the Middle Eastern context. These were globalisation, fragmentation, 'clash of civilizations' and democratic peace. It was argued that those who present the future of world politics as one of increasing globalisation treat the search for regional security as a side effect of increasing liberalisation and integration of production and finance. As a result, these approaches sideline issues such as the perpetuation of global inequality by the very same processes. The chapter further argued that both approaches gloss over the structural relationships between different parts of the world, and how state building, democratisation and security maintenance in one part of the world depends (to a certain extent) on keeping other parts of the world non-democratic and insecure. The literature on globalisation as well as democratic peace neglects issues such as the emphasis US policy-makers have put on encouraging 'low-intensity democracies' in the Middle East or the issue of arms transfers between North America, Western Europe and the Middle East.

The chapter also looked at Huntington's vision of the future as a 'clash of civilisations', and that of Kaplan as 'coming anarchy'. It was argued that Kaplan's 'problem-solving' approach to world politics, by overlooking the ways in which human agency has been complicit in creating the dynamics he has identified, has failed to see how human agency may again intervene and alter them. Huntington's thesis was criticised for adopting a similar fatalistic attitude (as well as his failure to understand the fluid character of civilisations and the porous nature of the boundaries between them). It was argued that both fail to reflect upon the potential constitutive effects of their own theorising.

Following an evaluation of other futures, Chapter 6 turned to the theme of 'desired' futures, and presented a preliminary inquiry into whether there exists a potential for the creation of a security community in the Middle East. Adopting the three-tier framework developed by Adler and Barnett as a checklist to assess the potential for the creation of a security community, the chapter pointed to the conditions that could indeed be viewed as conducive for such a development to take place. It was further argued that the very same conditions that could be viewed as propelling regional actors to look towards each other (such as the end of the Cold War, integration of world markets and global warming) could also be viewed as pushing them further apart from each other. In order for such factors to propel regional actors to turn towards each other, as Adler and Barnett expect them to do, actors would need to be presented with an alternative reading of their situation – a reading informed by an alternative conception of security which shows them as 'victims of regional security' rather than each other. The chapter noted that this would require the security community approach developed by Adler and Barnett to be re-worked from a critical perspective by adopting a broadened and deepened conception of security, and by paying more attention to the agency of non-state actors and the mutually constitutive relationship between theory and practice.

Part III, therefore, tried to further the aims of the book by presenting a critical perspective on thinking about the futures of regional security and a critique of other plausible future scenarios. Part III also considered whether unfulfilled potential exists in the Middle East for a security community to be created. Drawing upon the arguments developed in Parts I and II, which sought to point to unfulfilled potential in regional politics, it was argued that there indeed is some potential in terms of both material and human resources that could be tapped to create a security community in this of all regions. Indeed, even the very act of investigating the potential for the creation of a security community constitutes a first step towards its creation by way of pointing to unfulfilled potential immanent in regional politics and emphasising the problems that would have to be addressed on the way.

A security community may be formed by community-minded agents who agree to pool their resources to address security problems by adopting cooperative security practices. The creation of a security community does not require the pre-existence of physical, linguistic or cultural ties among potential members. As Deutsch and his colleagues emphasised, security communities may have humble origins. Actors' willingness to work together to form a community may constitute the necessary conditions initially required to form a security community. Getting the potential members to view regional insecurity itself rather than each other as the threat to their security, in turn, could generate this willingness. Nonstate actors such as intellectuals, who are in a mutually interactive relationship with social movements, could also play crucial roles in helping construct identities that cross physical and psychological borders.

Emphasising the mutually interactive relationship between intellectuals and social movements should not be taken to suggest that the only way for intellectuals to make a change is to get directly involved in political action. They can also intervene by providing a critique of the existing situation, calling attention to what future outcomes may result if necessary action is not taken at present, and by pointing to potential for change immanent in regional politics. Students of security could help create the political space for alternative agents of security to take action by presenting appropriate critiques. It should be emphasised however that such thinking should be anchored in the potential immanent in world politics. The hope is that non-state actors (who may or may not be aware of their potential to make a change) may constitute themselves as agents of security when presented with an alternative reading of their situation.

Thinking about the future becomes even more crucial once theory is conceptualised as constitutive of the 'reality' it seeks to respond to. In other words, our ideas about the future – our conjectures and prognoses – have a self-constitutive potential. What the students of Cold War Security Studies consider as a more 'realistic' picture of the future becomes 'real' through practice, albeit under circumstances inherited from the past. Thinking about what a 'desired' future would look like is significant for the very same reason; that is, in order to be able to turn it into a 'reality' through adopting emancipatory practices. For, having a vision of a 'desired' future empowers people(s) in the present.

Presenting pictures of what a 'desired' future might look like, and pointing to the security community approach as the start of a path that could take us from an insecure past to a more secure future is not to suggest that the creation of a security community is the most likely outcome. On the contrary, the dynamics pointed to throughout the book indicate that there exists a potential for descent into chaos if no action is taken to prevent militarisation and fragmentation of societies, and the marginalisation of peoples as well as economies in an increasingly globalising world. However, these dynamics exist as 'threats to the future' to use Beck's terminology; and only by thinking and writing about them that can one mobilise preventive action to be taken in the present. Viewed as such, critical approaches present not an 'optimistic', but a more 'realistic' picture of the future. Considering how the 'realism' of Cold War Security Studies failed not only when judged by its own standards, by failing to provide an adequate explanation of the world 'out there', but also when judged by the standards of critical approaches, as it was argued, it could be concluded that there is a need for more 'realistic' approaches to regional security in theory and practice.

The foregoing suggests three broad conclusions. First, Cold War Security Studies did not present the 'realistic' picture it purported to provide. On the contrary, the pro-status quo leanings of the Cold War security discourse failed to allow for (let alone foresee) changes such as the end of the Cold War, dissolution of some states and integration of some others. Second, notwithstanding the important inroads critical approaches to security made in the post-Cold War era, much traditionalist thinking remains and maintains its grip over the security practices of many actors. Third, critical approaches offer a fuller or more adequate picture of security in different parts of the world (including the Middle East). Cold War Security Studies is limited not only because of its narrow (military-focused), pro-status quo and state-centric (if not statist) approach to security in theory and practice, but also because of its objectivist conception of theory and the theory/practice relationship that obscured the mutually constitutive relationship between them. Students of critical approaches have sought to challenge Cold War Security Studies, its claim to knowledge and its hold over security practices by pointing to the mutually constitutive relationship between theory and practice and revealing how the Cold War security discourse has been complicit in constituting (in)security in different parts of the world. The ways in which the Cold War security discourse helped constitute the 'Middle East' by way of representing it as a region, and contributed to regional insecurity in the Middle East by shaping security practices, is exemplary of the argument that 'theories do not leave the world untouched'.

The implication of these conclusions for practice is that becoming aware of the 'politics behind the geographical specification of politics' and exploring the relationship between (inventing) regions and (conceptions and practices of) security helps reveal the role human agency has played in the past and could play in the future. An alternative approach to security, that of critical approaches to security, could inform alternative (emancipatory) practices thereby helping constitute a new region in the form of a security community. It should be noted, however, that to argue that 'everything is socially constructed' or that 'all approaches have normative concerns embedded in them' is a significant first step that does not by itself help one adopt emancipatory practices. As long as people rely on traditional practices shaped by the Cold War security discourse – which remains prevalent in the post-Cold War era – they help constitute a 'reality' in line with the tenets of 'realist' Cold War Security Studies. This is why seeking to address evolving crises through traditional practices whilst leaving a critical security perspective to be adopted for the long-term will not work. For, traditionalist thinking and practices, by helping shape the 'reality' 'out there', foreclose the political space necessary for emancipatory practices to be adopted by multiple actors at numerous levels. Hence the need for the adoption of a critical perspective that emphasises the roles human agency has played in the past and could play in the future in shaping what human beings choose to call 'reality'. Generating such an awareness of the potentialities of human agency could enable one to begin thinking differently about regional security in different parts of the world whilst remaining sensitive to regional actors' multiple and contending conceptions of security, what they view as referent(s) and how they think security should be sought in different parts of the world.

After decades of statist, military-focused and zero-sum thinking and practices that privileged the security of some whilst marginalising the security of others, the time has come for all those interested in security in the Middle East to decide whether they want to be agents of a world view that produces more of the same, thereby contributing towards a 'threat to the future', or of alternative futures that try to address the multiple dimensions of regional insecurity. The choice is not one between presenting a more 'optimistic' or 'pessimistic' vision of the future, but between stumbling into the future expecting more of the same, or stepping into a future equipped with a perspective that not only has a conception of a 'desired' future but is also cognisant of 'threats to the future'.

Notes

Introduction

1 The classic on neo-realism is Kenneth N. Waltz's *Theory of International Politics* (1979). For a constructivist critique, see Wendt (1992, 1999).
2 This is not to underestimate Walt's significant contribution to the literature on International Relations theory in general and balance of power in particular.
3 This argument builds upon the insights provided by Wæver (1989) and Booth and Wheeler (1992).
4 What is often meant by 'the end of Arabism' is the decline of interest in Arab unification as a project (see, for example, Faour 1993). Yet, as Shibley Telhami and Michael Barnett (2002: 18) point out, Arabism has been attached different meanings throughout history and 'to presume that Arabism has one particular meaning – for instance, unification – misses the central fact that Arabism has been attached to different projects at different moments'.
5 Briefly during the 1990s, Israel became a proponent of Middle Eastern regionalism. See Peres (1993). For further discussion, see Chapter 4.
6 For similar approaches to security in Europe, see Wæver (1989) and Booth and Wheeler (1992).
7 This, however, is not to suggest that the Middle East does not exhibit the characteristics of a single system. For a discussion, see Gause (1999).
8 See Chapter 2 for further discussion.
9 These four perspectives are ideal types and were adapted from Ibrahim (1996). The terms used to identify these perspectives are not necessarily the ones used by their proponents but were adopted for the sake of clarity. The proponents of these perspectives prefer to use the following terms: the 'Arab world/ homeland'; the 'Arab regional order/system'; the 'Islamic/Muslim world'; the 'Euro–Med/Mediterranean region'.

1 Pasts, presents and futures of security

1 It has become less and less meaningful to speak of the Third World since the term was first coined during the 1950s when their under-developed economies were thought to bring this otherwise diverse group of states together under the banner 'Third World'. Throughout the years, as they began to diversify in economic terms, and especially after the dissolution of the 'Second World', the use of the term 'Third World' has become increasingly problematic. It is equally problematic to use the term within the security context; despite certain similarities like low levels of social cohesion and weak political infrastructures, it still makes little sense to put India, Kuwait and Somalia all in the same basket. See Thomas (1987) for a discussion of the prob-

lematic character of the term. Also see the debate in *Third World Quarterly*, 1(1–3) (1979).

2 Michael Howard, one of the founders of the Institute of Strategic Studies noted that he initially suggested that the Institute be called the 'Institute for the Study of International Security'. Its current name was adopted, according to Howard, thinking that it would 'sell' better. See Howard (1989: 12). The Soviet Union, having its own 'nationalities question', opted for the term 'state security' instead of 'national security'. See Thomas (1989b: 176).

3 See Bull (1968) for a discussion of and response to some of the criticisms brought against academic strategists during the 1950s and 1960s. For other critics of Cold War Security Studies, see Green (1966, 1973) and Rapoport (1964).

4 On the impact of the Cold War on US academia, see Chomsky *et al.* (1997). Also see Booth (1997) for an autobiographical account.

5 Booth (1997: 118 n. 38) and Wyn Jones (1999: 94) distinguish between Traditional Security Studies and Critical Security Studies invoking Horkheimer's distinction between traditional and critical theory. See Horkheimer (1982: 188–243). Keith Krause (1998: 299) uses the terms 'mainstream', 'traditional', 'orthodox' and 'neo-realist' interchangeably to refer to the same body of thought. Bill McSweeney (1999: 23–78) looks at Cold War Security Studies together with some post-Cold War critics under the title 'Objectivist Approaches to International Security'.

6 See Independent Commission (1982), Møller (1992), Sharp (1980, 1985) and McInnes (1992: 130–1).

7 A significant exception to zero-sum thinking among the 'golden-age' strategic thinkers is Schelling (1963, 1966). Also see Lebow (1997).

8 Many of the ideas produced by Alternative Security thinkers were similar to those voiced by the feminists. See Tickner (1992).

9 For a brief overview of the debate on the concept of and conditions for peace, see Adler (1998a).

10 For a recent attempt to incorporate Critical Theory into Peace Research, see Broadhead (1997).

11 See *inter alia* Mathews (1990), Walker (1990a), Booth (1991a, 1991b), Buzan (1991a, 1991b), Kolodziej (1992), Shaw (1993), Lipschutz (1995) and Tickner (1995). See also Booth and Herring (1994: esp. pp. 120–38) for a critical overview of some of these works.

12 It is worth noting here that Ayoob, like Buzan, is influenced by the ideas of the International Society approach of Hedley Bull. See Ayoob (2002).

13 For critiques of Buzan, see Smith (1991) and McSweeney (1996: 81–93). For a recent critique of Ayoob, see Barnett (2002a). Pasha (1996) is critical of both Buzan and Ayoob.

14 This, however, should not be taken to suggest that the trajectory of Third World state formation is bound to follow that of Western state formation. As Barnett (2002a: 61) maintains, suggesting that would amount to 'historical determinism at its most teleological and simplest'.

15 For a neo-realist explanation of ethnic conflict see Posen (1993).

16 Ayoob is also aware of these interconnections. Yet his preferred approach is not that of re-thinking security relations in the world at large by paying due attention to the linkages between insecurities of Western and Third World states, but one which allows for Third World states to replicate the Western experience without the 'Amnesty International and the U.N. Human Rights Commission breathing down their necks' (2002: 45).

17 For a political economy perspective, see Sadowski (1993). For a feminist perspective, see Mernissi (1993: esp. pp. 1–10, 1996: vii–xv).

18 For example, female illiteracy rate in Morocco is 78.3 per cent, Algeria 63.1 per cent, Egypt 79.8 per cent, North Yemen 74.8 per cent, and South Yemen 96.6 per cent (note that the figures are from the pre-unification period). Iraq, the 'rogue state' of the Middle East, has 12.5 per cent female illiteracy. See Mernissi (1996: 58).
19 High illiteracy rate is included in Galtung's definition of 'structural violence'. See Galtung (1969: 169).
20 See Williams (1998) for an elucidation of the adoption of an objectivist conception of theory by neo-realists as a political practice that helped to constitute the world in line with their wishes.
21 Steve Smith (1997: 509) refers to those issues that are considered as 'problems' by policy-makers as merely 'the tip of the iceberg'.
22 For an exploration of this process within the Middle Eastern context, see Edward W. Said's trilogy: *Orientalism* (1978 [1995a]), *The Question of Palestine* (1992), *Covering Islam: How the Media and Experts Determine How We See the Rest of the World* (1997).
23 The Catholic Church is not exactly a powerless institution. The character of its power, however, is different from that of states.
24 It should be noted that states increasingly resort to collective defence and alliance warfare as experienced in the Gulf War (1991).
25 What roles states might assume in meeting a broader security agenda, however, is an empirical question and will be addressed in the following chapters with reference to empirical illustrations.

2 Representations of the Middle East during the Cold War

1 Wigen and Lewis (1997: 71).
2 On Mahan, see Crowl (1986).
3 According to Koppes (1976: 95), Mahan had very little knowledge of the affairs of this part of the world and had to be persuaded by the editor of *The National Review* to write this piece.
4 Still, there was considerable interest among US missionaries who began to regularly visit the Holy Lands starting from the early nineteenth century. Robert D. Kaplan's study entitled *The Arabists* (1993) tells the story of these individuals. On the *National Geographic*'s representations of the Middle East, see Little (2002: 9–42).
5 Said's *Orientalism* first came out in 1978. Page references are to the 1995 edition.
6 The School opened one year after the conclusion of the Sykes–Picot agreement between Britain and France partitioning the former Ottoman territories in the Middle East. See Adelson (1995: 62). On the Sykes–Picot agreement, see Monroe (1981: 32–7).
7 On the role played by some members of the Royal Geographical Society during the First World War, see Heffernan (1996).
8 It should nevertheless be noted that the 1950s (and to a certain extent the 1960s) were a period of transition not only for the Middle East but also the United States; it was during this period that the United States gradually took over the responsibility of maintaining regional security from Britain whose ailing economy led to a relinquishing of imperial responsibilities. On this period of transition, see Little (2002: esp. pp. 43–75).
9 On the 'Arabist' tradition, see Kaplan (1993).
10 See Kramer (2001) for a contrary view.
11 For an appreciation of Said's contribution to academic studies of the Middle East, see Abu-Laban (2001); for a sceptical overview of *Orientalism*'s impact, see Kramer (2001); for a critical review of Kramer's study, see Bilgin (2004b).

12 Cox's (1981: 182) formulation is 'all theories are *for* someone and *for* some purpose'.
13 For useful summaries, see Gause (1999: 13–17), Tibi (1993: 47–8) and Said Aly (1996: 26–8).
14 Dessouki and Matar included all members of the Arab League when drawing their mental map of the 'Arab Regional System', namely: Algeria, Bahrain, Djibouti, Egypt, Iraq, Jordan, Kuwait, Lebanon, Libya, Mauritania, Morocco, Oman, PLO, Qatar, Saudi Arabia, Somalia, Sudan, Syria, Tunisia, Yemen and the United Arab Emirates.
15 See Little (2002: 77–115) for a brief account of the emergence and development of the US–Israeli 'special relationship'.
16 See Rodinson (1981: esp. pp. 1–47). Fatima Mernissi (1995) relates how the Berber identity of Moroccan peoples was downplayed in favour of an Arab identity that was perceived to be a better tool to fight French colonialism.
17 For incisive overviews of Israel's security thinking see Horowitz (1993) and Evron (1993).

3 Practices of security during the Cold War

1 In 1954, the Anglo-Persian Oil Company became the British Petroleum Company.
2 My emphasis.
3 On Turkey's policies toward the Middle East during the 1960s, see Bağcı (1990) and Criss and Bilgin (1997).
4 It is interesting to note here that the draft of the treaty included a stronger clause on security cooperation, which was removed from the final agreement following objection by the British Foreign Office (Gomaa 1977: 7).
5 'The Alexandria Protocol'. Online. Available: <http://192.203.180.62/mlas/alexp.html> (accessed 8 October 1999).
6 'The Charter of the Arab League'. Online. Available: <http://192.203.180.62/mlas/charter.html> (accessed 9 October 1999).
7 In order to increase the number of listeners to his broadcasts, Nasser asked for the programmes of famous Egyptian singer Umm Khaltum to be scheduled immediately before or after his addresses. 'Distant Divas', on BBC Radio 4, 24 October 1998, 11:00 pm. See Lynch (1999: 61–2) for a discussion on the use of the radio in the Arab world during the 1950s and 1960s.
8 At this stage many Gulf states were not yet independent. Jordan, on the other hand, tried to balance the two groups.
9 On Saudi policies, see Safran (1988).

4 Representations of the Middle East in the post-Cold War era

1 See Bulut (2003) for a collection of articles published in the Arab press during the crisis and the war.
2 The terms 'East' and 'West' gained new meanings during the Cold War when they were used to refer to the two blocs headed by the United States and the Soviet Union.
3 Nasser himself emphasised the Arab, Islamic and African dimensions of Egypt's identity. See Dessouki (1989: 31–41). On the other hand, the 'Egyptian' identity could not openly be discussed. Karawan (2002: 157) notes that Hakim's book on Egyptian identity, where the author propounded a 'neutral' foreign policy, could not be published until after Nasser's death.
4 For an overview of the collective Euro–Arab relationship from 1973 onwards, see Jawad (1992), Calleja (1997) and Joffé (1999). For official EU

documentation, see http://europe.eu.int/comm/external-relations/euromed/ (accessed 14 July 2003).

5 Turkish policy-makers have their own reasons for hesitating to locate Turkey in the Mediterranean. For a discussion, see Bilgin (2004c).

6 See Galtung and Fischer (2003), for a more recent endorsement.

7 The actions taken outside the Middle East are no exception to this generalisation. For, in the aftermath of the September 11 attacks against targets in New York and Washington, DC, Osama bin Laden made it clear that the referent for his Islamist discourse on security was the Muslim Middle East; see Chapter 5.

8 The extent to which al-Qaida fits this generalisation is debatable. For a discussion, see Kaldor (2003b).

9 For a discussion, see Barnett and Gause (1998).

10 See Clark (2003) for a critique of the military focus in US policy-making toward Iraq.

5 Practices of security in the post-Cold War era

1 These are pre-war and pre-UN sanctions figures.

2 For a discussion on the reactions of Arab policy-makers and intellectuals to the end of the Cold War and the Gulf Crisis, see Karawan (1994: 433–54).

3 An exception to this tendency was the increasing collaboration between Israeli, Palestinian and other Arab peace movements and especially women's movements before the Peace Process was derailed. These groups of Arab women crossed the conceptual borders of the 'Arab regional order' to work with the Israeli women. See Sharoni (1996: 107–26).

4 For a discussion on civil society in theory and in practice in the Arab world, see Schwedler (1995: 1–30).

5 It is interesting to note here that Huveydi's article (2003) was published in the Saudi-financed daily newspaper *al-Sharq al-Awsat* (the Middle East).

6 Libya was excluded from the conference.

7 'Bulletin EU 6-1996'. Online. Available http://www.europa.eu.int/abc/doc/off/bull/en/9606/i1038.html (accessed November 25, 1998).

8 Available: http://europa.eu.int/comm/europaid/projects/med/financial/1995-2002.pdf (accessed 10 December 2003).

9 For discussions on the possible effects of European Security and Defense Policy on Euro–Mediterranean Partnership, see Youngs (2002) and Biscop (2003).

10 'In Osama bin Laden's own Words – Al-Jazeera TV – October 7, 2000'. Online. Available: www.september11.com/OsamaSpeeches.htm (accessed on 10 December 2003). See Esposito (2002) on Osama bin Laden and al-Qaida.

11 On the different uses of *jihad* by Muslims, see Esposito (2002) and Noor (2003).

12 On the attempts to engage in 'collective Islamic diplomacy' during the Gulf War, see Dessouki (1995: 259–60).

13 For an insider's account of the Madrid Conference and its aftermath, see Victor (1995).

14 Invitations to the bilateral track were issued to Lebanon, Syria, Jordan, Palestinian representatives, Egypt, Algeria, Tunisia, Morocco, Mauritania, Saudi Arabia, Kuwait, Bahrain, the United Arab Emirates, Qatar, Oman, Yemen, the European Union, Turkey, Canada, EFTA representatives, Japan and China.

15 Syria, Lebanon, Iran and the Sudan boycotted the summit.

16 This, however, is not to suggest that there was a direct relationship between progress in bilateral and multilateral tracks. For a discussion, see Kaye (2001, esp. pp. xviii–xx, 5–10, 23–9).

17 Kenneth Pollack (2003) proposed forming a similar institution but called it 'Middle Eastern NATO'.
18 This is not to argue that non-state actors have been able to influence the decisions of their policy-makers. As Jerrold D. Green (1986) has pointed out, the difference between 'popular *interest* in' policies and 'popular *influence* on' them cannot be underestimated. Yet, as Chapter 1 argued, the role non-state actors play in shaping the security agenda should not merely be seen as one of influencing governmental policy-making. These actors can be influential through their own actions (also referred to as 'grassroots statecraft', see Marsh 1995) or by drawing the limits of what is possible and what is not (for a discussion within the Jordanian context, see Lynch 1998–99, 1999, 2002; also see Lynch 2003 for a discussion regarding the broader Arab context).
19 On the impact of sanctions, see Arnove (2000).

6 Alternative futures for security in the Middle East

1 For an overview of neo-functionalism see Trankholm-Mikkelsen (1991); for a critique, see McSweeney (1999: 133–7).
2 On communication and knowledge as power, see Cox (1996c).
3 The economies of Gulf states are almost wholly oil-based. If oil is excluded from calculations, regional states' participation into global trade (with the exception of Israel, Tunisia and Turkey) is not very significant. The ratio of non-oil merchandise to gross domestic product (GDP) in the Middle East – excluding Turkey and Israel – is 6.1 per cent. Compared with 11.5 per cent in Latin America (another oil-producing region) this is very low. See Derviş and Shafik (1998) and Henwood (1993: 8).
4 Roger Owen (1999: 224) notes that Lebanon during the 1950s and 1960s is another exception.
5 This support is provided through economic aid as well as workers' remittances. See Kubursi (1999: 301–11) and Derviş and Shafik (1998).
6 Libya and Algeria are also oil and natural gas producers.
7 The 'Washington consensus' entails a series of measures such as fiscal discipline, tax reform, financial and trade liberalisation, privatisation and promotion of foreign direct investment that are designed to deal with the economic problems of developing countries. See Hunt (1999: 18).
8 Rosenau (1995) uses the term 'localisation' to refer to the process referred to here as fragmentation.
9 Robert D. Kaplan's article entitled 'The Coming Anarchy' (1994b) and book *The Ends of the Earth: A Journey at the Dawn of the 21st Century* (1996), despite their many shortcomings, received much acclaim in the mass media and were quoted by US policy-makers (including President Clinton) on numerous occasions. See Dalby (1996: 492 n. 12–14).
10 Kaplan bases his thesis on Homer-Dixon's conclusions in his 1991 article that had traces of environmental determinism. See Homer-Dixon (1991).
11 Robert W. Cox's conception of fragmentation as a form of 'resistance' to globalising forces is exemplary of the 'critical' (as opposed to 'problem-solving') approach to international phenomena. To put it in a nutshell, Cox's argument is that globalisation's perpetuation of inequalities worldwide could set social forces (such as social coalitions, labour movements, democratisation struggles) that might in the future lay down the groundwork for an alternative ('postglobalisation') world order. Although Cox is not unaware of the potential for disintegration and violent conflict dormant in the struggles led by such social forces, he maintains that the disintegration of some units could result in the formation of new alliances thereby bringing about a new order (see Cox

1996b: 156; for further elaboration on this point, see Cox 1999). What is significant about Cox's scenario is that it introduces an element of human agency to reverse the trends set by the forces of globalisation – a factor that is missing from Kaplan's approach. As Chapter 1 argued, critical theories of International Relations in general and critical security thinking in particular share Cox's stress on the role social forces could play as agents for change. However, if the efforts of these actors are to add up to constitute a transformative force, Cox's scenario would need to incorporate an image of a broader community to which these smaller groups could attach themselves. Cox indeed recognises the need to organise at the 'national, regional and world levels' for 'the creation of a vibrant civil society inspired by a strong spirit of solidarity at the community level and, by linkage with other strong communities in other countries, at the transnational or global level' (Cox 1999: 27). The point here is that, in the absence of (the image of) a broader political community to which social forces could attach themselves, the agency of non-state actors may fail to add up to create a counter-hegemonic bloc as Cox expects them to do.

12 Iraq, Syria and Turkey share the Tigris–Euphrates basin, Israel, Jordan and the Palestinian Authority share the Jordan basin, and Egypt and Sudan share the Nile basin. See Gleick (1994: 41–50) and Abu-Taleb (1994: 253).

13 It is argued that Middle Eastern countries have the highest median cost of water supply and sanitation in the world. See Abu-Taleb (1994: 254).

14 See Kaplan (2001) on Huntington.

15 On depictions of Islam and Muslims in the West, see Said (1997); on the problems involved in failing to distinguish between Islam and Islamism, see Tibi (1998b).

16 The term 'low-intensity democracy' is from Robinson (1996: 1–12).

17 'National Elections in the Middle East and the Arab World Since 1980', *Middle East Report* (Winter 1998) 16.

18 Adler and Barnett expect these three tiers as three phases in the building of a security community. Accordingly they expect the first tier to be set up before considering the second one. Yet, as Wiberg (2000) has argued, different dynamics exist in different parts of the world (as with Scandinavia) and what Adler and Barnett expect to see in the final stage may emerge first in some contexts. Accordingly, I have chosen to consider all three tiers when discussing the potential for the creation of a security community in the Middle East.

19 This, of course, is not to suggest that no attempts were made to construct security communities. Western Europe, for instance, is often viewed as close as it gets to a security community. See Wæver (1998: 69–118).

20 See Janice Bially Mattern (2000) on the roles 'gatekeepers' play in the creation of security communities.

21 The role Palestinian intellectual Edward W. Said has played over the years cannot be underestimated. See Khalidi (1998a) and Aruri and Shuraydi (2001).

22 A step in this direction has already been taken as a part of a project entitled 'The Search for Common Ground in the Middle East', undertaken by two non-governmental organisations: US-based 'Search for Common Ground' and 'The European Centre for Common Ground'. The title of the initiative is 'Vision 2020' and comprises a series of eleven newspaper articles written by intellectuals from across the Middle East on their visions of the region's future in the year 2020 and beyond. The articles were published over October–December 1999 simultaneously in nine newspapers and five languages and reaching millions across the Middle East. The series, funded by the Search for Common Ground together with UNESCO, was designed to enable peoples of the Middle

East to become aware of other regional peoples' hopes, dreams and fears about the future. It was also hoped that the series would raise peoples' awareness of their common humanity and common interests in cooperating for a better future. Building upon the experiences of this project, a similar one could also be launched to facilitate the creation of a security community in the future. See the first eight articles at http://www.sfcg.org/mideast_media/vision2020__index.html (accessed 10 October 1999).

23 A beginning has already been made in the field of inter-faith dialogue to try and find a common ground for believers of different religions to peacefully coexist. Communication on such issues could help develop the shared meanings and intersubjective understandings that could generate the knowledge on which the project of creating a security community could be based. This was the theme of the 1998 Conference entitled 'Religion and Pluralism' organised by the British Society for Middle Eastern Studies, held at the Centre for the Study of Islam and Christian–Muslim Relations, Selly Oak Colleges, Birmingham, UK.

24 The negotiations broke down in 1994 for reasons to do with the set up of the agenda (that did not include nuclear weapons).

25 Iver Neumann makes a similar point with reference to region building. See Neumann (1999: 139–40). Also see McSweeney (1999: 196).

26 The rate for the Middle East is 8.8 per cent. For the US it is 6.3, for Europe 6.1, for South Asia 3.8. See Sadowksi (1993: 12).

References

Aarts, P. (1999) 'The Middle East: A Region Without Regionalism or the End of Exceptionalism?' *Third World Quarterly*, 20(5): 911–25.

Abdel Aal, A.M.S.A. (1986) 'The Superpowers and Regional Security in the Middle East', in M. Ayoob (ed.) *Regional Security in the Third World: Case Studies From Southeast Asia and the Middle East*, London: Croom Helm.

AbuKhalil, A. (1992) 'A New Arab Ideology? The Rejuvenation of Arab Nationalism', *Middle East Journal*, 46(1): 22–36.

Abu-Laban, Y. (2001) 'Humanizing the Oriental: Edward Said and Western Scholarly Discourse', in N. Aruri and M.A. Shuraydi (eds) *Revising Culture, Reinventing Peace: the Influence of Edward W. Said*, New York: Olive Branch Press.

Abu-Rabi, I.M. (1996) 'Editor's Introduction', in I.M. Abu-Rabi (ed.) *Islamic Resurgence: Challenges, Directions and Future Perspectives – A Roundtable with Professor Khurshid Ahmad*, Lahore: Institute of Policy Studies.

Abū-Sulaymān, A.A. (1993) *Towards An Islamic Theory of International Relations: New Directions for Methodology and Thought*, Hendon, VA: The International Institute of Islamic Thought.

Abu-Taleb, M.F. (1994) 'Regional Cooperation in Water Resource Management', in E. Boulding (ed.) *Building Peace in the Middle East: Challenges for States and Civil Society*, Boulder, CO: Lynne Rienner.

Acharya, A. (1992) 'Regionalism and Regime Security in the Third World: Comparing the Origins of the ASEAN and the GCC', in B. Job (ed.) *The Insecurity Dilemma: National Security in the Third World States*, Boulder, CO: Lynne Rienner.

—— (1997) 'The Periphery as the Core: The Third World and Security Studies', in K. Krause and M. Williams (eds) *Critical Security Studies: Concepts and Cases*, London: UCL Press.

Adelson, R. (1995) *London and the Invention of the Middle East: Money, Power and War, 1902–1922*, New Haven: Yale University Press.

Adler, E. (1998a) 'Condition(s) of Peace', *Review of International Studies*, 24 (December): 165–91.

—— (1998b) 'Seeds of Peaceful Change: The OSCE's Security Community-Building Model', in E. Adler and M. Barnett (eds) *Security Communities*, Cambridge: Cambridge University Press.

Adler, E. and Barnett, M. (eds) (1998a) *Security Communities*, Cambridge: Cambridge University Press.

—— (1998b) 'Security Communities in Theoretical Perspective', in E. Adler and M. Barnett (eds) *Security Communities*, Cambridge: Cambridge University Press.

—— (1998c) 'A Framework for the Study of Security Communities', in E. Adler and M. Barnett (eds) *Security Communities*, Cambridge: Cambridge University Press.

Agnew, J. (1998) *Geopolitics: Re-visioning World Politics*, London: Routledge.

Agnew, J. and Corbridge, S. (1995) *Mastering Space: Hegemony, Territory and International Political Economy*, New York: Routledge.

Akşin, A. (1991) *Atatürk'ün Dış Politika İlkeleri ve Diplomasisi* [Atatürk's Principles in Foreign Policy-making and Diplomacy], Ankara: Türk Tarih Kurumu Basımevi.

Alagappa, M. (1995) 'Regionalism and Conflict Management: A Framework for Analysis', *Review of International Studies*, 21(4): 359–87.

Al-Amrani, I. (2003) 'Arab League Faces Uncertain Future', *Middle East Times*. Online. Available: http://www.metimes.com/2K3/issue2003-22/eg/arab_league_faces.htm (accessed 12 December 2003).

Aliboni, R. (1997–98) 'Confidence-building, Conflict Prevention, and Arms Control in the Euro–Mediterranean Partnership', *Perceptions*, (December–February): 73–86.

Allott, P. (1998) 'The Future of the Human Past', in K. Booth (ed.) *Statecraft and Security: The Cold War and Beyond*, Cambridge: Cambridge University Press.

Al-Mashat, A.M. (1985) *National Security in the Third World*, Boulder, CO: Westview Press.

Altunışık, M.B. (1999) 'Soğuk Savaş Sonrası Dönemde Türkiye-İsrail İlişkileri' [Turkish–Israeli Relations in the Post-Cold War Era] in M.B. Altunışık (ed.) *Türkiye ve Ortadoğu: Tarih Kimlik Güvenlik* [Turkey and the Middle East: History Identity Security], İstanbul: Boyut.

Ambler, R. (1995) 'Gandhian Peacemaking', in P. Smoker, R. Davies and B. Munske (eds) *A Reader in Peace Studies*, Oxford: Pergamon.

Anderson, B. (1991) *Imagined Communities: Reflections on the Origins and Spread of Nationalism*, London: Verso.

Anderson, L. (1990) 'Policy-making and Theory-building: American Political Science and the Islamic Middle East', in H. Sharabi (ed.) *Theory, Politics and the Arab World: Critical Responses*, New York: Routledge.

Arnove, A. (ed.) (2000) *Iraq Under Siege: The Deadly Impact of Sanctions and War*, Cambridge, MA: South End Press.

Aruri, N. and Shuraydi, M.A. (eds) (2001) *Revising Culture Reinventing Peace: The Influence of Edward W. Said*, New York: Olive Branch Press.

Asad, B. (2003) 'Esad: Tehlikenin Ortasındayız, Baş Hedefiz' [We Are in the Midst of Danger, We Are the Prime Target], in F. Bulut (ed.) *Arapların Gözüyle Irak İşgali: Binbir Gece Savaşları* [The Invasion of Iraq Through Arab Eyes: One Thousand and One Nights Wars], İstanbul: Berfin.

Ash, T.G. (1999) 'The Puzzle of Central Europe', *New York Review of Books*, (18 March): 19–23.

Ashton, N.J. (1993) 'The Hijacking of a Pact: The Formation of the Baghdad Pact and Anglo-American Tensions in the Middle East, 1955–1958', *Review of International Studies*, 25: 123–37.

Attali, J. (1999) *1492*, trans, M.A. Kılıçbay. Ankara: İmge Yayınları.

Attiyah, G. (2003) 'Wanted in Iraq: a Roadmap to Free Elections'. Online. Available: http://www.opendemocracy.net/debates/article-2-95-1541.jsp (accessed 28 November 2003).

Awad, I. (1994) 'The Future of Regional and Subregional Organization in the

Arab World', in D. Tschirgi (ed.) *The Arab World Today*, Boulder, CO: Lynne Rienner.

Ayoob, M. (1986) 'Regional Security in the Third World', in M. Ayoob (ed.) *Regional Security in the Third World: Case Studies From Southeast Asia and the Middle East*, London: Croom Helm.

—— (1994) 'Security in the Third World: Searching for the Core Variable', in N.A. Graham (ed.) *Seeking Security and Development: The Impact of Military Spending and Arms Transfers*, Boulder, CO: Lynne Rienner.

—— (1995) *The Third World Security Predicament: State Making, Regional Conflict and the International System*, London: Lynne Rienner.

—— (1997) 'Defining Security: A Subaltern Realist Perspective', in K. Krause and M. Williams (eds) *Critical Security Studies: Concepts and Cases*, London: UCL Press.

—— (2002) 'Inequality and Theorising in International Relations: The Case for Subaltern Realism', *International Studies Review*, 4(3): 27–48.

Azar, E.E. and Moon, C. (1988) 'Legitimacy, Integration and Policy Capacity: "Software" Side of Third World National Security', in E.E. Azar and C. Moon (eds) *National Security in the Third World: The Management of Internal and External Threats*, Aldershot: Edward Elgar.

Azzam, M. (1991) 'The Gulf Crisis: Perceptions in the Muslim World', *International Affairs*, 67(1): 470–87.

Bağcı, H. (1990) *Demokrat Parti Dönemi Dış Politikası* [Foreign Policy During the Democratic Party Era], Ankara: İmge.

Baldwin, D. (1995) 'Security Studies and the End of the Cold War', *World Politics*, 48(October): 117–41.

—— (1997) 'The Concept of Security', *Review of International Studies*, 23(1): 5–26.

Barber, B.R. (1992) 'Jihad vs. McWorld', *The Atlantic Monthly*, 269: 53–63.

—— (1995) *Jihad vs. McWorld: How Globalism and Tribalism Are Reshaping the World*, New York: Ballantine Books.

Barkawi, T. and Laffey, M. (1999) 'The Imperial Peace: Democracy, Force and Globalisation', *European Journal of International Relations*, 5(4): 403–34.

Barnett, M. (1996–97) 'Regional Security After the Gulf War', *Political Science Quarterly*, 111(4): 597–618.

—— (1998) *Dialogues in Arab Politics: Negotiations in Regional Order*, New York: Columbia University Press.

—— (2002a) 'Radical Chic? Subaltern Realism: A Rejoinder', *International Studies Review*, 4(3): 49–62.

—— (2002b) 'What Happened to the Big Bang? Arab Politics After 9/11', *Middle East Policy*, 9(4): 80–3.

Barnett, M. and Gause III, F.G. (1998) 'Caravans in Opposite Directions: Society, State, and the Development of Community in the Gulf Cooperation Council', in E. Adler and M. Barnett (eds) *Security Communities*, Cambridge: Cambridge University Press.

Beck, U. (1992) *Risk Society: Towards a New Modernity*, London: Sage.

—— (2003) 'The Silence of Words: On Terror and War', *Security Dialogue*, 34(3): 255–67.

Bedirhan, A. (2003) 'Araplar Solda Sıfır Kaldılar' [The Arabs were Surpassed], in F. Bulut (ed.) *Arapların Gözüyle Irak İşgali: Binbir Gece Savaşları* [The Invasion of Iraq Through Arab Eyes: One Thousand and One Nights Wars], İstanbul: Berfin.

Beinin, J. (1999) 'The Working Class and Peasantry in the Middle East: From Economic Nationalism to Neoliberalism', *Middle East Report*, 210: 18–22.

Bennett, B. (1990) 'Arab-Muslim Cases of Nonviolent Struggle', in R.E. Crow, P. Grant and S.E. Ibrahim (eds) *Arab Nonviolent Political Struggle in the Middle East*, Boulder, CO: Lynne Rienner.

Beriker-Atiyas, N. (1997) 'The Kurdish Conflict in Turkey: Issues, Parties, and Prospects', *Security Dialogue*, 28(4): 439–52.

Bernstein, S., Lebow, R.N., Stein, J.G. and Weber, S. (2000) 'God Gave Physics the Easy Problems: Adopting Social Science to an Unpredictable World', *European Journal of International Relations*, 6(1): 43–76.

Bially Mattern, J. (2000) 'Taking Identity Seriously', *Cooperation and Conflict*, 35(3): 299–308.

Bibi, G. (1995) 'The NGO Phenomenon in the Arab World – An Interview with Ghanem Bibi', *Middle East Report*, 193: 26–7.

Bigo, D. (2002) 'Security and Immigration: Toward a Critique of the Governmentality of Unease', *Alternatives*, 27 (special issue): 63–92.

Bilgin, P. (1999) 'Security Studies: Theory Practice', *Cambridge Review of International Affairs*, 12(2): 31–42.

—— (2000–01) 'The Middle East Peace Process in Wor(l)d Politics', *Arab Studies Journal*, 8(2)–9(1): 196–201.

—— (2002) 'Beyond Statism in Security Studies? Human Agency and Security in the Middle East', *The Review of International Affairs*, 2(1): 100–18.

—— (2003) 'Individual and Societal Dimensions of Security', *International Studies Review*, 5(2): 203–22.

—— (2004a) 'Whose Middle East? Geopolitical Inventions and Practices of Security', *International Relations*, 18(1): 17–33.

—— (2004b) 'Is the "Orientalist" Past the Future of Middle East Studies?' *Third World Quarterly*, 25(2) 423–33.

—— (2004c) 'A Return to "Civilisational Geopolitics" in the Mediterranean? Changing Geopolitical Images of the European Union and Turkey in the Post-Cold War Era', *Geopolitics*, 9(2): 269–91.

Bilgin, P. and Morton, A.D. (2002) 'Historicising Representations of Failed States: Beyond the Cold War Annexation of the Social Sciences?' *Third World Quarterly*, 23(1): 55–80.

Bilgin, P., Booth, K. and Wyn Jones, R. (1998) 'Security Studies: The Next Stage?' *Naçao e Defesa*, 84: 131–57.

Binyan, L. (1993) 'Civilization Grafting: No Culture is an Island', *Foreign Affairs*, 72(4): 19–21.

Biscop, S. (2003) 'Opening up the ESDP to the South: A Comprehensive and Cooperative Approach to Euro–Mediterranean Security', *Security Dialogue*, 34(2): 183–97.

Blackwill, R.D. and Stürmer, M. (eds) (1997) *Allies Divided: Transatlantic Policies for the Greater Middle East*, Cambridge, MA: MIT Press.

Bleiker, R. (2000) *Popular Dissent, Human Agency and Global Politics*, Cambridge: Cambridge University Press.

Bobrow, D.B. (1996) 'Complex Insecurity: Implications of a Sobering Metaphor', *International Studies Quarterly*, 40(4): 435–50.

Booth, K. (1991a) 'The Interregnum: World Politics in Transition', in K. Booth (ed.) *New Thinking About Strategy and International Security*, London: Harper Collins.

—— (1991b) 'Security and Emancipation', *Review of International Studies*, 17(4): 313–26.

—— (1991c) 'War, Security and Strategy: Towards a Doctrine for Stable Peace', in K. Booth (ed.) *New Thinking on Strategy and International Security*, London: Harper Collins.

—— (1994a) 'A Security Regime in Southern Africa: Theoretical Considerations', *South African Perspectives*, 30.

—— (1996) '75 Years On: Rewriting the Subject's Past – Reinventing its Future', in K. Booth, S. Smith and M. Zalewski (eds) *International Theory: Positivism and Beyond*, Cambridge: Cambridge University Press.

—— (1997) 'Security and Self: Reflections of a Fallen Realist', in K. Krause and M. Williams (eds) *Critical Security Studies: Concepts and Cases*, London: UCL Press.

—— (1998a) 'Cold Wars of the Mind', in K. Booth (ed.) *Statecraft and Security: The Cold War and Beyond*, Cambridge: Cambridge University Press.

—— (1998b) 'Security Within Global Transformation?' in K. Booth (ed.) *Statecraft and Security: The Cold War and Beyond*, Cambridge: Cambridge University Press.

—— (1999a) 'Nuclearism, Human Rights and Constructions of Security (Part I)', *The International Journal of Human Rights*, 3(2): 1–24.

—— (1999b) 'Three Tyrannies', in T. Dunne and N. Wheeler (eds) *Human Rights in Global Politics*, Cambridge: Cambridge University Press.

Booth, K. and Dowdy, L. (1982) 'Soviet Security Interests in the Indian Ocean Region', in D.R. Jones (ed.) *Soviet Armed Forces Review Annual*, 6: 327–77.

Booth, K. and Herring, E. (1994) *Keyguide to Information Sources in Strategic Studies*, London: Mansell.

Booth, K. and Vale, P. (1997) 'Critical Security Studies and Regional Insecurity: The Case of Southern Africa', in K. Krause and M. Williams (eds) *Critical Security Studies: Concepts and Cases*, London: UCL Press.

Booth, K. and Wheeler, N.J. (1992) 'Contending Philosophies About Security in Europe', in C. McInnes (ed.) *Strategy and Security in the New Europe*, London: Routledge.

Boulding, E. (1994) 'Hope for the Twenty-first Century: NGOs and People's Networks in the Middle East', in E. Boulding (ed.) *Building Peace in the Middle East: Challenges for States and Civil Society*, Boulder, CO: Lynne Rienner.

—— (1995) 'Image and Action in Peace Building', in E. Boulding and K.E. Boulding (eds) *The Future: Images and Processes*, London: Sage.

Boulding, K. (1978) *Stable Peace*, Austin: University of Texas Press.

—— (1995) 'Part I: Introduction', in E. Boulding and K.E. Boulding (eds) *The Future: Images and Processes*, London: Sage.

Bölükbaşı, S. (1992) *Türkiye ve Yakınındaki Ortadoğu* [Turkey and the Near Middle East], Ankara: Dış Politika Enstitüsü.

Brands, H.W. (1991) *Inside the Cold War: Loy Henderson and the Rise of the American Empire, 1918–1961*, New York: Oxford University Press.

Broadhead, L. (1997) 'Beyond the Traditions: Casting a Critical Light on Peace Research', in L. Broadhead (ed.) *Issues in Peace Research, 1997–98: Theory and Practice*, Bradford: Department of Peace Studies, University of Bradford.

Buheiry, M.R. (1989) *The Formation and Perception of the Modern Arab World: Studies by Marwan R. Buheiry*, L.I. Conrad (ed.), Princeton, NJ: The Darwin Press Inc.

Bull, H. (1968) 'Strategic Studies and its Critics', *World Politics*, 20(4): 593–605.

—— (1969) 'International Theory: The Case for a Classical Approach', in K. Knorr and J.N. Rosenau (eds) *Contending Approaches to International Politics*, Princeton, NJ: Princeton University Press.

Bulloch, J. and Darwish, A. (1993) *Water Wars: Coming Conflicts in the Middle East*, London: Gollancz.

Bulut, F. (ed.) (2003) *Arapların Gözüyle Irak İşgali: Binbir Gece Savaşları* [The Invasion of Iraq Through Arab Eyes: One Thousand and One Nights Wars], İstanbul: Berfin.

Bush, G. (2003a) 'President Bush Outlines Progress in Operation Iraqi Freedom', 16 April 2003. Online. Available: http://www.whitehouse.gov/news/releases/2003/04/iraq.20030416-9.html (accessed 28 July 2003).

—— (2003b) 'President Bush Discusses Freedom in Iraq and the Middle East', Remarks by the President at the 20th Anniversary of The National Endowment for Democracy. Online. Available: www.whitehouse.gov/news/releases/2003/11/primt/20031106-2.htm (accessed 18 December 2003).

Buzan, B. (1983; 2nd edn, 1991a) *People, States and Fear: An Agenda for International Security Studies in the post-Cold War Era*, London: Harvester Wheatsheaf.

—— (1991b) 'Is International Security Possible?' in K. Booth (ed.) *New Thinking on Strategy and International Security*, London: Harper Collins.

Buzan, B. and Roberson, B.A. (1993) 'Europe and the Middle East: Drifting Towards Societal Cold War?' in O. Wæver, B. Buzan, M. Kelstrup, P. Lemaitre (eds) *Identity, Migration and the New Security Agenda in Europe*, London: Pinter.

Buzan, B., Wæver, O. and de Wilde, J. (1998) *Security: A New Framework for Analysis*, Boulder, CO: Lynne Rienner.

Calleja, J. (1994) 'Educating for Peace in the Mediterranean: A Strategy for Peace-Building', in E. Boulding (ed.) *Building Peace in the Middle East: Challenges for States and Civil Society*, Boulder, CO: Lynne Rienner.

—— (1997) 'The Euro–Mediterranean Process After Malta: What Prospects?', *Mediterranean Politics*, 2(2): 1–22.

Campbell, D. (1992) *Writing Security: United States Foreign Policy and the Politics of Identity*, Manchester: Manchester University Press.

—— (1993) *Politics Without Principle: Sovereignty, Ethics, and the Narratives of the Gulf War*, Boulder, CO: Lynne Rienner.

Campbell, J.C. (1958) *Defence of the Middle East: Problems of American Policy*, New York: Harper and Brothers.

Chalk, P. (2003) 'Non-military Security in the Wider Middle East', *Studies in Conflict & Terrorism*, 26: 197–214.

Chaudhry, K.A. (1997) *The Price of Wealth: Economies and Institutions in the Middle East*, Ithaca, NY: Cornell University Press.

Chomsky, N., Kalznelson, I., Lewontia, R.C., Montgomery, D., Nader, L., Ohmann, R., Slever, R., Wallerstein, I. and Zinn, H. (1997) *The Cold War and the University: Toward an Intellectual History of the Postwar Years*, New York: The New Press.

Chubin, S. (1984) 'Soviet Policy Towards Iran and the Gulf', in C. Tripp (ed.) *Regional Security in the Middle East*, Aldershot: Gower with the IISS.

Clark, I. (1973) 'Collective Security in Asia: Towards a Framework for Soviet Diplomacy', *The Round Table* (October): 473–81.

—— (1997) *Globalisation and Fragmentation: International Relations in the Twentieth Century*, New York: Oxford University Press.

Clark, W.K. (2003) 'Iraq: What Went Wrong', *The New Work Review of Books*, (23 October): 52–4.

Clinton, W.J. (1993) 'Confronting the Challenges of a Broader World' (Address to the UN General Assembly, New York City, 27 September 1993) *Dispatch*, 4(39). Online. Available: http://www.state.gov/www/publications/dispatch/index.html (accessed 10 February 1999).

Cohen, R. (1994) 'Pacific Unions: A Reappraisal of the Theory that "Democracies Do Not Go to War with Each Other"', *Review of International Studies*, 20(3): 207–23.

'The Commission Document on Peace Building in the Middle East' (1994) in E. Boulding (ed.) *Building Peace in the Middle East: Challenges for States and Civil Society*, Boulder, CO: Lynne Rienner.

Cox, R.W. (1981) 'Social Forces, States and World Orders', *Millennium: Journal of International Studies*, 10(2): 126–58.

—— (1996a) 'Global *Perestroika*', in *Approaches to World Order*, Cambridge: Cambridge University Press.

—— (1996b) 'Towards a Posthegemonic Conceptualisation of World Order: Reflections on the Relevancy of Ibn Khaldun', in *Approaches to World Order*, Cambridge: Cambridge University Press.

—— (1996c) 'Civilizations in World Political Economy', *New Political Economy*, 1(2): 141–56.

—— (1999) 'Civil Society at the Turn of the Millennium: Prospects for an Alternative World Order', *Review of International Studies*, 25(1): 3–28.

Criss, N.B. and Bilgin, P. (1997) 'Turkish Foreign Policy Toward the Middle East', *Middle East Review of International Affairs* 1(1). Online. Available: http://meria.idc.ac.il/journal/1997/issue1/jvol1no1in.html (accessed 11 January 2004).

Crowl, P.A. (1986) 'Alfred Thayer Mahan: The Naval Historian', in P. Paret (ed.) *Makers of Modern Strategy: From Machiavelli to the Nuclear Age*, New York: Oxford University Press.

Cumings, B. (1998) 'Boundary Displacement: Area Studies and International Studies During and After the Cold War', in C. Simpson (ed.) *Universities and Empire: Money and Politics in the Social Sciences During the Cold War*, New York: New Press.

Dajani, S. (1998) 'Nonviolent Resistance in the Occupied Territories', in S. Zunes, L.R. Kurtz and B. Asher (eds) *Nonviolent Social Movements: A Geographical Perspective*, Oxford: Blackwell.

Dalby, S. (1990) *Creating the Second Cold War: The Discourse of Politics*, London: Pinter.

—— (1991) 'Critical Geopolitics: Discourse, Difference and Dissent', *Environment and Planning D: Society and Space*, 9: 261–83.

—— (1996) 'The Environment as Geopolitical Threat: Reading Robert Kaplan's "Coming Anarchy"', *Ecumene*, 3(4): 472–96.

David, S.R. (1991) 'Explaining Third World Alignment', *World Politics*, 43(2): 233–56.

Davison, R. (1960) 'Where is the Middle East?' *Foreign Affairs*, 38(4): 665–75.

Dawisha, A. (1982) 'The Soviet Union in the Arab World: The Limits to Superpower Influence', in A. Dawisha and K. Dawisha (eds) *The Soviet Union in the Middle East: Perspectives and Policies*, London: Heinemann.

—— (1984) 'Saudi Arabia's Search for Security', in C. Tripp (ed.) *Regional Security in the Middle East*, Aldershot: Gower with IISS.

Der Derian, J. (1992) *Antidiplomacy: Spies, Terror, Speed, and War*, Oxford: Blackwell.

—— (1995) 'The Value of Security: Hobbes, Marx, Nietzsche, Baudrillard', in R.D. Lipschutz (ed.) *On Security*, New York: Columbia University Press.

Derviş, K. and Shafik, N. (1998) 'The Middle East and North Africa: A Tale of Two Futures', *Middle East Journal*, 52(4): 505–16.

Dessouki, A.E.H. (1989) 'Nasser and the Struggle for Independence', in W.R. Louis and R. Owen (eds) *Suez 1956: The Crisis and its Consequences*, Oxford: Clarendon Press.

—— (1995) 'The Impact of Islamism on the Arab System', in L. Guazzone (ed.) *The Islamist Dilemma: The Political Role of Islamist Movements in the Contemporary Arab World*, Berkshire: Ithaca Press.

Deudney, D. (1990) 'The Case Against Linking Environmental Degradation and National Security', *Millennium: Journal of International Studies*, 19(3): 461–76.

Deutsch, K.W., Burrell, S.A., Kann, R.A., Lee, Jr. M., Lichterman, M., Lindgren, R.E., Loewenheim, F.L. and Van Wagenen, R.W. (1957) *The Political Community in the North Atlantic Area: International Organization in the Light of Historical Experience*, Princeton, NJ: Princeton University Press.

Devetak, R. (1995) 'Incomplete States: Theories and Practices of Statecraft', in J. Macmillan and A. Linklater (eds) *Boundaries in Question: New Directions in International Relations*, London: Pinter.

—— (1999) 'Theories, Practices and Postmodernism in International Relations', *Cambridge Review of International Affairs*, 12(2): 61–76.

Doumato, E.A. (1999) 'Women and Work in Saudi Arabia: How Flexible Are Islamic Margins?' *Middle East Journal*, 53(4): 568–83.

Doyle, M.W. (1986) 'Liberalism and World Politics', *American Political Science Review*, 80(4): 1151–69.

Duffield, M. (1990) 'Absolute Distress: Structural Causes of Hunger in Sudan', *Middle East Report*, (September–October): 4–11.

Dunn, D.J. (1991) 'Peace Research versus Strategic Studies', in K. Booth (ed.) *New Thinking on Security and Strategy*, London: Harper Collins.

Eickelman, D.F. (1989) *The Middle East: An Anthropological Approach*, Englewood Cliffs, NJ: Prentice Hall.

—— (1997) 'Trans-state Islam and Security', in S.H. Rudolph and J. Piscatori (eds) *Transnational Religion and Fading States*, Boulder, CO: Westview Press.

Eickelman, D.F. and Piscatori, J. (1996) *Muslim Politics*, Princeton, NJ: Princeton University Press.

El-Erian, M.A. and Fischer, S. (1996) 'Is MENA a Region? The Scope for Regional Integration', IMF Working Paper, WP/96/30.

El Sayyid, M.K. (1994) 'The Third Wave of Democratisation in the Arab World', in D. Tschirgi (ed.) *The Arab World Today*, Boulder, CO: Lynne Rienner.

Emerson, M. and Tocci, N. (2003) 'The Rubic Cube of the Wider Middle East'. Online. Available: http://www.ceps.be/Commentary/Apr03/EmersonTocci.php (accessed 29 November 2003).

Enloe, C. (1990) *Bananas, Beaches and Bases: Making Feminist Sense of International Politics*, Berkeley, CA: University of California Press.

—— (1993) *The Morning After: Sexual Politics at the End of the Cold War*, Berkeley, CA: University of California Press.

—— (1996) 'Margins, Silences, and Bottom Rungs: How to Overcome the Under-estimation of Power in the Study of International Relations', in K. Booth, S. Smith and M. Zalewski (eds) *International Theory: Positivism and Beyond*, Cambridge: Cambridge University Press.

Esposito, J.L. (1990) *The Iranian Revolution, Its Global Impact*, Miami: Florida International University Press.

—— (1993) 'Islamic Movements, Democratisation and U.S. Foreign Policy', in P. Marr and W. Lewis (eds) *Riding the Tiger: The Middle East Challenge After the Cold War*, Boulder, CO: Westview Press.

—— (1995) *The Islamic Threat: Myth or Reality?* New York: Oxford University Press.

—— (2002) *Unholy War: Terror in the Name of Islam*, Oxford: Oxford University Press.

Evron, Y. (1993) 'Deterrence Experience in the Arab–Israeli Conflict', in A. Kleiman and A. Levite (eds) *Deterrence in the Middle East: Where Theory and Practice Converge*, Boulder, CO: Westview.

Ezzat, D. (2003) 'What Collective Arab Order?' *Al Ahram Weekly*, 24–30 April.

Faksh, M.A. (1993) 'Withered Arab Nationalism', *Orbis*, (Summer): 425–38.

Faour, M. (1993) *The Arab World After Desert Storm*, Washington, DC: United States Institute of Peace Press.

Farber, H.S. and Gowa, J. (1995) 'Polities and Peace', *International Security*, 20(2): 123–46.

Farrell, T. (2002) 'Constructivist Security Studies: Portrait of a Research Program', *International Studies Review*, 4(1): 49–72.

Fawcett, L. and Hurrell, A. (eds) (1995) *Regionalism in World Politics: Regional Organization and International Order*, New York: Oxford University Press.

Feldman, S. and Toukan, A. (1997) *Bridging the Gap: A Future Security Architecture for the Middle East*, Oxford: Rowman & Littlefield.

Fergany, N. (1994) 'Arab Labor Migration and the Gulf Crisis', in D. Tschirgi (ed.) *The Arab World Today*, Boulder, CO: Lynne Rienner.

Forgacs, D. (ed.) (1988) *A Gramsci Reader: Selected Writings, 1916–1935*, London: Lawrence and Wishart.

Foucault, M. (1980) 'Interview with Michel Foucault, "Questions of Geography"', in C. Gordon (ed.) *Power/Knowledge: Selected Interviews and Other Writings, 1972–1977*, Sussex: The Harvester Press.

Fraser, C. (1997) 'In Defence of Allah's Realm: Religion and Statecraft in Saudi Foreign Policy Strategy', in S.H. Rudolph and J. Piscatori (eds) *Transnational Religion and Fading States*, Boulder, CO: Westview Press.

Freedman, L. and Karsh, E. (1991) 'How Kuwait Was Won: Strategy in the Gulf War', *International Security*, 16(2): 5–41.

Friedman, T.L. (1999a) '*DOS*capital', *Foreign Policy*, (Fall): 110–16.

—— (1999b) '*DOS*capital 2.0', *Foreign Policy*, (Fall): 121–5.

—— (2002a) *Longitudes and Attitudes: The World in the Age of Terrorism*, New York: Anchor Books.

—— (2002b) 'Techno Logic', *Foreign Policy*, (March–April): 64–5.

—— (2002c) 'State of Progress', *Foreign Policy*, (March–April): 66–7.

Fromkin, D. (1989) *A Peace to End All Peace: Creating the Modern Middle East, 1914–1922*, London: Andre Deutsch.

Galtung, J. (1969) 'Violence, Peace and Peace Research', *Journal of Peace Research*, 6(3): 167–92.

—— (1989) *Nonviolence and Israel/Palestine*, Honolulu: Institute of Peace, University of Hawaii.

—— (1995) 'Europe 1989: The Role of Peace Research and the Peace Movement', in R. Sunney and M.E. Salla (eds) *Why the Cold War Ended: A Range of Interpretations*, Westport, CT: Greenwood Press.

—— (1996) *Peace by Peaceful Means: Peace and Conflict, Development and Civilization*, London: Sage with PRIO.

Galtung, J. and Fischer, D. (2003) 'A Peace Proposal for the Middle East', *Peace Review*, 15: 67–9.

Gamble, A. and Payne, A. (eds) (1996) *Regionalism and World Order*, London: Macmillan.

Garnett, J. (1987) 'Strategic Studies and its Assumptions', in J. Baylis, K. Booth, J. Garnett and P. Williams (eds) *Contemporary Strategy*, vol. I, New York: Holmes and Meier.

Garrison, J. and Phipps, J. with Shivpuri, P. (1989) *The New Diplomats: Citizens as Ambassadors for Peace*, Devon: Green Books.

Gause III, F.G. (1999) 'Systemic Approaches to Middle East International Relations', *International Studies Review*, 1(1): 11–31.

Gleick, P.H. (1994) 'Reducing the Risks of Conflict Over Fresh Water Resources in the Middle East', in J. Isaac and H. Shuval (eds) *Water and Peace in the Middle East*, Amsterdam: Elsevier.

Gomaa, A.M. (1977) *The Foundation of the League of Arab States: Wartime Diplomacy and Inter-Arab Politics, 1941 to 1945*, London: Longman.

Gordon, T.E. (1900) 'The Problems of the Middle East', *The Nineteenth Century*, xlvii(277): 413–24.

Grant, P. (1990) 'Nonviolent Political Struggle in the Occupied Territories', in R.E. Crow, P. Grant and S.E. Ibrahim (eds) *Arab Nonviolent Political Struggle in the Middle East*, Boulder, CO: Lynne Rienner.

Gray, C. (1992) 'New Directions for Strategic Studies? How Can Theory Help Practice?' *Security Studies*, 1(4): 610–35.

Green, J.D. (1986) 'Are Arab Politics Still Arab?' *World Politics*, 38(4): 611–25.

—— (1999) 'The Information Revolution and Political Opposition in the Middle East', *MESA Bulletin*, 33: 21–7.

Green, P. (1966) *Deadly Logic: The Logic of Nuclear Deterrence*, Ohio: Ohio University Press.

—— (1973) 'Strategy, Politics and Social Scientists', in M.A. Kaplan (ed.) *Strategic Thinking and its Moral Implications*, Chicago, IL: The University of Chicago Press.

Guazzone, L. (1997) 'A Map and Some Hypotheses for the Future of the Middle East', in L. Guazzone (ed.) *The Middle East in Global Change: The Politics and Economics of Interdependence Versus Fragmentation*, London: Macmillan.

Gubser, P. (2002) 'The Impact of NGOs on State and Non-State Relations in the Middle East', *Middle East Policy*, 9(1): 139–48.

Gulf Cooperation: The Path to Progress and Unity, (1983) n.p.: Ministry of Information, State of Qatar.

Gusterson, H. (1999) 'Missing the End of the Cold War in International Security', in J. Weldes, M. Laffey, H. Gusterson and R. Duvall (eds) *Cultures of Insecurity: States, Communities, and the Production of Danger*, Minneapolis, MN: University of Minnesota Press.

Hadley, G. (1971) *CENTO – The Forgotten Alliance: A Study of the Central Treaty*

226   *References*

Organization, Sussex: Institute for the Study of International Organisation, University of Sussex.

Haftendorn, H. (1991) 'The Security Puzzle: Theory-building and Discipline-building in International Security', *International Studies Quarterly*, 35(1): 3–17.

Haidar, R. (1996) 'Women and Food Security', *Civil Society*, 55(6). Online. Available: http://www.ned.org/page_3/ICDS/1996/aug/woman.html (accessed 3 March 1998).

Hajjar, L. and Niva, S. (1997) '(Re)Made in the USA: Middle East Studies in the Global Era', *Middle East Report*, 205: 2–9.

Halliday, F. (1987) 'State, Society and International Relations: A Second Agenda', *Millennium: Journal of International Studies*, 16(2): 215–29.

—— (1990) 'The Ends of the Cold War', *New Left Review*, 180: 5–23.

—— (2002) 'New World, but the Same Old Disorder', *Observer*, 10 March.

Hamad, W. (2003) 'Who Speaks for the Iraqi People', *Eclipse*, 15. Online. Available: http://www.eclipsereview.org/issue15/iraqipeople.htm (accessed 12 December 2003).

Hanafi, H. (2000) 'The Middle East, in Whose World? (Primary Reflections)', in B.O. Utvik and K. Vikør (eds) *The Middle East in a Globalized World*, Bergen: Nordic Society for Middle Eastern Studies.

Hassouna, H.A. (1975) *The League of Arab States and Regional Disputes: A Study of Middle East Conflicts*, New York: Oceana Publications.

Haşane, R. (2003) 'Yeni Bağdat Paktı' [The New Baghdad Pact], in F. Bulut (ed.) (2003) *Arapların Gözüyle Irak İşgali: Binbir Gece Savaşları* [The Invasion of Iraq Through Arab Eyes: One Thousand and One Nights Wars], İstanbul: Berfin.

Hay, D. (1968) *Europe: The Emergence of An Idea*, Edinburgh: Edinburgh University Press.

Heffernan, M. (1996) 'Geography, Cartography and Military Intelligence: The Royal Geographical Society and the First World War', *Transactions of the Institute of British Geographers*, 21(3): 504–33.

Heikal, M.H. (1978) 'Egyptian Foreign Policy', *Foreign Affairs*, 56(4): 714–27.

—— (1992) *Illusions of Triumph An Arab View of the Gulf War*, London: Harper Collins.

—— (1996) *Secret Channels: The Inside Story of Arab–Israeli Peace Negotiations*, London: Harper Collins.

Heisbourg, F. (1997) 'The United States, Europe, and Military Force Projection', in R.D. Blackwill and M. Stürmer (eds) *Allies Divided: Transatlantic Policies for the Greater Middle East*, Cambridge, MA: MIT Press.

Held, D. (2001) 'Violence and Justice in a Global Age'. Online. Available: http://www.opendemocracy.net/debates/article-2-49-144.jsp (accessed 17 December 2003).

Held, D. and McGrew, A. (1999) 'The End of the Old Order? Globalisation and the Prospects for World Order', *Review of International Studies*, 24(December): 219–43.

Hentsch, T. (1996) *Hayali Doğu: Batı'nın Akdenizli Doğu'ya Politik Bakışı* [Imagining the Middle East]. Translated by Aysel Bora. İstanbul: Metis.

Henwood, D. (1993) 'Global Economic Integration: The Missing Middle East', *Middle East Report*, 184: 7–8.

Hettne, B. and Inotai, A. (eds) (1994) *The New Regionalism: Implications for Global Development and International Security*, Helsinki: Forssan Kirjapaina Oy [UNU World Institute for Development Economics Research].

Hettne, B. and Söderbaum, F. (1998) 'The New Regionalism Approach', *Politeia*, 17(3): 6–21.

Hobsbawm, E. and Ranger, T.O. (eds) (1983) *The Invention of Tradition*, Cambridge: Cambridge University Press.

Hodgson, M.G.S. (1974) *The Venture of Islam: Conscience and History in a World Civilization*, Vol. I, *The Classical Age of Islam*, Chicago: The University of Chicago Press.

Hoffman, M. (1987) 'Critical Theory and the Inter-paradigm Debate', *Millennium: Journal of International Studies*, 16(2): 231–49.

—— (1993) 'Agency, Identity and Intervention', in M. Hoffman and I. Forbes (eds) *Political Theory, International Relations and the Ethics of Intervention*, London: Macmillan.

Hoffman, S. (1995) 'An American Social Science: International Relations', in J. Der Derian (ed.) *International Theory: Critical Investigations*, London: Macmillan.

Hollis, R. (1994) 'Western Security Strategy in South West Asia', in A. Ehteshami (ed.) *From the Gulf War to Central Asia: Players in the New Great Game*, Exeter: University of Exeter Press.

—— (2003) 'Getting out of the Iraq Trap', *International Affairs*, 79(1): 23–35.

Homer-Dixon, T.F. (1991) 'On the Threshold: Environmental Changes as Causes of Acute Conflict', *International Security*, 16(1): 76–116.

Horkheimer, M. (1982) 'Traditional and Critical Theory', in *Critical Theory: Selected Essays*, trans. M.J. O'Connell and others, New York: Continuum.

Horowitz, D. (1993) 'The Israeli Concept of National Security', in A. Yaniv (ed.) *National Security and Democracy in Israel*, Boulder, CO: Lynne Rienner.

Hourani, C. (1947) 'The Arab League in Perspective', *Middle East Journal*, 1(2): 125–36.

Howard, M. (1989) 'IISS – The First Thirty Years: A General Overview', *Adelphi Papers*, 235: 10–19.

Hudson, M. (1999) 'Arab Integration: An Overview', in M. Hudson (ed.) *The Middle East Dilemma: The Politics and Economics of Arab Integration*, New York: Columbia University Press.

Hunt, D. (1999) 'Development Economics, the Washington Consensus and the Euro-Mediterranean Partnership Initiative', in G. Joffe (ed.) *Perspectives on Development: The Euro–Mediterranean Partnership*, London: Frank Cass.

Huntington, S.S. (1993) 'The Clash of Civilizations?' *Foreign Affairs*, 72(3): 22–49.

—— (1998) *The Clash of Civilizations and the Remaking of World Order*, London: Touchstone.

Hurd, N. (2003) 'Iraqi Food Security in Hands of Occupying Powers'. Online. Available: http://www.merip.org/mero/mero120203.html (accessed 2 December 2003).

Hurrell, A. and Woods, N. (1995) 'Globalisation and Inequality', *Millennium: Journal of International Studies*, 24(3): 447–70.

Huveydi, F. (2003) 'Arap Rejimleri Uyuyor mu?' [Are the Arab Regimes Asleep?] *Radikal*, 8 November.

Huysmans, J. (1995) 'Migrants As a Security Problem: Dangers of Securitizing Societal Issues', in R. Miles and D. Thränhardt (eds) *Migration and European Integration: The Dynamics of Inclusion and Exclusion*, London: Pinter.

—— (2002) 'Defining Social Constructivism in Security Studies: The Normative Dilemma of Writing Security', *Alternatives*, 27 (special issue): 41–62.

Ibrahim, S.E. (1994) 'Arab Elites and Societies After the Gulf Crisis', in D. Tschirgi (ed.) *The Arab World Today*, Boulder, CO: Lynne Rienner.
—— (1996) 'Future Visions of the Arab Middle East', *Security Dialogue*, 27(4): 425–36.
Ibrahim, Y.M., Cockburn, A. and Gopal, N. (2003) 'A Post-War Arab World – Three Views', *Washington Report on Middle East Affairs*, 22(4): 1–8.
Inbar, E. and Sandler, S. (eds) (1995) 'Special Issue: Middle Eastern Security: Prospects for an Arms Control Regime', *Contemporary Security Policy*, 16(1).
Independent Commission on Disarmament and Security Issues (1982) *Common Security: A Programme for Disarmament*, London: Pan Books.
Ismael, T.Y. and Ismael, J. (1990) 'Middle East Studies in the United States', in T.Y. Ismael (ed.) *Middle East Studies: International Perspectives on the State of the Art*, New York: Praeger.
Jacoby, T. and Sasley, B.A. (2002) 'Introduction: Redefining Security in the Middle East', in T. Jacoby and B.E. Sasley (eds) *Redefining Security in the Middle East*, Manchester: Manchester University Press.
Jawad, H. (1992) *The Euro–Arab Dialogue: A Study in Collective Diplomacy*, Reading: Ithaca Press.
Jentleson, B.W. and Kaye, D.D. (1998) 'Security Status: Explaining Regional Security Cooperation and its Limits in the Middle East', *Security Studies*, 8(1): 204–38.
Job, B.L. (1992a) *The Insecurity Dilemma: National Security of Third World States*, Boulder, CO: Lynne Rienner.
—— (1992b) 'The Insecurity Dilemma: National, Regime, and State Securities in the Third World', in B.L. Job (ed.) *The Insecurity Dilemma: National Security of Third World States*, Boulder, CO: Lynne Rienner.
Joffe, G. (ed.) (1999) *Perspectives on Development: The Euro–Mediterranean Partnership*, London: Frank Cass.
Joffe, J. (1984) 'Europe's American Pacifier', *Survival*, 26(4): 174–81.
Johnson, L.K. (1993) 'Smart Intelligence', *Foreign Policy*, 89: 53–69.
Johnson, P. and Tucker, J. (1975) 'Middle East Studies Network in the United States', *MERIP Reports*, 38: 3–20, 26.
Jones, D. (1999) *Cosmopolitan Mediation? Conflict Resolution and the Oslo Accords*, Manchester: Manchester University Press.
Jones, P. (1997) 'Arms Control in the Middle East: Some Reflections on ACRS', *Security Dialogue*, 28(1): 57–70.
Jouejati, M. (1996) 'Water Politics as High Politics: The Case of Turkey and Syria', in H.J. Barkey (ed.) *Reluctant Neighbour: Turkey's Role in the Middle East*, Washington, DC: United States Institute of Peace Press.
Jünemann, A. (2002) 'From the Bottom to the Top: Civil Society and Transnational Non-governmental Organisations in the Euro–Mediterranean Partnership', *Democratization*, 9(1): 87–105.
Kaldor, M. (1990) *The Imaginary War: Understanding East–West Conflict*, Oxford: Basil Blackwell.
—— (1997) 'The Revolutions of 1989', in G.A. Lopez and N.J. Myers (eds) *Peace and Security: The Next Generation*, Lanham, MD: Rowman & Littlefield.
—— (2003a) 'Iraq – the Democratic Option'. Online. Available: http://www.opendemocracy.net/debates/article-2-95-1579.jsp (accessed 28 November 2003).
——(2003b) 'Terrorism as Regressive Globalisation'. Online. Available: http://www.opendemocracy.net/debates/article-3-77-1501.jsp (accessed 12 December 2003).

Kaplan, F. (1983) *The Wizards of Armageddon*, Stanford, CA: Stanford University Press.

Kaplan, R. (1993) *The Arabists: The Romance of an American Elite*, New York: The Free Press.

—— (1994a) 'There is No "Middle East"', *The New York Times Magazine*, (February 20): 42–3.

—— (1994b) 'The Coming Anarchy', *Atlantic Monthly*, (February): 44–76.

—— (1996) *The Ends of the Earth: A Journey at the Dawn of the 21st Century*, London: Papermac.

—— (2001) 'Looking the World in the Eye', *The Atlantic Monthly*, (December): 68–82.

—— (2002a) 'Bad News is Next', *Foreign Policy*, (March–April): 65.

—— (2002b) 'Say Your Prayers', *Foreign Policy*, (March–April): 68–9.

—— (2002c) 'Freedom From Language', *Foreign Policy*, (March–April): 69–70.

Karaosmanoğlu, A.L. and Taşhan, S. (eds) (1987) *Middle East, Turkey and the Atlantic Alliance*, Ankara: Foreign Policy Institute.

Karawan, I.A. (1994) 'Arab Dilemmas in the 1990s: Breaking Taboos and Searching for Signposts', *Middle East Journal*, 48(3): 433–54.

—— (2002) 'Identity and Foreign Policy: The Case of Egypt', in S. Telhami and M. Barnett (eds) *Identity and Foreign Policy in the Middle East*, Ithaca: Cornell University Press.

Karpat, K. (ed.) (1975) *Turkish Foreign Policy in Transition*, Leiden: E.J. Brill.

Kaye, D.D. (2001) *Beyond the Handshake: Multilateral Cooperation in the Arab–Israeli Peace Process, 1991–1996*, New York: Columbia University Press.

Keddie, N. (1973) 'Is There a Middle East?' *International Journal of Middle East Studies*, 4(3): 255–71.

Kemp, G. (1991) *The Control of the Middle East Arms Race*, Washington, DC: Carnegie Endowment for International Peace.

Khadduri, M. (1957) 'The Problem of Regional Security in the Middle East', *Middle East Journal*, 11(1): 12–22.

Khadduri, M. and Ghareeb, G. (1997) *War in the Gulf, 1990–91: The Iraq–Kuwait Conflict and Its Implications*, New York: Oxford University Press.

Khalidi, R. (1998a) 'Edward W. Said and the American Public Sphere: Speaking Truth to Power', *Boundary 2*, 25(2): 161–77.

—— (1998b) 'The "Middle East" as a Framework for Analysis: Re-mapping a Region in the Era of Globalisation', *Comparative Studies of South Asia, Africa and the Middle East*, xviii(1): 74–81.

—— (2003) 'The Middle East as an Area in an Era of Globalisation', in A. Mirsepassi, A. Basu and F. Weaver (eds) *Localizing Knowledge in a Globalising World: Recasting the Area Studies Debate*, Syracuse, NY: Syracuse University Press.

Khalidi, W. (1991) 'Why Some Arabs Support Saddam', in M. Sifry and C. Cerf (eds) *The Gulf War Reader*, New York: Times Books and Random House.

Khalilzad, Z. (1997) 'Challenges in the Greater Middle East', in D.C. Gompert and F.S. Larrabee (eds) *America and Europe: A Partnership for a New Era*, Cambridge: Cambridge University Press.

Kharrazi, K. (2003) 'On Iranian Foreign Policy with Dr. Kamal Kharazzi'. Online. Available: http://www.mfa.gov.ir/News/English/documents/doc1265.htm (accessed 29 November 2003).

Khouri, R.G. (2002) 'Politics and Perceptions in the Middle East After September

11'. Online. Available: http://www.conconflicts.ssrc.org/mideast/khouri (accessed 14 December 2003).

Kirkpatrick, J.J. (1993) 'The Modernizing Imperative: Tradition and Change', *Foreign Affairs*, 72(4): 22–4.

Klein, B.S. (1994) *Strategic Studies and World Order*, Cambridge: Cambridge University Press.

Kolodziej, E.A. (1992) 'What is Security and Security Studies? Lessons from the Cold War', *Arms Control*, 13(1): 1–32.

Koppes, C.R. (1976) 'Captain Mahan, General Gordon, and the Origins of the Term "Middle East"', *Middle Eastern Studies*, 12(4): 95–8.

Korany, B. (1994) 'National Security in the Arab World: The Persistence of Dualism', in D. Tschirgi (ed.) *The Arab World Today*, Boulder, CO: Lynne Rienner.

—— (1997) 'The Old/New Middle East', in L. Guazzone (ed.) *The Middle East in Global Change: The Politics and Economics of Interdependence versus Fragmentation*, London: Macmillan.

—— (1999) 'The Arab World and the New Balance of Power in the New Middle East', in M. Hudson (ed.) *The Middle East: The Politics and Economics of Arab Integration*, New York: Columbia University Press.

Korany, B., Brynen, R. and Noble, P. (1993) 'The Analysis of National Security in the Arab Context: Restating the State of the Art', in B. Korany, P. Noble and R. Brynen (eds) *The Many Faces of National Security in the Arab World*, London: Macmillan.

Kramer, M. (1997) 'The Middle East, Old and New', *Daedalus*, 126(2): 89–112.

—— (2001) *Ivory Towers on Sand: the Failure of Middle Eastern Studies in America*, Washington, DC: Washington Institute for Near East Policy.

Krause, K. (1998) 'Critical Theory and Security Studies: The Research Programme of "Critical Security Studies"', *Cooperation and Conflict*, 33(3): 298–333.

Krause, K. and Williams, M. (1996) 'Broadening the Agenda of Security Studies: Politics and Methods', *Mershon International Studies Review*, 40(2): 229–54.

—— (eds) (1997a) *Critical Security Studies: Concepts and Cases*, London: UCL Press.

—— (1997b) 'From Strategy to Security: Foundations of Critical Security Studies', in K. Krause and M. Williams (eds) *Critical Security Studies: Concepts and Cases*, London: UCL Press.

Krippendorf, E. (1987) 'The Dominance of American Approaches in International Relations', *Millennium: Journal of International Studies*, 16(2): 207–14.

Kubálková, V. (1998) 'Reconstructing the Discipline: Scholars as Agents', in V. Kubálková, N. Onuf and P. Kowert (eds) *International Relations in a Constructed World*, New York: M.E. Sharpe.

Kubursi, A.A. (1999) 'Prospects for Arab Economic Integration After Oslo', in M.C. Hudson (ed.) *Middle East Dilemma: The Politics and Economics of Arab Integration*, New York: Columbia University Press.

—— (2001) 'The Arab Economy in Western Eyes', in N. Aruri and M.A. Shuraydi (eds) *Revising Culture Reinventing Peace: The Influence of Edward W. Said*, New York: Olive Branch Press.

Kugler, R.L. (1997) 'Military Force Projection', in R. Blackwill and M. Stürmer (eds) *Allies Divided: Transatlantic Policies for the Greater Middle East*, Cambridge, MA: MIT Press.

Kuniholm, B.R. (1980) *The Origins of the Cold War in the Near East: Great Power Con-*

flict and Diplomacy in Iran, Turkey, and Greece, Princeton, NJ: Princeton University Press.

Kürkçüoğlu, Ö. (1972) *Türkiye'nin Arap Ortadoğu'suna Karşı Politikası* [Turkish Policy Towards Arab Middle East], Ankara: Sevinç Matbaası.

Lacoste, Y. (1998) *Coğrafya Savaşmak İçindir* [Geography is for Waging War], trans. Ayşin Arayıcı, İstanbul: Özne.

Lake, A. (1993) 'From Containment to Enlargement' (Address at the School of Advanced International Studies, Johns Hopkins University, Washington, DC, September 21, 1993), *Dispatch*, 4(39). Online. Available: http://www.state.gov/www/publications/dispatch/index.html (accessed 10 February 1999).

—— (1994) 'Confronting Backlash States', *Foreign Affairs*, 73(2): 45–55.

Lake, D. and Morgan, P.M. (eds) (1997) *Regional Orders: Building Security in the New World*, Pennsylvania: The Pennsylvania State University Press.

Lambert, R.D. (1989) 'DoD, Social Science and International Studies', *ANNALS, AAPSS*, 502: 94–107.

Larsen, H. (2000) 'Concepts of Security in the European Union After the Cold War', *Australian Journal of International Affairs*, 54(3): 337–56.

Layne, C. (1994) 'Kant or Cant: The Myth of Democratic Peace', *International Security*, 19(2): 5–49.

Lebow, R.N. (1997) 'Thomas Schelling and Strategic Bargaining', *International Journal*, 51(3): 555–76.

Lebow, R.N. and Risse-Kappen, T. (eds) (1995) *International Relations Theory and the End of the Cold War*, New York: Columbia University Press.

Lemann, N. (2003) 'After Iraq: The Plan to Remake the Middle East', *The New Yorker*, February 17–24. Online. Available: http://newyorker.com/fact/content/?030217fa_fact (accessed 24 September 2003).

Lenczowski, G. (1980) *The Middle East in World Affairs*, Ithaca: Cornell University Press.

Lewis, B. (1990) 'The Roots of Muslim Rage', *The Atlantic Monthly* (September 1990). Online. Available: http://www.theatlentic.com/issues/90sep/rage.htm (accessed 12 November 1999).

—— (1994) *The Shaping of the Modern Middle East*, New York: Oxford University Press.

Lewis, E.L. (2003) 'In the Aftermath of the Presidential Visit: The Gulf Emirates and American Interests in the Middle East'. Online. Available: http://www.inthenationalinterest.com/Articles/Vol2Issue17Lweispfw/html (accessed 12 December 2003).

Linklater, A. (1990a) *Men and Citizens in the Theory of International Relations*, London: Macmillan.

—— (1990b) *Beyond Realism and Marxism: Critical Theory and International Relations*, London: Macmillan.

—— (1995) 'Community', in A. Danchev (ed.) *Fin de Siècle: Meaning of the Twentieth Century*, London: Tauris Academic Press.

—— (1998) *The Transformation of Political Community: Ethical Foundations of the Post-Westphalian Era*, Cambridge: Polity.

Lipschutz, R.D. (ed.) (1995) *On Security*, New York: Columbia University Press.

Little, D. (2002) *American Orientalism: The United States and the Middle East Since 1945*, Chapel Hill: The University of North Carolina Press.

Lopez, G.A., Smith, J.G. and Pagnucco, R. (1997) 'The Global Tide', in G.A. Lopez and N.J. Myers (eds) *Peace and Security: The Next Generation*, Lanham: Rowman & Littlefield.

Lukes, S. (1974) *Power: A Radical View*, London: Macmillan.

Lynch, M. (1998–99) 'Abandoning Iraq: Jordan's Alliances and the Politics of State Identity', *Security Studies*, 8(2/3): 347–88.

—— (1999) *State Interests and Public Spheres: The International Politics of Jordan's Identity*, New York: Columbia University Press.

—— (2002) 'Jordan's Identity and Interests', in S. Telhami and M. Barnett (eds) *Identity and Foreign Policy in the Middle East*, Ithaca: Cornell University Press.

—— (2003) 'Taking Arabs Seriously', *Foreign Affairs*, 82(5): 81–94.

Maddy-Weitzman, B. (1993) 'A New Arab Order? Regional Security After the Gulf War', *Orient*, 34(2): 221–30.

Mahan, A.T. (1902) 'Persian Gulf and International Relations', *The National Review*, (September): 27–45.

Mahbubani, K. (1993) 'The Dangers of Decadence: What the Rest Can Teach the West', *Foreign Affairs*, 72(4): 10–14.

Makowsky, A. (1996) 'Israeli–Turkish Relations: A Turkish "Periphery Strategy"?' in H.J. Barkey (ed.) *Reluctant Neighbor: Turkey's Role in the Middle East*, Washington, DC: United States Institute of Peace Press.

Mansfield, P. (1991) *A History of the Middle East*, London: Penguin.

Maoz, Z. (1997) 'Regional Security in the Middle East: Past Trends, Present Realities and Future Challenges', in Z. Maoz (ed.) *Regional Security in the Middle East: Past, Present and Future*, London: Frank Cass.

Marfleet, P. (2000) 'A New Orientalism: Europe Confronts the Middle East', in T.Y. Ismael (ed.) *International Relations of the Middle East in the 21st Century: Patterns of Continuity and Change*, Aldershot: Ashgate.

Marsh, P. (1995) 'Grassroots Statecraft and Citizens' Challenges to U.S. National Security Policy', in R. Lipschutz (ed.) *On Security*, New York: Columbia University Press.

Martin, L.G. (ed.) (1998) *New Frontiers in Middle East Security*, London: Palgrave Macmillan.

Marx, K. (1997) 'The Eighteenth Brumaire of Louis Bonaparte', in D. McLellan (ed.) *Karl Marx: Selected Writings*, Oxford: Oxford University Press.

Mathews, J.T. (1990) 'Redefining Security', *Foreign Affairs*, 68(2): 162–77.

McCaughey, R.A. (1984) *International Studies as an Academic Enterprise: A Chapter in the Enclosure of American Learning*, New York: Columbia University Press.

McGhee, G. (1990) *The US–Turkish–Middle Eastern Connection*, New York: St. Martin's Press.

McGwire, M. (1986) 'Deterrence: The Problem, Not the Solution', *International Affairs*, 62(1): 55–70.

—— (1987) *Military Objectives in Soviet Foreign Policy*, Washington, DC: The Brookings Institution.

McInnes, C. (1992) 'Alternative Defence', in C. McInnes (ed.) *Security and Strategy in the New Europe*, London: Routledge.

McSweeney, B. (1996) 'Identity and Security: Buzan and the Copenhagen School', *Review of International Studies*, 22(1): 81–93.

—— (1999) *Security, Identity and Interests: A Sociology of International Relations*, Cambridge: Cambridge University Press.

Mernissi, F. (1993) *Islam and Democracy: Fear of the Modern World*, trans. M.J. Lakeland, Reading, MA: Perseus Books.

—— (1995) *Peçenin Ötesi: İslam Toplumunda Kadın-Erkek Dinamikleri* [Beyond the Veil: Male–female Dynamics in Muslim Society], trans. Mine Kürkçü, İstanbul: Yayınevi Yayıncılık.

—— (1996) *Women's Rebellion and Islamic Memory*, London: Zed.

Mikhail-Ashrawi, H. (1995) *This Side of Peace*, New York: Touchstone and Simon & Schuster.

Miller, G. (1992) 'An Integrated Communities Approach', in G. Nonneman (ed.) *The Middle East and Europe: An Integrated Communities Approach*, London: Federal Trust for Education and Research.

Milliken, J. (1999) 'Intervention and Identity: Reconstructing the West in Korea', in J. Weldes, M. Laffey, H. Gusterson and R. Duvall (eds) *Cultures of Insecurity: States, Communities and the Production of Danger*, Minneapolis: University of Minnesota Press.

Miskin, A. (pseud.) (1995) 'Globalisation and Its Discontents', *Middle East Report*, 193: 28.

Mitchell, T. (2003) 'Deterritorialization and the Crisis of Social Science', in A. Mirsepassi, A. Basu and F. Weaver (eds) *Localizing Knowledge in a Globalising World: Recasting the Area Studies Debate*, Syracuse, NY: Syracuse University Press.

Møller, B. (1992) *Common Security and Non-offensive Defence*, Boulder, CO: Lynne Rienner.

Møller, B. and Wiberg, H. (1994) 'Introduction', in B. Møller and H. Wiberg (eds) *Non-offensive Defence for the Twenty-first Century*, Boulder, CO: Westview Press.

Monroe, E. (1981) *Britain's Moment in the Middle East, 1914–1971*, London: Chatto and Windus.

Mosjov, L. (1985) 'Common Security and the Third World', in R. Vayrynen (ed.) *Policies of Common Security*, London: Taylor & Francis with SIPRI.

Mustafa, A. (1998) 'Regionalism: Disease of the 20th Century', *Khalifah Magazine*, 9(1). Online. Available: http://www.khalifah.com/nauframe2.htm (accessed 31 May 1999).

Nachmani, A. (1987) *Israel, Turkey and Greece: Uneasy Relations in the Eastern Mediterranean*, London: Frank Cass.

Nasr, S. (1997) 'Interview with Salim Nasr – A View From the Region: Middle East Studies in the Arab World', *Middle East Report*, 205: 16–18.

Nasser, G.A. (1955) 'The Egyptian Revolution', *Foreign Affairs*, 32(2): 199–211.

Neumann, I.B. (1999) *Uses of the Other: 'The East' in European Identity Formation*, Manchester: Manchester University Press.

Niblock, T. (1992) 'Towards a Conference on Security and Cooperation in the Mediterranean and the Middle East (CSCM)', in G. Nonneman (ed.) *The Middle East and Europe: An Integrated Communities Approach*, London: Federal Trust for Education and Research.

Niva, S. (1999) 'Contested Sovereignties and Postcolonial Insecurities in the Middle East', in J. Weldes, S. Niva, M. Laffey, H. Gusterson and R. Duvall (eds) *Cultures of Insecurity: States, Communities, and the Production of Danger*, Minneapolis, MN: University of Minnesota Press.

Noble, P. (1984) 'The Arab System: Pressures, Constraints, and Opportunities', in B. Korany and A.E.H. Dessouki (eds) *The Foreign Policies of Arab States: The Challenge of Change*, Boulder, CO: Westview Press.

Noor, F.A. (2003) 'The Evolution of "Jihad" in Islamist Political Discourse: How a Plastic Concept Became Harder'. Online. Available: www.ssrc.org/sept11/essays/noor.htm (accessed 14 December 2003).

Norton, A.R. (1993) 'Special issue: Civil Society in the Middle East', *Middle East Journal*, 47(2).

Nuri, A. (2003) 'April to November: an Iraqi Journey'. Online. Available: http://www.opendemocracy.net/debates/article-2-95-1589.jsp (accessed 28 November 2003).

Nye, J.S. (1989) 'The Contribution of Strategic Studies: Future Challenges', *Adelphi Papers*, 235: 20–34.

—— (2000) *Understanding International Conflicts: An Introduction to Theory and History*, New York: Longman.

Ohmae, K. (1994) *The Borderless World: Power and Strategy in the Global Marketplace*, London: HarperCollins.

Ortaylı, İ. (1983) *İmparatorluğun En Uzun Yüzyılı* [The Longest Century of the Empire], İstanbul: Hil.

Osseiran, S. (1994) 'The Democratisation Process in the Arab-Islamic States of the Middle East', in E. Boulding (ed.) *Building Peace in the Middle East: Challenges for States and Civil Society*, Boulder, CO: Lynne Rienner.

Ó Tuathail, G. (1998) 'Samuel Huntington and the "Civilizing of Global Space"', in G. Ó Tuathail, S. Dalby and P. Routledge (eds) *The Geopolitics Reader*, London: Routledge.

Ó Tuathail, G. and Agnew, J. (1992) 'Geopolitics and Discourse: Practical Geopolitical Reasoning in American Foreign Policy', *Political Geography*, 11(2): 190–204.

Ó Tuathail, G. and Dalby, S. (eds) (1998) *Rethinking Geopolitics*, London: Routledge.

Ó Tuathail, G., Dalby, S. and Routledge, P. (eds) (1998) *The Geopolitics Reader*, London: Routledge.

Ovendale, R. (1998) *The Longman Companion to the Middle East Since 1914*, London: Longman.

Owen, R. (1999) 'Inter-Arab Economic Relations During the Twentieth Century: World Markets vs. Regional Market?' in M.C. Hudson (ed.) *Middle East Dilemma: The Politics and Economics of Arab Integration*, New York: Columbia University Press.

Palmer, A. (1992) *The Decline and Fall of the Ottoman Empire*, London: John Murray.

Parfitt, T. (1997) 'Europe's Mediterranean Designs: An Analysis of the Euro–Med Relationship with Special Reference to Egypt', *Third World Quarterly*, 18(5): 865–81.

Pasha, M.K. (1996) 'Security as Hegemony', *Alternatives*, 21(3): 283–302.

Paz, R. (2003) 'Islamists and Anti-Americanism', *Meria Journal*, 7(4). Online. Available: http://meria.idc.ac.il/journal/2003/issue4/jv7n4a5.html (accessed 9 January 2004).

Pelletrau, R., Schlagintweit, R., Noyami, Y. and Moïsi, D. (1998) *Advancing Common Purposes in the Broad Middle East*, New York: The Trilateral Commission.

Peres, S. with Naor, A. (1993) *The New Middle East*, Dorset: Element.

Perthes, V. (1997) 'Europe, the United States and the Middle East Peace Process', in R.D. Blackwill and M. Stürmer (eds) *Allies Divided: Transatlantic Policies for the Greater Middle East*, Cambridge, MA: MIT Press.

Peters, J. (1996) *Pathways to Peace: The Multilateral Arab–Israeli Peace Talks*, London: Royal Institute for International Affairs.

Pfeifer, K. (1993) 'Does Food Security Make a Difference? Algeria, Egypt and Turkey in Comparative Perspective', in B. Korany, P. Noble and R. Brynen (eds) *The Many Faces of National Security in the Arab World*, London: Macmillan.

—— (1999) 'How Tunisia, Morocco, Jordan, and Even Egypt Became IMF "Success Stories" in the 1990s', *Middle East Report*, 210: 23–7.

Philip, G. (1994) *The Political Economy of International Oil*, Edinburgh: Edinburgh University Press.

Pipes, D. and Garfinkle, A. (eds) (1991) *Friendly Tyrants: An American Dilemma*, Houndmills, Basingstoke: Macmillan.

Piscatori, J.P. (1986) *Islam in a World of Nation-States*, Cambridge: Cambridge University Press.

Pitner, J. (2000) 'NGO's Dilemmas', *Middle East Report*, 214: 34–7.

Pollack, K.M. (2003) 'Securing the Gulf', *Foreign Affairs*, 82(4): 2–16.

Posen, B. (1993) 'The Security Dilemma and Ethnic Conflict', *Survival*, 35(1): 27–47.

Pripstein-Posusney, M. (1998) 'Behind the Ballot Box: Electoral Engineering in the Arab World', *Middle East Report*, 210: 12–15.

Ramazani, R.K. (1976) 'Iran and the United States: An Experiment in Enduring Friendship', *Middle East Journal*, 30(3): 322–34.

—— (1988) *The Gulf Cooperation Council: Record and Analysis*, Charlottesville: University Press of Virginia.

—— (1998) 'The Emerging Arab–Iranian Rapprochement: Towards an Integrated U.S. Policy in the Middle East', *Middle East Policy*, 6(4): 45–62.

Rapoport, A. (1964) *Strategy and Conscience*, New York: Schocken.

Rasmussen, M.V. (2002) ' "A Parallel Globalisation of Terror": 9–11, Security and Globalization', *Cooperation and Conflict*, 37(3): 323–49.

Ray, J.L. (1995) 'The Future of International War: Global Trends and Middle Eastern Implications', in D. Garnham and M. Tessler (eds) *Democracy, War and Peace in the Middle East*, Bloomington: Indiana University Press.

Reitzel, W. (1948) *The Mediterranean: Its Role in America's Foreign Policy*, New York: Harcourt, Brace & Company.

Rhein, E. (1997) 'Europe and the Greater Middle East', in R.D. Blackwill and M. Stürmer (eds) *Allies Divided: Transatlantic Policies for the Greater Middle East*, Cambridge, MA: MIT Press.

Richards, A. (1999) 'The Global Financial Crisis and Economic Reform in the Middle East', *Middle East Policy*, 6(3): 62–71.

Risse-Kappen, T. (1995a) 'Democratic Peace – Warlike Democracies? A Social Constructivist Interpretation of the Liberal Argument', *European Journal of International Relations*, 1(4): 491–517.

—— (1995b) 'Ideas do not Float Freely: Transnational Coalitions, Domestic Structures and the End of the Cold War', in R.N. Lebow and T. Risse-Kappen (eds) *International Relations Theory and the End of the Cold War*, New York: Columbia University Press.

Roberson, B.A. (ed.) (1998) *The Middle East and Europe: The Power Deficit*, London: Routledge.

Robinson, W.I. (1996) *Promoting Polyarchy: Globalisation, US Intervention, and Hegemony*, Cambridge: Cambridge University Press.

—— (1998) 'Beyond Nation-state Paradigms: Globalisation, Sociology and the Challenge of Transnational Studies', *Sociological Forum*, 13(4): 561–94.

Rodinson, M. (1981) *The Arabs*, trans. Arthur Goldhammer, London: Croom Helm.

Rosecrance, R. (1991) 'Regionalism and the Post-Cold War Era', *International Journal*, 46(3): 373–93.

Rosenau, J.N. (1995) 'Distant Proximities: The Dynamics and Dialectics of Globalisation', in B. Hettne (ed.) *International Political Economy: Understanding Global Disorder*, London: Zed.

Rubenstein, R.E. and Crocker, J. (1994) 'Challenging Huntington', *Foreign Policy*, 96: 113–28.

Rubin, B. (1995) *The New Middle East: Opportunities and Risks*, Israel: BESA Center for Strategic Studies.

Russett, B. with the collaboration of Antholis, W., Ember, C., Ember, M. and Maoz, Z. (1995) *Grasping the Democratic Peace: Principles for a Post-Cold War World*, Princeton, NJ: Princeton University Press.

Sadowski, Y. (1992) 'Scuds versus Butter: The Political Economy of Arms Control in the Arab World', *Middle East Report*, 177: 2–13.

—— (1993) *Scuds or Butter? The Political Economy of Arms Control in the Middle East*, Washington, DC: The Brookings Institution.

—— (2002) 'The Evolution of Political Identity in Syria', in S. Telhami and M. Barnett (eds) *Identity and Foreign Policy in the Middle East*, Ithaca: Cornell University Press.

Safran, N. (1988) *Saudi Arabia: The Ceaseless Quest for Security*, Ithaca, NY: Cornell University Press.

Said, A.A. (1994) 'A Middle Eastern Peace Strategy', in R. Ellis and J. Turpin (eds) *Rethinking Peace*, Boulder, CO: Lynne Rienner.

Said, E.W. (1991a) 'Intellectuals and the War: Interview with Edward Said', *Middle East Report*, 171: 15–20.

—— (1991b) 'American Intellectuals and Middle East Politics', in B. Robins (ed.) *Intellectuals: Aesthetics, Politics and Academics*, Minneapolis: University of Minnesota Press.

—— (1992) *The Question of Palestine*, London: Vintage.

—— (1994a) *Representations of the Intellectual – The 1993 Reith Lectures*, London: Vintage.

—— (1994b) *The Politics of Dispossession: The Struggle for Palestinian Self-determination, 1969–1994*, London: Chatto & Windus.

—— (1978; reprint 1995a) *Orientalism: Western Conceptions of the Orient*, London: Penguin.

—— (1995b) *Peace and its Discontents: Gaza-Jericho 1993–1995*, London: Vintage.

—— (1997) *Covering Islam: How Media and Experts Determine How We See the Rest of the World*, London: Vintage.

—— (2001) *Power, Politics and Culture: Interviews with Edward W. Said* (ed.) Gauri Viswanathan, New York: Vintage.

Said Aly, A.M. (1996) 'The Shattered Consensus: Arab Perceptions of Security', *The International Spectator*, 31(4): 23–52.

Salamé, G. (1994) 'Torn Between the Atlantic and the Mediterranean: Europe and the Middle East in the Post-Cold War Era', *Middle East Journal*, 48(2): 226–49.

Salem, P.E. (1997) 'Arab Political Currents, Arab–European Relations and

Mediterraneanism', in L. Guazzone (ed.) *The Middle East in Global Change: The Politics and Economic of Interdependence versus Fragmentation*, London: Macmillan.

Sanjiyan, A. (1997) 'The Formulation of the Baghdad Pact', *Middle Eastern Studies*, 33(2): 226–66.

Sardar, Z. (1985) *Islamic Futures: The Shape of Ideas to Come*, London: Mansell.

Satha-Anand, C. (1990) 'The Nonviolent Crescent: Eight Theses on Muslim Nonviolent Action', in R.E. Crow, P. Grant and S.E. Ibrahim (eds) *Arab Nonviolent Political Struggle in the Middle East*, Boulder, CO: Lynne Rienner.

Satloff, R. (1997) 'America, Europe and the Middle East in the 1990s: Interests and Policies', in R.D. Blackwill and M. Stürmer (eds) *Allies Divided: Transatlantic Policies for the Greater Middle East*, Cambridge, MA: MIT Press.

Sayigh, Y. (1990) 'Confronting the 1990s: Security in the Developing Countries', *Adelphi Papers*, 251.

—— (1991) 'The Gulf Crisis: Why the Arab Regional Order Failed', *International Affairs*, 67(1): 487–507.

—— (1999) 'Arab Economic Integration: The Poor Harvest of the 1990s', in M. Hudson (ed.) *Middle East Dilemma: The Politics and Economics of Arab Integration*, New York: Columbia University Press.

Schaffer, M.B. (1998) 'Speculations About Geopolitics in the Late 21st Century', *Futures*, 30(5): 443–52.

Schelling, T. (1963) *The Strategy of Conflict*, New York: Oxford University Press.

—— (1966) *Arms and Influence*, New Haven: Yale University Press.

Scholte, J.A. (1996) 'Beyond the Buzzword: Towards a Critical Theory of Globalisation', in E. Kofman and G. Youngs (eds) *Globalisation: Theory and Practice*, London: Pinter.

Schwedler, J. (1995) *Toward Civil Society in the Middle East? A Primer*, Boulder, CO: Lynne Rienner.

Seabury, P. (1949) 'The League of Arab States: Debacle of a Regional Arrangement', *International Organization*, 3(4): 633–42.

Seale, P. (2003) 'Is the Arab System Dead?' *Al Hayat*. Online. Available: http://English.daralhayat.com/comment/10-2003/Article-20031002-fe318cO.../story.htm (accessed 10 December 2003).

Selim, M.E. (1997) 'Mediterraneanism: A New Dimension in Egypt's Foreign Policy', *Kurasat Istratijiya* [Strategic Papers of the Al-Ahram Center for Political and Strategic Studies] 4(27). Online. Available: http://www.acpss.org/ekuras/ek27/ek27a.html (accessed 19 September 1999).

Shafik, N. (1999) 'Labour Migration and Economic Integration in the Middle East', in M. Hudson (ed.) *The Middle East Dilemma*, New York: Columbia University Press.

Sharabi, H. (1988) *The Next Arab Decade: Alternative Futures*, Boulder, CO: Westview Press.

Sharoni, S. (1993) 'Middle East Politics Through Feminist Lenses: Toward Theorising International Relations From Women's Struggles', *Alternatives*, 18: 5–28.

—— (1995) *Gender and the Israeli–Palestinian Conflict: The Politics of Women's Resistance*, Syracuse, NY: Syracuse University Press.

—— (1996) 'Gender and the Israeli–Palestinian Accord: Feminist Approaches to International Politics', in D. Kandiyoti (ed.) *Gendering the Middle East: Emerging Perspectives*, London: I.B. Tauris.

Sharp, G. (1980) *The Politics of Nonviolent Action*, Boston: Porter Sargent.

—— (1985) *Making Europe Inconquerable: The Potential of Civilian-based Deterrence and Defence*, London: Taylor & Francis.

Shaw, M. (1993) 'There is No Such Thing as Society: Beyond Individualism and Statism in International Security Studies', *Review of International Studies*, 19(2): 159–75.

Shehadi, K. (1997) 'The Poverty of Arab Diplomacy: Conflict Reduction and the Arab League', in P. Salem (ed.) *Conflict Resolution in the Arab World: Selected Essays*, Beirut: American University of Beirut.

Shehadi, K.S. (1998) 'Middle East', in P.B. Stares (ed.) *The New Security Agenda: A Global Survey*, Tokyo: Japan Center for International Exchange.

Shukrullah, H. (2003) 'The Gates of Hell', *Al Ahram Weekly*, March 20–26.

Sidaway, J.D. (1994) 'Geopolitics, Geography, and "Terrorism" in the Middle East', *Environment and Planning D: Society and Space*, 12: 357–72.

Singham, A.W. (1993) 'The National Security State and the End of the Cold War: Security Dilemmas for the Third World', in J. Singh and T. Bernauer (eds) *Security of Third World Countries*, Aldershot: Darmouth with UNIDIR.

Sirriyeh, H. (2000) 'A New Version of Pan-Arabism', *International Relations*, 15(3): 53–66.

Smith, C.G. (1968) 'The Emergence of the Middle East', *The Journal of Contemporary History*, 3(3): 3–17.

Smith, S. (1987) 'Paradigm Dominance in International Relations: The Development of International Relations as a Social Science', *Millennium: Journal of International Studies*, 16(2): 189–206.

—— (1991) 'Mature Anarchy, Strong States and Security', *Arms Control*, 12(2): 325–39.

—— (1996) 'Positivism and Beyond', in K. Booth, S. Smith and M. Zalewski (eds) *International Theory: Positivism and Beyond*, Cambridge: Cambridge University Press.

—— (1997) 'Power and Truth: A Reply to William Wallace', *Review of International Studies*, 23(4): 507–16.

—— (1999) 'The Increasing Insecurity of Security Studies: Conceptualising Security in the Last Twenty Years', *Contemporary Security Policy*, 20(3): 72–101.

Smoker, P., Davies, R. and Munske, B. (eds) (1995) *A Reader in Peace Studies*, Oxford: Pergamon.

Sosland, J. (2002) 'Understanding Environmental Security: Water Scarcity, the 1980s' Palestinian Uprising and the Implications for Peace', in T.A. Jacoby and B.E. Sasley (eds) *Redefining Security in the Middle East*, Manchester: Manchester University Press.

Sørensen, G. (1996) 'Individual Security and National Security: The State Remains the Principal Problem', *Security Dialogue*, 27(4): 371–86.

Spencer, C. (2001) 'The Mediterranean Matters – More Than Before', *The World Today*, 57(3): 15–17.

Spiro, D.E. (1994) 'The Insignificance of the Liberal Peace', *International Security*, 19(2): 50–86.

Stamnes, E. and Wyn Jones, R. (2000) 'Burundi: A Critical Security Perspective', *Peace and Conflict Studies*, 7(2). Online. Available: http://www.gmu.edu/academic/pcs/WJonesSt72PCS.htm (accessed 11 January 2004).

Starr, J. (1991) 'Water Wars', *Foreign Policy*, 82: 17–36.

Stork, J. (1995) 'The Middle East Arms Bazaar After the Gulf War', *Middle East Report*, 197: 14–19.

Sullivan, P. (2000) 'The Gulf War, Economic and Financial Linkages, and Arab Economic Development: Iraq – the Pivot?' in T. Ismael (ed.) *The International Relations of the Middle East in the 21st Century: Patterns of Continuity and Change*, Aldershot: Ashgate.

Sylvester, C. (1994) *Feminist Theory and International Relations in a Postmodern Era*, Cambridge: Cambridge University Press.

Tamkoç, M. (1976) *The Warrior Diplomats: Guardians of National Security and Modernization of Turkey*, Salt Lake City: University of Utah Press.

Tanenhaus, S. (2003) 'Bush's Brain Trust', *Vanity Fair*, (July): 114–18, 164–9.

Taylor, P.J. (1991) 'A Theory and Practice of Regions: The Case of Europes', *Environment and Planning D: Society and Space*, 9: 183–95.

Telhami, S. and Barnett, M. (2002) 'Introduction: Identity and Foreign Policy in the Middle East', in S. Telhami and M. Barnett (eds) *Identity and Foreign Policy in the Middle East*, Ithaca: Cornell University Press.

Thomas, C. (1987) *In Search of Security: The Third World in International Relations*, Brighton: Wheatsheaf.

—— (1989a) 'Introduction', in C. Thomas and P. Saravanamuttu (eds) *Conflict and Consensus in South/North Security*, Cambridge: Cambridge University Press.

—— (1989b) 'Southern Instability, Security and Western Concepts – On an Unhappy Marriage and the Need for a Divorce', in C. Thomas and P. Saravanamuttu (eds) *The State and Instability in the South*, London: Macmillan.

—— (1991) 'New Directions in Thinking About Security in the Third World', in K. Booth (ed.) *New Thinking About Strategy and International Security*, London: Harper Collins.

—— (1997) 'Globalisation and the South', in C. Thomas and P. Wilkin (eds) *Globalisation and the South*, London: Macmillan.

—— (2000) *Global Governance, Development and Human Security: The Challenge of Poverty and Inequality*, London: Pluto Press.

Thomas, C. and Wilkin, P. (eds) (1999) *Globalization, Human Security and the African Experience*, Boulder, CO: Lynne Rienner.

Tibi, B. (1993) *Conflict and War in the Middle East, 1967–91: Regional Dynamics and the Superpowers*, trans. Clare Krjzl, London: Macmillan.

—— (1998a) *Conflict and War in the Middle East: From Interstate War to New Security*, London: Macmillan.

—— (1998b) *The Challenge of Fundamentalism: Political Islam and the New World Order*, Berkeley, CA: University of California Press.

—— (1999) 'From Pan-Arabism to the Community of Sovereign States: Redefining Arab and Arabism in the Aftermath of the Second Gulf War', in M. Hudson (ed.) *The Middle East Dilemma: The Politics and Economics of Arab Integration*, New York: Columbia University Press.

Tickner, J.A. (1992) *Gender in International Relations: Feminist Perspectives on Achieving Global Security*, New York: Columbia University Press.

—— (1995) 'Re-visioning security', in K. Booth and S. Smith (eds) *International Relations Theory Today*, Oxford: Polity Press.

—— (1997) 'You Just Don't Understand: Troubled Engagements Between Feminists and IR Theorists', *International Studies Quarterly*, 41(4): 611–32.

Toukan, A. (1997) 'Arab National Security Issues: Perceptions and Policies', in S. Feldman and A. Toukan, *Bridging the Gap: A Future Security Architecture for the Middle East*, Lanham: Rowman & Littlefield.

240   *References*

Trankholm-Mikkelsen, J. (1991) 'Neo-functionalism: Obstinate or Obsolete? A Reappraisal in the Light of the New Dynamism of the EC', *Millennium: Journal of International Studies*, 20(1): 1–22.

Tucker, J. (1988) 'Middle East Studies in the United States: The Coming Decade', in H. Sharabi (ed.) *The Next Arab Decade: Alternative Futures*, Boulder, CO: Westview Press.

Turner, S. (1998) 'Global Civil Society, Anarchy and Governance: Assessing an Emerging Paradigm', *Journal of Peace Research*, 35(1): 25–42.

UNRISD (1995) *States of Disarray: The Social Effects of Globalisation*, London: UNRISD.

Victor, B. (1995) *Hanan Ashrawi: A Passion for Peace*, London: Fourth Estate.

Wæver, O. (1989) 'Visions of Conflict: Conflicts of Vision', in O. Wæver, P. Lemaitre and E. Tromer (eds) *European Polyphony: Perspectives Beyond East–West Dialogue*, New York: St Martin's Press.

—— (1994) 'Insecurity and Identity Unlimited', Centre for Peace and Conflict Research Working Paper, no. 14.

—— (1995) 'Securitization and Desecuritization', in R.D. Lipschutz (ed.) *On Security*, New York: Columbia University Press.

—— (1998) 'Insecurity, Security and Asecurity in the West European Non-War Community', in E. Adler and M. Barnett (eds) *Security Communities*, Cambridge: Cambridge University Press.

Walker, R.B.J. (1990a) 'Security, Sovereignty and the Challenge of World Politics', *Alternatives*, 15(1): 3–28.

—— (1990b) 'Sovereignty, Identity, Community: Reflections on the Horizons of Contemporary Political Practice', in R.B.J. Walker and S. Mendlowitz (eds) *Contending Sovereignties: Redefining Political Community*, Boulder, CO: Lynne Rienner.

—— (1997) 'The Subject of Security', in K. Krause and M. Williams (eds) *Critical Security Studies: Concepts and Cases*, London: UCL Press.

Wallerstein, I. (1997) 'The Unintended Consequences of Cold War Area Studies', in N. Chomsky *et al.* (eds) *The Cold War and the University: Toward an Intellectual History of the Postwar Years*, New York: The New Press.

Walt, S.M. (1987) *The Origins of Alliances*, Ithaca: Cornell University Press.

—— (1991) 'The Renaissance of Security Studies', *International Studies Quarterly*, 35(2): 211–39.

Waltz, K.N. (1979) *Theory of International Politics*, Random House: New York.

Weldes, J., Laffey, M., Gusterson, H. and Duvall, R. (1999) 'Introduction: Constructing Insecurity', in J. Weldes, M. Laffey, H. Gusterson and R. Duvall (eds) *Cultures of Insecurity: States, Communities, and the Production of Danger*, Minneapolis, MN: University of Minnesota Press.

Wendt, A. (1992) 'Anarchy is What States Make of It: The Social Construction of Power Politics', *International Organization*, 46(2): 391–425.

—— (1999) *Social Theory of International Politics*, Cambridge: Cambridge University Press.

Wenger, M. and Stark, J. (1990) 'The Food Gap in the Middle East', *Middle East Report*, 166: 15–20.

Wheeler, N.J. (1996) 'Guardian Angel or Global Gangster: The Ethical Claims of International Society Revisited', *Political Studies*, 44(1): 123–36.

Whitelam, K.W. (1996) *The Invention of Ancient Israel: The Silencing of Palestinian History*, London: Routledge.

Wiberg, H. (2000) 'Security Communities: Emanuel Adler, Michael Barnett and Anomalous Northerners', *Cooperation and Conflict*, 35(3): 289–98.

Wigen, K.E. and Lewis, M.W. (1997) *The Myth of Continents: A Critique of Metageography*, Berkeley, CA: University of California Press.

Williams, M. (1998) 'Identity and the Politics of Security', *European Journal of International Relations*, 4(2): 204–25.

Winder, R.B. (1987) 'Four Decades of Middle Eastern Study', *Middle East Journal*, 41(1): 40–63.

Wolfers, A. (1962) *Discord and Collaboration: Essays on International Politics*, Baltimore, MD: The Johns Hopkins University Press.

Wyn Jones, R. (1995a) ' "Message in a Bottle"? Theory and Praxis in Critical Security Studies', *Contemporary Security Policy*, 16(3): 299–319.

—— (1995b) ' "Travel Without Maps": Thinking About Security After the Cold War', in J. Davis (ed.) *Security Issues in the post-Cold War World*, Cheltenham: Edward Elgar.

—— (1999) *Security, Strategy and Critical Theory*, Boulder, CO: Lynne Rienner.

Yapp, M. (1982) 'Soviet Relations with Countries of the Northern Tier', in A. Dawisha and K. Dawisha (eds) *The Soviet Union in the Arab World: The Limits to Superpower Influence*, London: Heinemann.

Youngs, R. (2002) 'The European Security and Defence Policy: What Impact on the EU's Approach to Security Challenges?' *European Security*, 11(2): 101–25.

Zaharna, R.S. (2003) 'Repeat: Iraq is not a Modern-day Germany', *Christian Science Monitor* 95(187). Online. Available: http://www.csmonitor.com (accessed 11 January 2004).

Zalewski, M. (1994) 'The Women/"Women" Question in International Relations', *Millennium: Journal of International Studies*, 23(2): 407–23.

Zunes, S. (1998) 'Unarmed Resistance in the Middle East and North Africa', in S. Zunes, L.R. Kurtz and B. Asher (eds) *Nonviolent Social Movements: A Geographical Perspective*, Oxford: Blackwell.

—— (2002) 'Redefining Security in the Face of Terrorism', *Peace Review*, 14(2): 233–9.

—— (2003) *Tinderbox: U.S. Middle East Policy and the Roots of Terrorism*, London: Zed Books.

Index